One More for the Road

Special thanks to Jim Ziegener, computer genius if there ever was one, for his
technical wizardry

Cover Photo by Patricia Flinn
ISBN: 1-4196-4839-X
Library of Congress Control Number: 2006910266

To order additional copies, please contact us.
BookSurge, LLC
www.booksurge.com
1-866-308-6235
orders@booksurge.com

EUGENE C. FLINN

ONE MORE FOR THE ROAD

40 TALES FROM IRELAND, HOBOKEN, AND OTHER FARAWAY PLACES

2007

One More for the Road

TABLE OF CONTENTS

PREVIOUSLY PUBLISHED IN MAGAZINES

*T*he following stories by Eugene C. Flinn were previously published in literary magazines and/or anthologies in the United States, Canada, and Ireland.

"One More for the Road" in *The Potomac Review*, Rockville, Maryland

"The Butterfly Ride" in *Kaleidoscope*, The International in Magazine of Literature and Fine Arts, Akron, Ohio; *Tabula Rosa*, London, Ontario, Canada; and Brick Publications *Peeks and Valleys*, South Bend, Indiana

"Driftwood" in *Glass Tessarant*, Agoura Hills, CA.

"Elmer's General Store" in Black Mountain Review, Ballclaire, Country Antrim, Ireland

"The Madwoman of Murray Hill" in *Vincent Brothers Review*, Riverside, Ohio

"November Rain" in *Spring Hill Review*, Brush Prairie, Washington and *Rockford Review*, Loves Park, Il.

"The Cathouse on Fifth Avenue" in *Idiot Wind*, Occoquan, Virginia

"The People's Choice of Windy Hills in *Potpourri*, Prairie Village, Kansas; *Small Pond Review*, Stratford, Connecticut; and *The Pointed Circle*, Portland, Oregon

"The Carpenter, the Walrus, the Marathon Runner and Squinty, the Irish Setter" in *The San Diego Writers Monthly*, San Diego, California.

"Uncle Morty and Misery, the Jewish Cat" in *The Roanoke Review*, Salem, Virginia; *Gertrude*, Portland, Oregon; *DeKalb College, Clarkston, Georgia*; and *Spring Hill Review*, Brush Prairie, Washington

"A Shrewd Bite" in *Green's Magazine*, Regina, Saskatchewan, Canada

"A Mattress for Aunt Mary," *Dialogue*, Salem, Oregon; and *Recorder Publishing Co.* Bernardsville, NJ

PREVIOUSLY PUBLISHED IN MAGAZINES

The Viager at Happy Homer's Ice Cream Haven" in *Thin Ice*, Council Bluffs, Iowa and *Tyro Literary Magazine* in Sault Ste Marie, Ontario, Canada

"Bottoms Up, Strawberries Down" in *I, the First Person, Zeugma Press*, Gratan, California; *Heartland Journal*, Madison, Wisconsin; and *Concho River Review*, San Angelo, Texas

"Matching Earrings" in *The Lamp-Post of the Southern California C.S. Lewis Society*, Santa Ana, CA

"Watch Out for Mrs. Prongay," *Telestar Publishers*, Parma, Ohio

"The Cemetery Lady" in *Bibliophilos, A Journal of History, Literature and the Liberal Arts*, Fairmont, WV

"What I Did for Soup" in *Midday Noon*, Waite Park, Minnesota; *Clockwatch Review: A Journal of the Arts*. Illinois Wesleyan University, Bloomington, Illinois; *Rockford Review*, Rockford, Illinois; *Leapings*, Santa Rosa, California; and Piedmont Literary Review, Forest, Virginia

"A Bottle of Whiskey for Denny" in *Pangolin Papers*, Turtle Press, Nordland, Washington and *The Recorder Publishing Company*, Bernardsville, New Jersey

"Christmas in a Barn" in *The Raven Chronicles*, Seattle, Washington; *The Independent Review*, Independence, Missouri; and *Tabula Rosa: A Journal of Politics and Literature*, London, Ontario, Canada;

"DADS' Day" in *Lynx Eye*, Los Angeles, California: *Satire*, C&K Publications, Hancock, Maryland; *First Class: Four-Sep Publications*, Friendship, Indiana; *Star Route Journal*, Redway, California; and *Zoiks Magazine*, Raleigh, North Carolina

"Shine, Mister?" in *Mindprints*, Santa Maria, California

"The Butterfly Ride" in *Kaleidoscope, The International Magazine of Literature and Fine Arts*, Akron, Ohio; *Vignettes*, Wenatchee, Washington; and *Next Phase*, New Haven, Connecticut

"A Little Adultery in the Fifth Grade" in *Koyo*, Branford, Ontario, Canada

"Layover in Halifax Airport" in *Kaleidoscope, The International Magazine of Literature,* Akron, Ohio

Many thanks to April Bogdon of BookSurge, LLC, an Amazon company, for skillfully guiding this manuscript through the publishing process. Your expertise and professionalism are greatly appreciated.

For Patricia
The day begins with you
Kiss away the stardust,
The Moon has had her fling.
Open wide the windows
And hear the robins sing:
"Patricia,"
They whistle through the trees.
The bluebirds are singing love songs
too,
And roses are smiling at the sun.
Patricia, the day begins with you.
With all my love

And for my brother, John Dermod Flinn, and his wife, Betty, dual citizens of Ireland and the United States, and the inspiration of the Irish stories in this collection.

INTRODUCTION

In a sense the writing of Eugene C. Flinn spans three centuries. He is still writing in the twenty-first, has spent most of his long life in the twentieth, and spins tales firmly rooted in the tradition of some of the great short story writers of the nineteenth, the likes of Anton Chekhov and Guy de Maupassant. He shares the straight-forwardness of their prose style, speaking in the language of the common man mostly about ordinary people in both ordinary and extraordinary situations. Flinn has the gift of spotting the unique in the apparently commonplace and transforming it into entertaining and even moving short stories.

Many of the stories in this collection are told in the first person, and most of them are told from a single point of view, drawing the reader into a kind of intimacy with the narrators, making it easy to suspend one's disbelief. We follow the story-teller into Finneran's Pub in Ireland and get a sample of Flinn's fine ear for dialect in *A Bottle of Whiskey for Denny* and discover nonagenarian Finneran's makeshift bar in a nursing home in *One More for the Road*. The innocent boy in *A Little Adultery in the Fifth Grade* is accused by his teacher nun and is forced to confess a mortal sin he doesn't begin to understand. In *Uncle Morty and Misery, the Jewish Cat* we are in the head of a young Catholic boy praying at the behest of his family for an ever-growing list of strangers. In fact the Catholic Church crops up quite frequently and the ubiquitous "Our Lady of Perpetual Chastity" appears in a number of stories where and when required.

A more serious note is struck when Flinn makes moving, rather than comic, use of his own Catholic background as in *Christmas in a Barn*, in which a Polish priest provides comfort to soldiers who have no other common language by performing a Christmas Mass in Latin during the Battle of the Bulge in World War II. Flinn also reveals his tender side in the "Love Comes in Different Packages" and "Remembrances of Things Past" sections. *The Cemetery Lady* is protected after she collapses by the stray dogs she has been feeding in a graveyard. A beloved golden retriever who has gone to heaven thinks of a way to comfort his bereaved owners in *From Flaubert with Love*. A dear life-long friend is fondly remembered in *Bannon*.

Though only one section of the collection is entitled "Comic Tales," Flinn's humor touches most of the stories in the collection, especially those in "A Touch of the Irish," "On the Satirical Side," and "From a Child's Point of View" sections. Thus a painful dog bite has funny consequences in *A Shrewd Bite*, and a little boy's unsuccessful attempt to kill his beloved grandmother on her way from confession so she can go straight to heaven makes us smile. The satire in "On the Satirical Side" is never the harsh, bitter satire of a Jonathan Swift, but more like the gentle mockery of a James Thurber. Thus a surprise election victory addresses political corruption and voter ignorance in *The People's Choice of Windy Hills*, and *Watch Out for Mrs. Prongay* deals with gossip and internal politics in a nursing home. Flinn seems especially to enjoy poking fun at his characters who are pretentious or snobbish and spoiled, as in *The Cathouse on Fifth Avenue* and *The Viager at Happy Homer's Ice Cream Haven*.

A few of the tales deal with the fantastic or supernatural, as when people learn to fly in *Layover in Halifax Airport* or a ghost-like apparition interacts with the narrator in *The Woman in a Faded Camisole*.

This collection of stories is pleasant light reading and offers a refreshing break from the slick fiction so often encountered today. They reveal a sensibility that is essentially kind, fun-loving, animal-friendly, occasionally mischievous, sometimes nostalgic and even sentimental, but never cynical.

Many of Eugene C. Flinn's stories have been previously published in the United States, Canada, Ireland, and Australia, and in a collection entitled *It Happened in Hoboken: Comic Tales from the Waterfront City*. Dr. Flinn lives in an eighteenth century country house in New Jersey with his wife Patricia, author of *The Listerine Lunatic and Other Strange Stories*, and three large dogs.

> Maria S. Rost
> *Professor Emeritus of English*
> *and American Literature*

I.
A Touch of the Irish

"You gave me the key to your heart, my Love,
Then why do you make me knock?"
"Ah, but that was yesterday and—Saints above
Last night I changed the lock."
—John Boyle O'Reilly

JACK FLINN, KING OF THE BLARNEY

I'll give ye the line of discussion.
  I've oft kissed the auld Blarney Stone.
I have and I'll tell ye a story:
  I've often kissed Mother Malone.
The byes when they go out a-courtin'
  They haven't the spunk of a mouse.
They'll stand on the corner and whistle;
  They're afraid to go into the house.
But I always walk in with me swagger,
  As if the auld place were me own,
And I'll sit meself down on the sofa
  And it's "Good evening, dear Mother Malone."
Then I'll kiss the auld woman, I'll hug the auld man,
  Give Dennis a shilling and shake hands with Dan
Fight for his sister and do all I can. And do all I can,
  And then I'll walk out with me gal, Betty Ann.
I've only been courtin' a fortnight,
  But her heart and her hand I had won,
And the next toime I walk in the cottage
  The auld woman—she calls me her son.
When I asked the auld man for his daughter,
  His son-in-law soon I would be,
He said, "By me soul, Jackie Flinn, shure
  Ye can have both me daughter and me.
                    —Old Irish folk song, slightly revised

A BOTTLE OF WHISKEY FOR DENNY

Rainy weather was good for business in Finneran's Pub in Taughmaconnel. The more it rained, the more depressed the boys got, and the more depressed they got, the more they drank. And the more they drank the better were Mike Finneran's chances of winning the Guinness Gold Medal awarded to the publican who sold the most pints of stout in County Roscommon in 2001. And, of course, it almost always rained in Taughmaconnel. On days like this Mike was glad he had not followed his mother's advice to study for the priesthood. He had found his niche here in the pub in the grandeur behind the shiny mahogany bar with God knows how many bottles of Irish whiskey within easy reach. A dream come true. And yet in a way, he had probably done as his mother had bidden him, because the stories he heard from his vantage point on the other side of the bar were probably no less heart-wrenching than those a priest listened to on long Saturday afternoons in the confessional.

St. Malachy's Church was just around the corner from the pub and the boys with heavy consciences usually stopped by to see Mike before they made their confessions. And then when it was finally over, after they had recounted, blow by blow, the awful details of every single one of their transgressions, especially the sins of lust and gluttony, most of the boys would troop back to Finneran's to celebrate their return to innocence by downing a few shots of Powers Irish whiskey. So it was Finneran to Malachy to Finneran. If Saturday afternoons were sandwiches, St. Malachy's would be the corned beef and mustard in the middle and Finneran's Pub the two pieces of buttered rye bread on each side.

This particular Saturday, having been blessed with a steady light rain, should have been a perfect day for Finneran. However, there was one rub: Dennis O'Callaghan. There was practically no way to keep O'Callaghan out of his pub and, once he got in, there was absolutely no way to get him out. Oh, Mike could have called Constable Burke, but Denny was an old friend. Hadn't they played football together for Roscommon when they were young? And besides, O'Callaghan had the decency to always come to his pub sober. Some of Finneran's other customers got themselves stoned at Flaherty's, two miles away in Dysart, and stopped at Finneran's only to glom the nightcap and to use the facilities. O'Callaghan would never do such a thing, Finneran told himself. No, his friend had the common courtesy to get drunk, from beginning to end, in his pub.

"Hey, Finneran," O'Callaghan shouted, somehow managing to slur two words that did not have sibilant sounds, "how's about another pint of Guinness and a shot of Jamison's? I'm dying of thoist, I am."

"The only way you'd die of thirst, Dennis O'Callaghan, would be for thunder and lightning to strike down every Guinness brewery in Ireland and England."

"That would be a tragedy indeed," Patrick Doyle agreed, looking up from The Irish *Times*. "Heaven forbid, Mike, you shouldn't even be saying sooch things. It might put the idea in the Almighty's head. And then where would we be?"

"Do you hear me, Mike?" Finneran called out. "I need a drink."

Finneran made no effort to respond to his old friend.

"For God's sakes, Mike, are you deef? I might as well be on a desert drinking camel pee."

"You've had enough for one day, Denny," Mike admonished. "Your old woman will be knocking down me doors bitching to the heavens, if you come staggering home again."

"Shure, an' I think Mike has a good point, Denny," Doyle declared. "Ye know yerself when your woman gets riled she can shout the rafters off this place."

But O'Callaghan had never been sidetracked by logic in his life. Unless it was logic he could put to good use.

"My God, man, I've known ye since we was in the IRA together. How can you abandon me now?"

Finneran hesitated. He knew what O'Callaghan was going to remind him of next: that he had saved him from drowning in the River Suck when they were kids forty years ago. Finneran also had a long file on the things he had done for O'Callaghan over the years, but he wasn't in the mood for debating.

"All right, Denny. One more and that's it. And then home you go to that foine woman of yours who's probably right now warming the bed for ye."

"You're a good man, Michael Finneran. And when I'm dead and gone, I'll remember you took care of a man in need."

"How can you remember him when you're dead?" Doyle wanted to know.

But by this time O'Callaghan had gulped down his shot of Jamison's and was swilling down his stout and as if he was worried that Finneran might change his mind and take it back. It was an idle fear, for at that moment Cavanaugh, Horgan, and Kelly, three of the heaviest drinkers in Taughmaconnel, popped in from Sean McDermott's wake. Finneran grinned. An evening with these boys and he'd have a grand chance of taking the lead among publicans who featured Guinness Stout. For the next two hours he did little but fill pints and attempt to agree with all three of his big spenders at the same time, as they argued over the state of the Irish economy and the wealth of the Catholic Church. He was so busy trying to keep the trio drinking and spending that he didn't hear the phone ring. Doyle reached behind the bar and answered it.

"It's Mrs. O'Callaghan, Mike," he called out, cupping his hand over the phone. "She wants to know if her husband is here."

Finneran, who had forgotten about O'Callaghan, looked across the room to see his old friend and nemesis slumped over the bar.

"Tell her he just left and should be home shortly," Mike said.

As soon as Doyle hung up, Finneran signaled to him to get O'Callaghan up.

"Can you drive him home, Patrick? You just told his missus he had already left."

Doyle nodded. He didn't particular like the assignment, which would cut down on his stout-drinking time, but he thought a favor like this ought to be worth a few drinks on Finneran when he was caught short. He walked over to O'Callaghan and shook him gently.

"Wake up, Denny. Your chauffeur has arrived. We are off to see the Queen."

But O'Callaghan did not budge. Doyle took a firm grip on his shoulder, lifted it from the bar, and gave it a healthy shake.

"Let's go, man. The word just came in that you won a case of John Jamison's whiskey."

But as soon as Doyle let go, O'Callaghan's slumped down on the bar again.

"Jaysus, Doyle, can't you get him out of here? I don't want no truck with his old woman."

"He won't wake up, Mike."

Impatient, Finneran collected the empty pints of the hard-drinking trio from the wake and walked over towards his old nemesis.

"I should never have given him that last stout," he mumbled, half to himself. "That's what put him to sleep all right."

Doyle, who was bending over O'Callaghan touching his wrist, suddenly regarded him curiously.

"I-I don't think he's asleep, Mike."

"You mean the blatherskite is faking? Step back, Patrick, I'll—"

But the look on Farrington's face caused him to hesitate.

"Y-you mean he's—"

Doyle nodded his head in agreement.

"Deader than a doornail."

***

The next three days were precarious ones for Finneran, even though everything seemed to be going his way. Constable Burke, who was a frequent visitor to Finneran's Pub, cleared him of all wrong-doing. He said he was satisfied with Coroner Duffy's report that "death was caused by failure of the heart's action." However, to give it more of an official ring, the Constable suggested the coroner make his finding a little more "medical-sounding." Duffy, who earned most of his livelihood driving a fish lorry, obliged by adding that "it was quite likely a case of coronary thrombosis." The Constable liked that. From his experience he had found that people rarely asked questions about anything they didn't understand, especially if it had a nice official sound to it. He had heard that coronary thrombosis was a blood clot in the heart, but he suspected it was another one of those terms that sounded important but didn't really mean much, like saying *expectorate* when all you meant was *spit*.

It was the general opinion of Taughmaconnel that official reports notwithstanding, O'Callaghan, like several of his townsfolk, had simply drunk himself to death. No one attached any onus on Finneran because folks reasoned that if a man wants to drink, who is there to stop him? Roscommon was fresh out of everything from sunny weather to decent libraries, but there was no dearth of Irish whiskey and Guinness Stout.

And if Finneran didn't supply him, there were others who would. Might as well let him have a few jars in a pleasant pub filled with friendly faces.

That left Finneran off the hook with the law and with Taughmaconnel society, but there was always Mrs. O'Callaghan to deal with. He was convinced that she was just waiting to start a civil suit against him, accusing him of taking her husband's life in order to win the Guinness Publican of the Year Award. That she said nothing to him other than to acknowledge his presence with a dazed nod when he attended the wake on the first night only deepened his belief that when she recovered from the trauma of the wake, she was going after him with the best barrister in County Roscommon.

He confided his fears to Patrick Doyle, who managed a night of free drinking by assuring his friend that Mrs. O'Callaghan was more likely to salute him than sue him.

"How can you say that, Doyle?" he asked while rinsing out glasses on the night before O'Callaghan was to be buried. "Shure an' I lied by saying Denny had left for home when he was probably already dead. I tell you, I'm going to have a few stiff shots of Jamison's before I make me confession at St. Malachy's this Saturday."

Doyle downed his Guinness and moved his pint glass to the edge of the bar for a refill.

"You don't have a thing to worry about, Man. Everybody in Taughmaconnel knows that Molly O'Callaghan had little use for Denny. In a way, you can't blame her. I've heard it said that she was praying that the banshees would take poor Denny away. After all, she rarely saw him to talk to, and when she did, he was so polluted that she didn't have the damnedest notion of what he was saying. And I've heard tell he tried to use his mitts on her once in awhile. So all of that's gone and, as they say, Molly is a liberated woman again."

"You-you think she'll actually be grateful to me that Denny is de—? Aw, come now Patrick, you can't mean that. Denny was not a bad soul."

"You know that and I know that, Michael, but we're men, and women don't understand us the way we do. Shure an' Molly felt a little bad when she got the news. But after the shock wore off, she probably said to herself, 'Well, 'tis a shame the old bugger is gone, but I have to tell meself the truth and admit that he was an albatross around me bloody neck.' So you see, Mike, she probably has nothing but gratitude for you."

Finneran nodded, becoming beguiled by the easy rhythms of Doyle's logic. There was some truth in what he is saying, he mumbled to himself, feeling a sense of relief for the first time since O'Callaghan drooped his head on his bar and died. Almost at that very instant, as if in response to his musings, the door swung open and Molly O'Callaghan walked in, dressed in her black Sunday hat and dark blue cloth coat.

***

Finneran was so nervous he knocked over a row of stout glasses as he moved to the end of the bar to greet Mrs. O'Callaghan.

"A thousand welcomes to you, missus. I can't tell you how sorry I am about the demise of your husband, me old friend, Denny."

Mrs. O'Callaghan took a seat at the bar next to Patrick Doyle. She didn't say a word, but just kept staring at the massive array of whiskey bottles behind Finneran's head.

"Yes, indeed," Doyle said, hoping to help his friend out, "it was a great tragedy all right. Dennis was sooch a good man. As right as the mail, he was, that's for sure."

Mrs. O'Callaghan unbuttoned her coat and fidgeted with her fingers on the bar. Finneran took that as a signal that she wanted a drink.

"What'll ye have, Molly? On the house, of course. Just name your poi—just name it and its yours."

Mrs. O'Callaghan stared him straight in the eyes. "I don't drink."

"Well, maybe you'd like a little soda pop? We have six flavors— strawberry, cream, orange—"

"No thank you." Although he realized that this was probably the worst thing he could do, Finneran was so nervous he couldn't help himself. He reached for the Jamison's and poured himself a stiff shot while Mrs. O'Callaghan glared at him.

"The doctor's orders," he stammered. "Me congestion is acting up. Look, Mrs. O'Callaghan, I don't want ye to think I am responsible for your husband's death. Ye wouldn't believe the number of times I've cut him off and told him to go home. Isn't that right, Doyle?"

On cue, his friend stood up and verified the bartender's account of his innocence in the death of O'Callaghan. The woman stared at him as if she were watching a fly slowly drowning in a pot of boiling hot tea. Finally she spoke.

"Mr. Finneran..."

"Yes, Mrs. O'Callaghan."

"It was John Jamison's Irish Whiskey that Denny drank, was it not?"

Not knowing what to expect, Finneran reluctantly nodded his head in agreement.

"You have a brand new bottle behind you, do you not?"

"Yes, ma'm."

"Give it here."

"Oh yes, Mrs. O'Callaghan. Right away."

Finneran reached up and pulled down the bottle. To calm the nervous tension raging inside of him, he dusted it off a bit with his apron. Doyle tried to subdue a snicker. The last thing that gathered dust in Finneran's Pub was Irish whiskey.

Mrs. O'Callaghan examined the label carefully, reading the description of the contents half aloud.

"How much is this?" Doyle gestured quickly to Finneran, but it was hardly necessary.

"Oh, I wouldn't think of taking your money, Mrs. O'Callaghan."

"All right then. Have you a little satchel?"

Finneran carefully placed the bottle in a white paper bag and handed it to Mrs. O'Callaghan. She accepted it without a word, turned, and walked resolutely out the pub.

"Jaysus! What do you make of that, Doyle?"

"It can't be that she is suddenly so grief-stricken that she going to take to drink."

"Denny told me she hated the taste of it," Finneran said. "I can't believe she would start drinking now at this late stage of her life."

"Well, Mike, at any rate she didn't threaten to sue ye." Finneran nodded.

"You know, Patrick, I almost wisht that she had. She seemed awfully peculiar, wouldn't you say?"

"Well, 'tis true her eyes seemed a wee bit strange. But she always looked a little quare to me. The main thing, Michael, is she's gonna leave ye alone. Say, if you're going down towards the end of the bar ye might bring me the bottle of Powers Irish whiskey. Maybe you'll have a sip with me. In memory of old Denny."

Finneran brought back the bottle and set two whiskey tumblers down on the bar.

"I can't put me finger on it, Patrick, but something peculiar is going on," he said. "Something awfully quare. I can feel it in me bones."

***

By the end of the short mass at St. Malachy's that Sunday just about everybody in Taughmaconnel knew why Mrs. O'Callaghan had wanted that bottle of John Jamison. Timmy Nolan who worked on the fish lorry with Coroner Duffy saw the whole thing and he told Bridie O'Donnell while she was pitching hay, and when Bridie rode into town she saw Artie Deering who told...In other words, it did not take long before Mary McElaney, who runs the rectory for Father Brennan, got wind of it. From that time on the news whistled around town like a balloon caught in a stiff wind.

To the amazement of everyone and to the consternation of Father Brennan, Mrs. O'Callaghan had broken with Catholic burial rites and had her husband cremated. When Margan, the Protestant funeral director, gave her Denny's ashes in a little green urn, she poured them into the bottle of John Jamison's Irish whiskey, corked it up, and buried it in her backyard next to the grave of Cassandra, her favorite cat. A few brave souls ventured to her house, presumably to see if Molly was cracking up, but the old woman would have none of it. She put a padlock on the gate of the white picket fence that surrounded her cottage. A group of women from the St. Malachy's Rosary Society appeared at the gate with the hope of establishing a brief dialogue with her as "good Christians concerned with the state of her soul." She appeared and gave them a four-word statement:

"The matter is closed." Till this day Finneran wonders whether he should have given her the bottle in the first place. It would have been more honorable simply to have accepted the responsibility for her husband's death, he told Doyle.

"Aw, how can ye say that, Michael?"

"Denny was me pal. I never should have let her get even with his poor ashes like that."

Doyle took a long sip of his whiskey. "I don't know, Mike. Maybe she gave him the finest final resting place imaginable, don't ye think? Look at it from Denny's point of view. What did he like better than Irish whiskey?"

Finneran had to admit that Doyle had a point there. +++++

THE SHREWD BITE
The air bites shrewdly

Hamlet I, iv 1

We were spending a two-month holiday in Dun Laoghaire, and neither of us had had a drink in six weeks. Now when people decide to go on the wagon and visit Ireland at the same time, you know they have to be serious. Every morning Sheila and I were up with the tinkers and washwomen and we'd jog ten kilometers around the quays of Dun Laoghaire before breakfast. The we'd walk around the countryside, or take the train into Dublin to do a little research in the library of Trinity College. We'd go to a fine pub for lunch—corned beef and cabbage, salad and soda bread, but, of course, nothing stronger than a pot of tea. After a while we were getting to actually *like* the taste of tea and wondered how we could have spent so many years drinking sour stuff like bitters and beer.

We were staying near Martello's Tower where they have the James Joyce Museum. Each morning we'd jog past it and wave to the ghost of Joyce fleeing from its parapets on a dark rainy night when one of his pals decided to have a shoot-em-ups in the crowded confines of the tower. Still, what happened to Joyce was mild compared to what was in store for us.

Behind the museum we would pick up a little dirt road that followed the bend of the sea and ran through the mist towards Dalkey. One Sunday morning when it forgot to rain we saw something we had not noticed since coming to Ireland, probably because it had been enshrouded in a heavy mist on the days we jogged past it. Behind a huge stone wall and partially hidden by trees was a towering castle, hanging over the sea and gleaming in the reflection of the sun.

"Isn't that beautiful?" Sheila sighed. "Wouldn't you like to live there for a few days?"

The occasion for our holiday in Ireland was the celebration of our fifth wedding anniversary. What the heck, I told myself, why not splurge for once?

"I bet we can get lodging there. They rent out rooms in Irish castles, y'know."

"But this doesn't look like *that* kind of a castle. There are no signs or anything."

"We'll never know unless we ask."

That was the biggest mistake of our holiday. We jogged down a long dirt road, right up a small moat to the castle door. I banged on a large brass knocker while Sheila looked at me apprehensively. "I don't know, Neil. This could be—"

The door swung open. A stout woman in a long brown dress and white apron looked at us curiously. I was just about to ask about the availability of rooms in the castle when a gray dog—the kind that has long white whiskers and stands only a few inches off the ground—shot through the woman's legs like a furry torpedo and began circling us and barking in angry falsetto.

"Mind you," the woman warned, "he bites."

At first we were disinclined to defend ourselves, for the dog—if that's what he was—looked more like a bloated mouse. However, he suddenly sprung almost two feet into the air and sunk his nasty little teeth into Sheila's bare leg. As I tried to grab him, he lunged for my foot. After that, things happened so quickly I am not sure of their sequence, but I do remember that a minute later Sheila was flat on the moat, crying in pain, and the woman in the white apron with the little monster dog had vanished into her medieval past. I pounded on the castle door several times, but got no response. I offered to carry Sheila, but she said she could hobble by leaning on my shoulder.

"I'll get you to a hospital," I said. "We'll walk towards town and maybe somebody will stop."

"Screw the hospital," Sheila said. "My leg feels as if it has been sliced by a knife. Did he get you?"

I looked at my foot. He had got a good chunk of my left *Nike*, but missed my foot.

"What I need is a drink," she said. "Take me to a pub."

I had our sacred vow of abstinence to consider, of course, but I did not feel that this was the appropriate time to bring it up with Sheila. Considering everything, it *did* seem like an emergency. After all, those St. Bernard dogs became famous by bringing people brandy when they were suffering from injuries. And if Sheila had a drink it would be downright inhospitable of me to make her drink alone. I told her that the circumstances did indeed seem to make a drink necessary, much as we were both reluctant to break our pledges.

Sheila had given me a simple assignment. I was sure it would be a lot easier to locate a pub than a hospital in Ireland. We walked a block and found Duffy's. I tried the door. It was locked. That baffled me. It was almost one in the afternoon. Seconds later the publican opened the door an inch or two.

"Another ten minutes, lad."

"What the devil for?"

"We can't open until the last mass is over."

Sheila said she'd rather hobble to the next pub than wait and think about her leg. When we arrived at Holloran's, the publican there was just opening up. But as we were about to enter, he reached an arm in front of Sheila, blocking her passage.

"No ladies. Today's Sunday, y'know."

Not having been drinking, neither of us had bothered to learn the rules.

"Could I get a drink for her then? She's been bitten by a dog."

"Ah, an' haven't we all?" he laughed and shut the door in our face.

We tried three more pubs and received the same response in each case: no women served on Sunday in this part of Ireland. I suppose if I hadn't said anything about the dog bite and just ambled up to the bar and asked for a stiff one, I might have somehow smuggled it out to Sheila. But once they turned her down, they watched me like a hawk. You may have heard a great deal about all the drinking that goes on in Ireland, but you couldn't prove it by Sheila and me. No matter what they say, you've got to know your way around to get a drink over there.

In desperation we decided to go to the hospital. They told Sheila she had nothing to worry about because there were no rabies in Ireland. Having said that, the nurse gave her a stiff shot in the you-know-where. It was the only shot that she got all day.

The next day Sheila was so stiff she couldn't walk. We didn't know if she was suffering from the dog bite or the tetanus shot. In the evening we called a doctor's office to make an appointment for the next day. The doctor answered the phone himself and told us he would be right over to our boarding house. It was a strange country: a woman couldn't get a drink on Sundays, but the doctors made house calls at night.

Dr. Rogers looked as if he had just stepped out of a Dickens novel. He was a chubby little man with a Homburg, a gold watch on a long chain, a natty three-piece brown worsted suit. He examined Sheila's leg with a magnifying glass the size of a cantaloupe and gave her some pills.

"Now get right to bed," he said, as he returned his stethoscope and magnifying glass to his little black satchel. "I shall be back the first thing in the morning, and when I return, young lady, I shall expect you to be wearing a proper nightgown."

"What's this proper nightgown business?" I asked Miss Harris, the proprietress of our boarding house.

"Ah, Dr. Rogers is a something of a moralist. He doesn't like examining women in their street clothes." I explained that by Dr. Rogers' standards we were probably immoral because we slept in our birthday suits. Miss Harris told Sheila she might borrow one of her nightgowns for the morning examination. It was white flannel with little purple flowers and Sheila had enough room in to invite a friend or two to share it. Miss Harris weighed about 300 pounds.

Dr. Rogers was pleased by it, though, and apparently also with Sheila's leg. He checked it carefully with his magnifying glass at the point of the bite, gave her a medication, and returned after high tea. Once again he nodded his head sagely and announced:

"Very fine. Very fine."

We didn't know if that meant Sheila's leg, the shape of the dog bite or her prospect of a quick recovery. He told Sheila to stay in bed and that he would be checking her early in the morning.

After the third day Sheila stopped wearing the nightgown with the purple flowers for Dr. Rogers' twice-a-day examinations. He was apparently so enraptured by the shape of the dog bite that he didn't seem to notice she was not fitted out like a tent. He would stare at her leg for a few minutes each time he visited and then tell her it was "Very fine" but that she still had to remain in bed. He wouldn't let us ask questions before he began his scrutiny with the magnifying glass, and, when he finished, he ran off without really answering them.

"How long do I have to stay in bed, Doctor?"

"Till your leg is better."

"And when do you think that will be?"

"It's up to the good Lord."

Even when I tried to pay him, he rushed off, leaving me with my checkbook in my hand. He was a strange doctor. After the fourth day, when Sheila's back began to hurt, we asked Miss Harris about him.

"Do you think he really knows what he's doing?" Sheila asked.

"Oh, indeed. Isn't he Lady Wicklow's doctor." "Who's Lady Wicklow?"

"Don't you know? Why, she's the richest woman in County Dublin. Sure, and it's her dog that took a piece out of your leg."

And that explained Dr. Rogers. It occurred to us that he might be more interested in his wealthy patron than in Sheila's leg. When he visited us after high tea, Sheila told him that her back was hurting.

"Hmmm," he said, and turned his magnifying glass on the dog bite.

"What about my back?" she asked.

"Fine, just fine," he said, packing his bag and getting ready to leave.

"Look, Doc," I said. "We want a second opinion." "Impossible."

"Why?"

"It just isn't done here. You're not in the States, y'know."

I lunged for him, but he was too quick for me. All I got was his homburg, which flew from his head when he escaped through the door.

That afternoon I began calling doctors, but as soon as I told them that Dr. Rogers had been our doctor, they told me they were too booked up to handle the case.

"Lady Wicklow has considerable influence around here," Miss Harris said. "You would do better hiring a solicitor."

On the fifth call I located one who did not represent Lady Wicklow and could thus do business with us. The first thing he did was to locate Dr. McDermott, who had also managed to grow up without being part of Lady Wicklow's entourage.

Dr. McDermott had neither a homburg nor a magnifying glass, but he was willing to listen to Sheila's complaints about her back.

"Best thing you can do for your back is to get out of bed and walk about a bit."

"But Dr. Rogers told me to stay in bed."

"He was probably concerned with the remote possibility that you could infect your leg where the dog bit you. It was his client's dog, y'know. But by lying in bed so much you have probably atrophied the sacroiliac cartilage." "Is that serious?"

"You could have problems with your back for a while," he said. "You don't want it to become chronic, so you had best move it about as soon as you can."

Sheila got up and tried to walk. I could see that her first steps pained her, but as she began to slowly circle the room, she gained more confidence.

"Take a walk around the quays," Dr. McDermott advised. "I'll stop back to see you tomorrow." Sheila was so glad to be able to walk again that we circled the quays for almost two hours. As we were passing the Dun Laoghaire railroad station on our way back to Miss Harris' boarding house we saw a familiar silhouette in a homburg near the entrance to the platform. As soon as he spied us, he picked up his bag and ran off into the dusk. Obviously he had found out. News travels fast in Ireland.

A week later when Sheila's back had improved, but not enough for jogging or carrying anything heavier than a light suitcase, we asked our solicitor, Patrick Campbell, Esq., about the possibility of suing Dr. Rogers and Lady Wicklow.

"Neither of them ever even apologized," Sheila said. "Lady Wicklow's maid shut the door in our face." Campbell agreed to take the case, but said it wouldn't be easy.

"It's not like the States, y'know. The awards are small and it will be probably difficult to prove that the dog bite was the cause of your problem. It could have been the tetanus shot. And it will take awhile to get a trial date, especially with the influence Lady Wicklow has around here. She'll get the Judge to keep postponing it until it's time for you to return home."

He was right on all counts, but we had grown to love the countryside around Dun Laoghaire despite the Sunday saloon laws and Lady

Wicklow's dog, so we corresponded with Campbell for nearly a year and as the summer season approached we finally got a trial date. We left for Ireland for another holiday, hoping that this time Lady Wicklow would be paying for it. If not, at least we would be able to jog together along the quays again for Sheila's back had recovered, except for an occasional twinge now and then. We were still on the water wagon, but since we had withstood the temptation of Ireland's pubs once and under rather extenuating circumstances, we felt confident we could do it again.

We finally got to see Lady Wicklow, a grand dame in her eighties, I would say. She sat in the second row of the courtroom in a long brown dress that almost touched her toes, a huge hat with fake flowers and a pince-nez, which she would rest reflectively on her rather long thin nose from time to time. One of her four solicitors called on her to testify and she marched to the witness box like Queen Victoria about to review the changing of the guard at Buckingham Palace.

"Would you describe your dog, Brandy, to the Judge, Lady Wicklow?" she was asked.

"Oh, he is such a delightful little doggie," she said. "It disturbs me—and probably him—that he is at the center of this nasty business."

"Was he well on the date in question—the date of the alleged attack? You recall that date, do you not?"

"Yes, indeed. It was just a fortnight after he had been to the hospital to have his ulcers looked after. He had been feeling out of sorts for nearly a month."

"Do you think Brandy's indisposition caused the er—accident?"

"Oh, yes. Normally he's so gentle—just like that American doggie of the films, Benji I believe he is called." "Thank you, Lady Wicklow."

All through lunch Campbell looked pretty grim. "Lady Wicklow's influence covers Dun Laoghaire like a snow storm," he said. "We would have to have an air-tight case to expect any chance of winning. She has everyone afraid of testifying that her dog is mean."

"But what more proof does the Judge need?" Sheila asked. "I was bitten on the leg and put in bed. Her own doctor treated me."

"Oh, she doesn't deny it. But in Ireland every dog is entitled to one bite."

"You're kidding?"

"I wish I weren't, but that's the law."

The image of that little monster going after Sheila flashed across my mind as clearly as a picture postcard. I saw the castle, the moat and the stout maid in the long brown dress and white apron screaming at us.

"I've got an idea," I told Campbell. "Put her maid on the stand."

***

Miss Sullivan was her name and she was a nervous wreck as she looked down at Lady Wicklow staring hard at her from the second row.

"Now tell me," Campbell asked, "when Brandy charged in the direction of the plaintiff, did you not call out to her, 'Mind you, he bites.'?"

The witness dropped her eyes. She dared not look at Lady Wicklow. But she was a devout Catholic too, and she had just placed her hand on the Bible and had sworn to tell the truth, so help her God.

"That I did, sir," she said finally, "but you see—"

"May I respectfully remind the court that in Ireland every dog is entitled to one bite? Lady Wicklow's Brandy has already had his share, your Honor."

We were awarded 5,000 pounds, not enough to buy a castle in Ireland to be sure, but after we had paid our expenses to Campbell, his staff and expert witnesses like Dr. McDermott, we had enough money to spend the rest of the summer in Ireland in style. After the trial Campbell drove us to Duffy's, the pub near the James Joyce Museum that hadn't yet opened the Sunday afternoon that Sheila was bitten. Campbell insisted we have a drink with him. "We haven't touched the stuff in more than a year," we told him. "Ah, but you'll have just one to toast good old Lady Wicklow and her dog?"

Sheila looked at me and I at her.

"Just one—a sip of brandy in honor of your canine benefactor?" Campbell pleaded, waving to Duffy to pour shots for everyone in the house.

Sheila and I clicked glasses. The brandy went down like pure silk.+++++

INTERFACING OFF GALWAY BAY

I won the Aran Islands in a lottery.

Before Framingham put my name in the hat, I had never heard of them. The next thing I knew I had $25,000 in expenses and $100,000 in rented computer equipment at my disposal.

"See if you can get a plane tomorrow," Framingham said.

"For the Aran Islands?"

"Are you kidding, Markiewicz? You might as well ask a jet to land on Alcatraz. Those islands are exaggerated piles of rocks sitting in the ocean thirty miles west of Galway. You'll have to take a jet to Shannon and get to Aran the best way you know how. Hire somebody to help you carry your gear."

"O.K. Frame, I'll get right on it."

I hadn't bluffed him. He must have seen in my eyes that I hadn't the foggiest idea of what I was going to be doing.

"Look, Markiewicz, we got more than a half-million dollars on this grant and your research is a big chunk of it. The boss wants a report in three days. Here's the literature on the project. If I were you I'd go to the library right away and at least get a little idea of where you're going. Check back issues of the National Geographic; they always carry stories on weird, out-of-the-way places."

"Gotcha, Frame."

"And whatever you do, cable us your report. It doesn't matter if you found out anything—just as long as it looks like you're doing research. Mention your desire to share your discoveries with all of mankind. Crap like that. You know the big fuss the Boss makes about reports, how he loves to have them set up in large type and pin them to our bulletin board with gold thumbtacks to impress the senators and congressmen when they come around."

"I'm on my way, Frame."

I could tell by the way he persisted that he wished Borchiazzo had got the Aran Islands and I had picked Chateroy Holler in West Virginia instead. But it was too late now.

"Remember if you screw up the Aran Islands, you will hurt our chances on the grant to study how the Borneo orangutans manage sex without their tails. That one should be good for seven hundred grand, at least."

By the time I landed in Shannon I had completed some of my homework and had begun to see how Framingham had wriggled still another grant out of the government. His project was to examine the reactions of people living in 18th century environments to our computerized society. Then the senators and congressmen could vote on whether it was better to keep moving on ahead or go back to the simpler days. Frame warned me not to let the facts interfere with the results. The Congressmen were not interested in Thoreau's philosophy; they wanted the findings to favor progress because progress meant more spending, more lobbying and, of course, eventually more government grants. He had made a wise choice in the Aran Islands. Here was a place without highways, gas stations, factories, shopping centers, hospitals, police departments, hotels, and even a solitary MacDonald's. Telephones were rare, television and automobiles were virtually non-existent, and the principal source of entertainment was the pubs and churches. Presidents and Kings could be assassinated and these people might not know about it for days. And even when they did find out, sudden death would scarcely be news. Fishermen from Aran were constantly drowning in these rough seas. The crazy thing was that few of them could swim.

I rented a van at the airport, tossed in my computers, and headed north. I had a little trouble getting used to driving on the left side of the road and narrowly missed hitting two sheep, a cow, and an old woman carrying a basket of wash on the outskirts of the little town of Crusheen.

"I'm sorry, ma'm; I'm not used to the road."

She smiled at me.

"Ah, 'tis a caution all right."

She set her basket down and started pulling out shirts, shifts, socks and long johns and setting them on the turf. At the bottom of the basket was a gaily wrapped package. She handed it to me.

"It's fer me niece, Bridey. She's twinty-six today. Just drop it in Finneran's Pub in the town of Derrybrien up the road a bit."

I stared at her uncertainly.

"Mind McGinty's pigs just around the bend," she said, and started picking up her wash.

It turned out Bridey was the barmaid at Finneran's. I asked her the best way to get to the Aran Islands. Before she could answer an elderly man in a brown tweed cap and a long black coat, spoke up. He had watched my entrance into the pub as a cat eyes a fish wagon.

"The best way to get there, ye say?"

"I'd appreciate your advice, sir."

He looked at me as a shrink might observe a new patient.

"As for meself, I'd rather spend a winter in the bottom of a well, but if ye have yer heart set on it, I'll tell ye. That's a foine vehicle ye have outside, young fellow."

"Thank you."

"I'm going your way meself."

"Can I give you a lift?"

"Grandeur. Timothy Connolly's the name. From County Mayo, God help us."

"Felix Mickiewicz here."

"Ye don't say?"

He pumped my hand vigorously. I had heard the Irish were friendly, but I had never expected a guy with a Polish name to knock anyone dead here.

"Related to the Countess, are ye?"

"What countess?"

"Are ye putting me on, lad? Countess Mickiewicz, of course. Great Irish patriot. Nearly lost her life for the ould sod in the Easter uprising of 1916."

"She sounds Polish."

"Ah, Irish as Dugan's goats she was. But her husband was a Polish Count. A grand man himself."

After that I didn't feel so much like a stranger in a foreign land.

Connolly directed me to Mulligan's Pub on Wharf Road in Galway City, where he said I might run into some fishermen with a boat to take me to Aran. The three islands were due west of us, about a four-hour sail into Galway Bay.

"On a clear day ye can see the biggest one, Inishmore, from Connemara up to the North," he said. "I'd jine ye for a bitters, but me bladder's been bothering me latterly. Thanks fer the ride. I do be hopin' ye change yer mind. It's foine here in Galway, y'know."

After my second drink I asked the bartender if he knew anyone going out to the islands.

"Shure, an' what do ye want to go there for?"

I hesitated.

"To meet the people."

"Hey, Michael," he called out. "Here's a fellow who wants to see the A-rabs."

From the back of the pub a stocky guy with blond hair and a seaman's cap sitting on the back of his head raised his glass in the air.

"Here's to the A-rabs," he said.

He approached the bar, apparently ready to begin a discussion. I obliged.

"You mean the people who live on those islands are Arabs?" I asked.

The man in the seaman's cap laughed.

"Naw. Shure 'tis just the name we give 'em."

"Why?"

The stocky guy looked at me, puzzled.

"Why?" he asked. "I don't know why. I don't have answers for every bloody question in life."

"Would you have a drink with me?"

He nodded. I thought I would try out my new title.

"Name is Mickiewicz," I said.

He looked at me with a new interest.

"Popular name around here," he said.

I was ready for him. One thing I had learned from my experiences in the grant business and as a tobacco institute spokesman: the importance of a well-placed lie.

"Ah yes. I'm a distant relative of the Countess.

"Well, now. You must have been over to the Lisadell House then?"

I hadn't the slightest idea of what he was talking about. The Lisadell House could have been a pub, restaurant, or part of the Galway red-light district. My best guess was that the Countess had lived there. Here goes, I told myself. I had to get out to those islands as fast as I could.

"The Lisadell House? Oh, yes. My relatives just had a kielbasa festival there."

It seemed to have worked.

"Sure, you're right as the mark. 'Tis an honor indeed to be in the company of a relative of the Countess. So you want to see the A-rabs?"

Except for the battles in the North, I had assumed that all the Irish were of a single philosophy. I could see that at least the people in this pub regarded those on the Aran Islands as different.

"Are they very superstitious?" I asked, trying to hide my eagerness. Michael grinned.

"The truth of the matter is 'twould be hard to find an Irishman who wasn't. But the A-rabs believe just about everything. They hear the banshees singing on the rocks and, even without a drop of Jameson taken, on a misty night on Aran they can see leprechauns making shoes for the fairies by the furzy bushes."

"You're putting me on," I protested, hoping against hope that he was telling the truth."

He crossed his heart solemnly with both arms.

"As true as me ould mother is having a cup of tay with St. Brendan and St. Brigit and the other saints of God right now. Y'know St. Brendan lived on Aran. He left from there whin he discovered America."

He downed his bitters and I signaled the bartender for another round.

"I suppose it's the isolation from the mainland that make these people believe so much in the supernatural," I suggested.

"Well, the A-rabs are peculiar, but I'd have to admit if I were living there where the nights are dark, the dogs are barking, the calves mooing and the wind howling through the furzy bushes, me own teeth would be rattling with fear, and I might be seeing a few banshees and leprechauns meself. It's a lonely place out there on the rocks and after awhile, y'know, your mind can start imagining things."

All the little pieces fell together neatly in my head. I knew now that I could come up with the kind of report that Framingham and the Senators wanted.

"They tell me the steamer doesn't leave for five days," I said. "It's worth a couple hundred pounds to me to get a ship there."

"Ah, the Mickiewicz family is one that never had to fret the spuds. That's fer sure."

"I'll double it if you can come back in a week to get me off."

Michael laughed.

"By thin even a Mickiewicz will have had enough of the A-rabs, right?"

I nodded.

"Lissen," he said, "I'll take ye there meself. Tomorrow morning with the tide. Meself and a few of the lads are going past there with our diving gear. There's sunken treasure in those waters, y'know. Meet me here at seven in the morning."

I cabled Framingham and told him he would have his first report from the Aran Islands in less than 24 hours.

***

A fine mist lay on the deck of Michael's small craft, the Purple Eagle, but he wasn't dismayed.

"Ah 'tis like this many a morning," Michael said, "that's how we wash the streets in Galway City. By half-nine ye'll see the sun climb up the back of Inishmaan."

It took us about five minutes to load all my gear onto Michael's ship. I knew he wanted to ask me questions about it, but he maintained the same polite indifference I had noticed other Irish folks had displayed since I arrived here. But he had his way of asking for hints.

"Looks like you've got enough stuff in there to blow the islands into the sea," Michael observed.

"That I have," I smiled. "But I'm not interested in anything like that."

Michael looked at me curiously.

"All the way from the United Sates of America with a ton of equipment, and you're bringing it all to the A-rabs?"

I smiled. That never gets you in trouble, Framingham had told me.

First they were long stretches of flat gray rock sitting solemnly in the sea. As we came closer I could see little dots that must have been random houses, following a winding road up a hill. I didn't see any trees, just rows and rows of brilliant yellow vegetation, following the path of the stone walls on each side of the road. These must be the furzy bushes Michael had spoken of. At the end of hill the cliffs reached out to the sky.

"That's Dun Angus," Michael said. "Built by the Romans before Christ was born."

Inishmore, the largest island, was a study in isolation. On the plane I had read where the people on these remote islands had survived, barely, from the sea—from the fish they caught and the kelp they cut from the rocks. I wondered how they would find life on a Times Square subway. Or how the occupants of a crowded elevator at Bloomingdale's would react if they were suddenly set down on these barren rocks. I congratulated myself. I was getting into the spirit of my assignment. As long as my computers weren't damaged when we loaded them ashore, I might be able to provide Framingham with the data he needed.

"There's no real harbor in Inishmore—just a pier we can slide into," Michael said. "We'll give you a hand with the unloading. If you wait here you will no doubt attract a few A-rabs to lug your stuff for you. There are no hotels, but if you slip them a few pounds they'll give you a place to sleep and breakfast, too. Actually, they're not as bad as I've been making them out. Give my regards to the Mickiewicz family next time you see them."

I sat on my crates and watched the small diving craft lose itself in the horizon. Although I had the feeling that unseen eyes were watching me, I did not see anyone on the small dock.

"Caed mila faltha."

I turned in the direction of the voice. It was a little boy who couldn't be more than seven or eight. A brown setter was walking behind him.

"Do you speak English?"

"Sure."

"Then why the Gaelic?"

"It's our way of saying welcome."

"Thanks, kid. Do you know where I can find a place to stay? And someone to help me move these crates?"

He ran off, followed by the dog. For a moment I was afraid that I had frightened him away, but in a few minutes a pony and trap turned the bend of the road leading to the dock.

"This is my brother, Sean," the kid said.

An hour later I was sitting by a turf fire of an old country kitchen with a dozen people, young and old, surrounding me. We had just polished off a simple, but filling, meal of fish and potatoes, cooked in the roaring fire. The kid, whose name was Kevin, finally asked the question that all the others must have been thinking about.

"Whatcha got in them cases, Mister?"

They gathered around on the floor in front of me in a semi-circle. My computers were set on an old pine table a safe distance from the fire. I'm glad I thought of bringing high-powered batteries because there was no electricity in the house.

I turned a couple of dials. The computers moved from the main menu to a program designed to pick up noises in the room, translate them into digits, and then into sounds. Everyone was impressed by the activity on the screen except Salty, the setter, who lay down by the fire.

"Will you lookit that?"

"Shure, ain't it a wander?"

I took out all my cameras—still, camcorder, and digital—and got a few shots of their expressions. Eyes wide open, jaws at parade rest, wonderment everywhere among the shadows of the fire-lit room. I had brought ultra-rapid film so I didn't have to use flashes. I did not want to break the spell. Framingham would have these pictures on the bulletin board minutes after they arrived.

"Now watch this."

I turned a few more levers. They followed the flickering lights in open admiration. Suddenly a gravel voice from one of the computers broke the silence.

"Hello, everybody."

They stared at the computer in amazement.

"Did you hear the machine talk?" Mrs. Flaherty, Kevin's mother, asked her husband..

"That I did," he answered nervously.

"Mrs. Flaherty, can you hear me?" one of my computers asked.

"Y-yes," she replied nervously, half-wondering if she should reveal her presence in the room.

"That was a grand supper you cooked for all of us," the computer groaned like a man in a well. "Grand indeed."

"Did you hear that, Nora?" Mrs. Callaghan, her neighbor from down the road, asked.

"I whisht to God I didn't," Mrs. Flaherty replied.

I pushed another button to make sure I was taping everything they were saying. Framingham would love this.

"That's a foine trick you're doing with those cases, Mister," Sean pointed out in admiration.

"Oh, it's no trick," I said.

"But a box can't talk."

"Can a leprechaun?" I asked.

"Bejasus," Mrs. Flaherty gasped. "Have you one of the wee people inside?"

Mr. Flaherty was scrutinizing one of the largest computers.

"Would you like to talk to it?" I asked.

"Well—"

"Go ahead. Say anything you want."

He cleared his throat as if he were making a political speech. With everyone's eyes on him, he bent over the computer the way one does when talking to a small child.

"Shure, an' how did ye get trapped in a box?"

There was a pause. Mr. Flaherty looked at the monitor screen, and then at the other people in the room, uncertainly. I hit the Return button.

"Trapped in a box," the computer repeated mechanically. "Trapped in a box...trapped in a box." Mrs. Callaghan had been listening to the staccato sound carefully.

"He doesn't sound Irish to me," she said. "Not even English."

"Not even English...not even English," the computer rasped robotically.

Mrs. Callaghan jumped back from it as if she were recoiling from a snake.

Before the night thinned out into morning everyone in that room had carried on a conversation with my computers. At first they had been shy and hesitant, but the more of their questions that each computer answered, the more my hosts treated it like a person. Even when they had exhausted their curiosity, they still sat staring, alternately at the computers and at me. Finally Mr. Flaherty spoke up.

"It's a foine trick, Mr. Markiewicz, but don't you think you should let him out?"

"Let who out?"

"The little man you have in the box."

"I have no little man in there. You don't really think there is a little man in this box, do you?"

They stared at me in silence. I knew they didn't believe me. This was just what I wanted. The more they doubted me, the more they would show their faith in the wee people. The more they believed in the leprechauns, the more I could demonstrate the triumph of progress and show what happens when the people of the earth wittingly or unwittingly follow the advice of Henry Thoreau. And, of course, the more Framingham, his Boss, and the congressmen would like my work.

Sean and Kevin wandered over to the computers and lifted one of the smaller ones up in the air and tried to see through the back of it.

"There's a lot out there beyond Galway Bay that you haven't heard of," I told them. "Would any of you like to come back to the United States with me?

There was just that same curious silence again. Mrs. Flaherty came down the stairs.

"I've warmed your bed for ye, Mr. Mickiewicz."

I didn't know what she meant until I saw the hot water bottle in her hand. I turned off my computers and taping machines, replaced my cameras in their cases and climbed the stairs, grateful for the rest because it had been a long day. As I turned around to wave good-night I saw that they were still staring at the tangle of wires, monitors and instrument boards of my computers and laptops.

***

The room was facing east and the sun streamed through to wake me up. I didn't hear any stirring in the house, so I guessed everyone was still asleep. As soon as Sean got up I would ask him to take my equipment to the section of the island near Dun Angus. I had gotten great reactions last night, but I knew I ought to get a good cross- section of this and the other two islands while I was here. Still, I felt that it would be difficult to improve upon what I already had on those disks. Framingham had to love the contrast: people who had never flicked the channels of a television set observing for the first time some of today's most sophisticated computers.

Mrs. Flaherty had told me to make myself some tea, should I get up before she did. It would be fun to go to the outside pump for the water and then put it in that big black pot over the fire that seemed to be going day and night

I laced up my shoes and made my way out the little hallway. All was still; everyone was asleep all right. I found the stairs and made my way down, trying to walk gently so they would not creak. With my eyes on the steps, I didn't notice it until I reached the landing and looked down in the direction of the turf fire.

The floor was strewn with thousands of little wires, fuses, broken glass, and huge gray chunks of plastic hacked into so many grotesqueries they resembled a piece of modern sculpture. My computers had been raped. I wondered if they did it because they felt sorry for the little man or because they wanted the pot of gold he would give them for setting him free. +++++

A MATTRESS FOR AUNT MARY

Tim Dooley kept his engineer's cap and his gray overalls hanging on the back of the bedroom door from the day they made him retire. Molly, of course, objected and would remove them and slip them over a nail in the back of his section of the closet, even threatening to pack them up in the attic in the family trunk. But Tim, who had seldom got his way in their 40 years of marriage, kept taking them off the old nail and restoring them to the brass hook behind the door.

"You're not working on the railroad any more, Timothy Dooley," Molly would complain. "For God's sake, let me donate those moldy old clothes to the Salvation Army."

"I've been a railroader all my life, Woman. The least you can do is let them hang from the door in peace."

Molly would sigh and give in for the time being. It wasn't worth getting into a snit about, especially since there had been so many other areas in which Tim Dooley had been ornery ever since he retired. One thing was sure: she was not traipsing around the nation on any train, or even into Pennsylvania for that matter. The railroad had given Dooley a gold pass, which enabled him and a guest to travel any place in the continental United States. Dooley had been itching to get her on a train, but she had too much to do at home than to be gallivanting all over the country- side.

There wasn't too much the two of them agreed on those days except that perhaps the most pleasant hours of their life were from noon to 3 p.m. on the third Saturday of every month. That was when Tim was sure to be out of the house, attending the regular meeting of his chapter of the International Brotherhood of Railroad Trainmen. Dooley hadn't missed one since he retired, looking forward to the opportunity to play a few games of checkers while ex- changing railroad gossip with some of the other old-timers. Molly was glad to be finally rid of him for a few hours, but she still insisted he get back by 5:30, because she began to worry when he was out after dark since his eyes weren't what they used to be.

It was usually after six when Tim got home because he would stop and see Bertha and Leo Latchford before getting on the 5:19 for the trip back to Molly. Bertha was his granddaughter. The Latchfords had an apartment about a half-mile from the meeting hall of the Brotherhood, so it was convenient for Dooley. Leo was convinced that Tim would do anything to forestall renewing his acquaintance- ship with Molly.

The Latchfords would mark the calendar to remind themselves to be home that third Saturday since they knew it meant a great deal to Tim. For the first year after his retirement, neither Tim nor the Latchfords forgot the day of his monthly visits. Tim, with his engineer's temperament for reliability, would probably never have forgotten. Fortunately on the one occasion the Latchfords slipped up, they were able to pass the blame onto Aunt Mary.

***

It was one of those misty and uncertain Saturday afternoons in February. Had it been a person instead of a day, it would surely have been assigned to the vestibule in Dante's Hell set aside for people who can't make up their minds. Leo had been awakened at 6 a.m. by his Aunt Mary, who lived in an old brownstone in the heart of the Flatbush section of Brooklyn. He had been in such a sound sleep that the jangling of the bedside phone sounded like a Mack truck crashing into a concrete pillar.

"This would be a good day for the mattress and chairs," she said.

"All of them?" Leo asked.

"And the table, naturally."

"Aunt Mary, that stuff will never fit in my old Ford."

"God will find a way."

That was Aunt Mary for you, Leo reflected. She acted as if God were lingering around in Leo's back pocket, thinking of ways to get him through the down side of life.

Leo's mistake had been telling Aunt Mary that Bertha and he were planning on buying new furniture. Aunt Mary was in charge of the collections committee for the St. Jude Relief Fund. Her job was to accumulate as many old things as she could for St. Jude's warehouse, where it was either sold or given to people in need. St. Jude was the apostle of the hopeless, Aunt Mary said, and if you ever turn your back on the hopeless, you're in for it. That's why Leo couldn't argue with Aunt

Mary, even though Bertha and he hadn't gotten around to shopping for the new furniture. But, he reasoned, responding to Aunt Mary right away had its good side: about to be deprived of their mattress, they were quite likely to buy a new one at the first opportunity.

"You had better give me the address again, Aunt Mary," Leo said, rubbing the sleep out of his eyes. "I always get lost going to your place."

It took two hours to get everything tied to the roof and loaded in the trunk. Leo was sure they were going to look like the Okefenokees as they made their way through Brooklyn, but as Bertha kept reminding Leo, it was for a good cause. They had to climb in the windows to get in the car because they had roped the doors closed. Just as Leo boosted Bertha in head-first and was about to undertake the same undignified action himself, Tim Dooley stepped down from the Number 7 bus. In the confusion they had forgotten that this was his Brotherhood of Railroad Trainmen Day. The meeting had ended a little earlier than usual.

"Hi, folks," he said casually, as if Bertha and Leo went around with mattresses hanging from their roof every day of the week.

Bertha explained about Aunt Mary and St. Jude, the hope of the hopeless. Tim Dooley looked a little hopeless himself.

"I-I wouldn't have come, if I had known."

"Oh, Grandfather, it's just something that happened out of the blue," Bertha tried to explain. "I'm really sorry. But next time..."

Tim Dooley appeared crestfallen. The color had drained from his face and his eyes were as woeful as those of a whipped dog.

"All right, then. I guess I can see you after the next meeting of the Brotherhood."

"Now, now, Grandfather. Let's see—"

It was bad enough traveling to Brooklyn in a foggy mist. Neither Leo nor Bertha wanted to start the trip by leaving the old trainman shuffling his feet sadly on the pavement.

"Mr. Dooley," Leo began, "would you like to come to Aunt Mary's with us?"

Tim stared hard at Leo. For a moment it looked like he would smile a polite "No thank you." He pulled out his gold trainman's watch, shook it, checked its sound, and finally arrived at his conclusion.

"Sure," he said. "Why not?"

***

Once Dooley decided to go, he seemed completely relaxed. He was still thin and wiry and had no problem working his way through the window into the back seat. As they drove across the Brooklyn Bridge and down busy Flatbush Avenue, he kept waving to everyone whose attention he could attract. Not many people were returning his friendly greetings because the traffic was horrendous, and the mood of most motorists and pedestrians seemed to match the gray of the day. Bertha had the directions and kept feeding them to Leo every time he stopped for a light.

"Did you say something about making a turn at a big church?"

"Yes," she answered, "and I think it's over there on the left."

The trouble was Leo was on the right. He tried to work his way to the left, but every time he inched over a little, he was greeted by a barrage of angry horns.

"The bastards behind me aren't going to let me turn."

"You better go straight then, Leo. Try turning at the next corner."

But the drivers behind him still wouldn't let him move. Cars and minds were bumper-to-bumper. Leo finally made his way to the left, only to be confronted with a sign proclaiming "Don't even *think* of taking a left turn here."

"We're lost," Leo wailed.

He felt a foot on his shoulder. It was Mr. Dooley.

"Where are you going, Grandfather?" Bertha asked.

"I'll be right back," Dooley said, taking the sheet of directions from Bertha. "There's a policeman directing traffic in the middle of the street. I'm going to have a little chat with him."

With horns blazing on both sides of him Mr. Dooley snaked his way through the traffic to the harassed cop, who was blowing his whistle and swinging his arms furiously.

"Good afternoon, Officer," he said, holding up the paper with the directions he had just taken from Bertha. "Timothy Dooley's the name. Hail from Union Village, New Jersey. Was an engineer for the Jersey Central for nigh onto 25 years. Started with the railroad as a coal-shoveler. Seems we're off to see Aunt Mary and—"

The frustrated motorists near the cop had their eyes glued for his hand signal so they could finally move on. The sight of an elderly man suddenly beginning a casual conversation with one of the busiest cops in Brooklyn boggled their minds.

"Look, Buddy," roared the cop, "Don't be giving me any shit about your Aunt Mary. Can't you see I've got me hands full?"

Mr. Dooley apprised the army of vehicles spewing noise, smoke and filth in every direction.

"Yes, indeed. We never had anything like this at the Jersey Central. In my day we'd get maybe—"

At that point a dozen or so motorists put their hands on their horns at the same time, drowning out the last of Mr. Dooley's sentence. This infuriated the cop, who blew his whistle and waved his arms until most of the honking came to a halt. Suddenly he looked down at this thin, bespectacled old-timer who seemed unruffled by the commotion. The cop's eyes flickered as an idea was born.

"You say your name is Dooley?"

"Timothy Patrick Aloysius Dooley. Born in County Roscommon, Ireland, land of the sheep-stealers."

A smile creased the cop's face.

"Dennis Finneran here. County Mayo, God help us."

"'Tis true," Mr. Dooley said, nodding his head sympathetically. "The ground is barren there. Hard to grow potatoes."

The honking started again slowly, then built to a crescendo. Officer Finneran pulled out his service revolver and fired two shots in the air. The drivers nearby took their hands off their horns. Finneran checked the safety and fired a third shot into the Brooklyn skies. There was a funereal silence. He stood on the bumper of the car in front of him and braced himself on the hood.

"The first Yahoo that makes a sound is going down to the station house. And the rest of you will be stuck here while we are waiting for the Paddy wagon."

He jumped down from the fender and turned to Mr. Dooley.

"So you're on your way to see your Aunt Mary? She must be getting up there, Mr. Dooley. Well, let's take a look at these directions you've got here. O.K., this is where you are. Now I'm going to let you take a left turn at this corner because you need to go down for about a half mile till you come to a Catholic Church. St. Brigit of the Martyrs, it is called. Well, at St. Brigit's you hang a—"

***

Mr. Dooley held Aunt Mary spellbound for nearly a half-hour telling the story of the cow at Bradford Junction that fell asleep on the railroad tracks and delayed the 8:22 out of New Brunswick for 16 minutes. He had a second helping of lemon meringue pie, a healthy belt of Bushmills Irish whiskey, and was invited by his hostess to say the grace after meals. Then when Bertha and three of Leo's cousins, who lived nearby and had stopped over for dinner, lined up to kiss Aunt Mary good- bye, Mr. Dooley took his place right behind them and gave Aunt Mary such a hug she had to come up for breath. But she seemed to like it and told Leo and Bertha to be sure to bring Mr. Dooley with them the next time they came to Brooklyn, whether they had furniture for St. Jude or not.

Mr. Dooley was still grinning like Alice's Cheshire cat when he got in the back of Leo's Ford. It was only after they had traveled about thirty miles west of the Holland Tunnel that the smile began to fade from Mr. Dooley's eyes. He wished now that he had called Molly and told her that he would be late. But he knew what she would have said. It would have spoiled everything. Molly didn't understand anything about the Brotherhood of Railroad Trainman and she certainly wouldn't have understood Aunt Mary and the chairs and mattress for St. Jude. +++++

THE IRISHMAN WHO BATHED IN VICKS VAPORUB

The first mass at Our Lady of Perpetual Chastity Roman Catholic Church in Jersey City was at six in the morning, but my grandfather prepared for it by getting up at four. As soon as he swung his legs over the side of the bed, he gave my grandmother a good solid swipe in the ribs to make sure she was awake as well.

"Get up, Woman," he would bray into her ears. He never called her Mary, her Christian name. Mary Mulligan, 91 at the time, happened to be a woman, so that's what she got called. He had no great sympathy for her because of her age: he was 96 himself.

Years later when I examined the cluttered cell in which they slept— one small bed, an island bordered north, east, south, and west by four altars dedicated to the Blessed Virgin, the Sacred Heart of Jesus, St. Joseph, and St. Patrick—I wondered how the two of them managed to dress in the dark at 4 a.m. without bumping into the statues. He never accepted the concept of electricity, and besides, even at his age he was too modest to let Mama, as the family called her, see him half-dressed. Sex to him must have been doing it in the dark with all his clothes on and praying that the Blessed Virgin et al were not watching. Mama probably didn't care one way or the other, for she had spent a lifetime of going along with Papa. Only when he had his pants and shoes on would he light one of the four vigil candles. The heavy odor of the church-scented wax would drift into my room and wake me up.

"Woman, bejasus, we'll be late for the holy mass if you don't stir your arse."

"But, Papa, it's only four o'clock and the church isn't far."

It was, in fact, two houses away. One of things my mother had insisted upon when buying a home was that it be close to a Catholic church so that Mama and Papa could walk to mass every day. My father had other criteria for selecting a house, but he was trapped. After all, how could he say speak out against two nice old people who enjoyed going to church? Father O'Donnell, the pastor, certainly liked the idea. On rainy days he would be there at the St. Joseph's altar with only the altar boys to keep him company, if it weren't for my grandparents.

I remember the sweet smell of the candles one particularly freezing day in December many years ago. I looked out the window and saw that Krumgold's postage-stamp lawn, my best haven in ring-a-leavio games, was covered with snow almost hedge-high. How was Mama ever going to make it through the blizzard?

"Hurry up, Woman," my grandfather growled, as he creaked his way down stairs using the St. Patrick's vigil candle to light his way.

"I'm coming, Papa."

What a disaster awaited the two of them that snowy morning! We might never have known, because Papa was close-lipped and resented anyone being privy to his movements. But Mama, taking a considerable risk, told all.

There the two of them were, ridiculous in the snow on the top steps of Our Lady of Perpetual Chastity's at 5:30 a.m. like punch-drunk pigeons, lost in the swirling flakes of winter. And Papa knew that John the Sexton didn't open the door until a quarter to six.

5:35.

5:40.

5:45—

My grandfather gave the huge brass knob a rough squeeze.

5:50.

Another squeeze; this time an angry one.

5:55.

"John, where the hell are you?"

"Oh, my!" ejaculated my grandmother.

6:00.

Papa's exasperation had reached its boiling point. He thought to himself that by this time he could have been in the front of the church fingering his rosaries as Father O'Donnell made his solemn, albeit sleepy, entrance in a long white skirt and alb.

6:05—"John, where—?"

6:10—Still no John.

6:15—"Damn that man. Damn him to h——-"

"Papa, shhhh!"

6:20—The sound of a lock moving. The doorknob turned from the inside. Papa grabbed it furiously and pulled it towards him, sending a tiny hill of freshly fallen snow cascading down the steps.

"John," he shouted hoarsely, "it's time ye got yer lazy arse out of bed."

But it wasn't John. The sexton had been suddenly stricken with the flu, and it was Father O'Donnell himself, considerably behind schedule, who had unlocked the door. Papa stared at the black cassock in disbelief. Suddenly he plunged both knees into the snow-covered top step.

"Begging yer pardon, Father," he cried out, blessing himself." Begging yer pardon."

Mama told my mother on the promise that she would not reveal Papa's embarrassment to anyone. My mother told my father, who told Uncle Tom, who told Uncle Mickey, who told my brother and me. Papa never knew officially that we knew, but the suppressed snickers he observed as he made his entrances and exits gave him a pretty good idea.

**

Although he was usually the only man in church besides Father O'Donnell and John the Sexton, Papa always formally dressed when he went to Mass—black suit, black tie, white starched shirt, and $20 ankle-high shoes from Coward's.

Nowadays twenty bucks might just about cover the cost of a fancy pair of socks. But at that time you could buy a name-brand suit with two pair of pants for less than that. And if you were a kid, you got the same deal for ten bucks and a free baseball bat. Sometimes a whistle too.

It may sound extravagant then for a nonagenarian to be going around buying twenty dollars shoes, but everybody suspected Papa was loaded. And Papa must have sensed our suspicions and did everything he could to throw us off the track. One way was to buy shoes only infrequently. By changing them shortly after the six o'clock mass and alternately putting on one of his four old pairs, he managed to make a pair of church shoes last him about fifteen years. Then he retired it to alternate day-time wear for another ten, tossing it out only when Borchiazzo the cobbler refused to put on another set of half-soles. Papa hated to throw anything away.

He met Mama by the River Suck, which divides his native Roscommon from her Galway. She said he came from "the land of the sheep stealers"; he retaliated by taking her to the fair in Ballygar and telling her of his dream to come to America.

And so they got married in a little thatched-roof church in Athlone and sailed for Jersey City, New Jersey.

He got a job on the waterfront as a longshoreman at $7. a week. By the time he was raising a family he was making $11, plus some stray bananas that he assured himself had fallen from the boat and were damaged. He gave Mama the bananas and $5 to run the flat, feed Uncle Tom, Aunt Caroline, Uncle Mickey and my mother and he banked the other $6. As his salary inched up he maintained just about the same ratio of money spent to money saved. When he retired he must have had close to a million dollars in the bank, thanks to the miracles of compound interest. Nevertheless, the older he became, the more suspicious he was of banks. The family had the feeling that after he finally was forced to retire from the docks he took most of his money out of the bank and hid it somewhere. Yet with thousands of dollars apparently within easy reach, he was still a reluctant shoe-buyer.

It was my father who took him to Coward's. Papa tried out several pairs of shoes, walking up and down the full length of the store. Back again to the patient salesman. Then down the long aisle again. Surreptitiously he wandered out into the street. He did not ask permission because he did not think they would trust him. Certainly he would not have trusted that young salesman with the red bow tie if the situation had been reversed. He slyly scraped the soles of the shoes against the curb, testing their durability. Inside the store again, he sat down and squinted at the inside of each shoe with the concentration of Estragon. Finally realizing the inevitable—that he was going to have to give up some money if he wanted to walk home with the shoes under his arm—he approached the salesman, who had been receiving an economic and sociological briefing on Papa from my father.

"They squeak a bit, y'know," he said, by way of wearing the salesman down.

"I'm sorry about that, sir," the salesman replied, catching my father's wink. "That's not our No. 1 shoe. Would you like to try a more expensive style?"

My grandfather turned white as a sepulcher. He hated to do business with these tinkers every fifteen years.

"N-no, no! These will be foine as long as they're the cheapest ones ye got."

He paused and sought to paint his face with its most forlorn, pathetic look. Despite his age, he was so healthy looking that it was only with extreme effort that he was able to appear helpless.

"Now how much money will ye be charging a poor ould man like me for these cheap shoes?"

"Twenty dollars."

Papa had thought his sad look would bring the price down to a least $19. He pretended to swoon.

"My God, man, twinty dollars! Do ye know that I have been out of work for nearly twinty years?"

Papa, ever aware of the punishment of God and Father O'Donnell, was telling the truth. He had been forced to retire from the docks at the age of 75.

"I'm sorry, sir," the salesman responded, returning my father's wink. "I don't set the prices."

"Ye don't, do ye now?" Papa answered angrily. "If ye don't, who does thin?"

"Why, Mr. Coward, sir."

"Hmmmmmp. Well, bring yer Mister Coward out here. Tell him an ould man would like a bit of a talk with him about the way he's taking advantage of the unemployed."

The salesman paused and looked for a signal from my father. It had been raining all morning, and the com- mission on rubbers was peanuts. He decided the adventure with my grandfather would tickle the boys at Dohoney's after the fourth round of drinks.

"I can't bring Mr. Coward here, sir."

"Oh, is that right? And why not if I may ask, young feller?"

From behind the galoshes rack my father began to slice the air with both arms, simulating a breaststroke. It was January.

"He's in Florida, sir."

This infuriated Papa. He realized that he was at a *cul de sac*. "In Flo-ree-da. Flo-ree-da, indeed! No wander the tinker can charge twinty dollars for a cheap pair of shoes."

He stared hopelessly at the shoes. He had been certain his walking stiffly and his furious pinching at the leather would have knocked off at least a dollar and a half from the price. But with Mister Coward in—

"All right, all right. I'll take them, even if I have to die a poor man. But make sure ye put an extra pair of shoe- laces in the box."

The salesman waved his thanks to my father. It was not every day that the customer's companion was on the side of the salesman. He was tempted to invite my dad to Dohoney's to give the story a bit more authenticity.

"And a shoe harn, too," Papa called after him.

***

Papa never took a bath in his life: he used Vicks *VapoRub* instead.

Vicks probably wasn't around when he was young, but neither were bathtubs in his part of Ireland. When he discovered Vicks, he fell in love with the little blue bottle and considered bathing an anathema. I know, because he began Vicks-ing himself in my bedroom every morning, starting about seven o'clock.

As soon as he came in, he quickly got out of his church clothes, folded them carefully for the next morning and placed them in the drawer beneath the St. Patrick's altar. He stored his precious Coward shoes in a cabinet under the Sacred Heart of Jesus altar and locked it securely. Then he gathered up his jumper, old trousers and shoes, sewing kit and bottle of Vicks. Having the same confidence in the integrity of his family as Gregory Samoa, he locked the bedroom door with the only key. Why he never had one made for Mama, I'll never know; it couldn't be that he thought she would swipe his good shoes because he always locked them up separately. Now, clad only in tattered red long johns, which he wore summer and winter, and a pair of black socks that had been relegated to casual wear after ten years of service at the six o'clock mass, he padded his way down the hall to my room.

No matter how sound asleep I was, the pungent smell of the Vicks and the grunts and groans from Papa as he shoveled gobs of the greasy stuff underneath his longjohns always woke me up. He was a frenetic Vicks-er, convinced that heavy doses of it smeared generously—a strange word for him—about his body guaranteed longevity. He stank considerably, what with the heavy combination of body odor and Vicks.

I never knew why of all the family I was so honored by Papa, but it may have been because in those days I had a good eye and fairly steady hands, and he needed me to thread his needle. As soon as he finished Vicks-ing, he wiped his hands on my sheets and tugged at my feet. Papa wasn't much for unnecessary words. Usually after I wearily guided the thread through the tiny eyelet with Papa tapping his feet impatiently, neither of us being much into sexual significances in those days, I escaped for a try at the bathroom. But sometimes I would hold my nose and watch Papa sew, so fascinated was I with his multi-colored jumper.

In the beginning it was probably a regular blue denim shirt. However, each time it sprang a hole, Papa sewed it. When years spread the hole as big as his fist, he scrounged around for a vagrant piece of material—part of an old red handkerchief, a piece of brown rug, a slice of Mama's old purple drawers, it didn't matter—and he filled the void. As the years went by there were so many eclectic patches that it was impossible to find a piece of the original blue denim. Papa had reached the status of one who makes rainbows, but he was less interested in aesthetics than he was in escaping the haberdasher. He had several of these multi-colored jumpers, which he wore and repaired for decades, walking about the neighborhood looking very much like a human quilt, much to the embarrassment of my mother.

Mom was a hard-working, easy-going woman in just about every respect but one: Papa. When it came to her father, Mother was a snob. She was so worried that the neighbors would discover the man Papa really was that she felt it necessary to cover his tracks and pass him off as a likeable old Irish eccentric whose grandparents lived in a castle and who traced his ancestry back to the days of the Kings of Ireland. Thus when Papa's red flannel underwear became caked with Vicks and he gave it a casual rinse—soap and water was apparently all right for clothes but not people—and hung it on the line, Mother hurriedly reeled it in and dried it out in the cellar. She begged him to wear his church clothes all day, to stop scrounging the streets looking for junk to sell, and to desist from haggling with the Hungarian ragman when people were watching, but Papa simply told her to mind her own business.

Papa couldn't care less what people thought of him, except perhaps Father O'Donnell, and that was only from 6 to 6:20 a.m. as he raced through the mass, fudging on some of the Latin. Papa's philosophy on what the neighbors thought was direct and simple. "Thinking is for tinkers," he would say and never alter his position. On the other hand, Mother was not only obsessed with maintaining the good opinion of the people around Boyd Avenue, but she was also convinced that she had successfully hoodwinked the whole neighborhood, despite Papa's daily jaunts up and down the streets in his tattered jumpers and trousers in search of old tinfoil from discarded cigarette packages to sell to Oscar, the Hungarian junkman.

***

To maintain her image of Papa, Mother felt it imperative to keep the neighbors out of the house for fear of their seeing Papa's trappings, smelling his Vicks, or hearing one of his candid remarks. She still shuddered every time she recalled how Papa had almost blown the marriage of her sister, Caroline, to a wealthy dental supplies magnate.

Aunt Caroline had been remarkably successful in keeping her intended, Art, away from Papa. She would meet him on the corner in a more fashionable neighborhood five blocks away. But one day Art insisted on meeting her parents.

"I want to see if your mother is as pretty as you," Art had argued.

As they climbed the stairs of the urine-drenched cold-water flat to the sixth floor, where Mama and Papa and their four children lived at the time, Aunt Caroline hoped for a quick cup of tea and a fast good-bye. Arriving out of breath, Art smiled graciously and seemed not to notice the stench from Papa's snuff boiling on the wood-burning stove. He stirred his spoon through the tea leaves and stared admiringly at Mama's strong, yet sweet, features. Then he turned to Papa.

"May I have the milk, Mr. Mulligan?"

"Go to the tylet, the second door down the hall," Papa advised him. "Ye'll find it on the fire escape. And take it aisy on the milk. The robber in the delicatessen downstairs charges me two cents a quart for it."

There were no refrigerators in those days, and Papa only bought ten-cent pieces of ice on summer days when the temperature approached 90.

***

On one occasion Mother abandoned her game plan. She had a distant cousin who was a monsignor, a rank she placed somewhere among the Dukes and certainly higher than Father O'Donnell. When she noticed that Papa had been taking longer and longer scavenger hunts, especially in the late afternoons, she wrote to the monsignor to invite him to a mid-afternoon tea. Once he accepted, she invited my teacher and our committeeman's wife to impress them with the royalty in our family. She and Mama baked raisin cakes all morning. She got out the special linen tablecloths and gold-tinged dishes, usually reserved for after-funeral snacks. She polished the brass knobs on the dining room door and soaked the banister, which skirted the west end of the dining room on its way upstairs, with 436 furniture oil, the most expensive stuff that Joe-the-Gyp sold.

Her part was a success. Miss Godell, my teacher, and Mrs. Carey, the committeeman's wife, were awestruck by the solemnity with which Monsignor Donovan said grace. He stretched it out so long that it seemed like the mass on Holy Thursday. After promising to scrub my fingernails, I was invited to join the group for dessert. I remember the silver dishes looking so shiny that I could see the reflection of the monsignor's white starched collar between the raisin muffins.

It happened so suddenly that Mother did not have a chance to improvise. Papa pulled on the brass knob of the dining room door and entered, wearing his raggediest jumper—it looked like it was made of the flags of a dozen countries—and carrying a sack filled with old cigarette wrappings and bits and pieces of wire on his back. He headed for the stairs without a word and began to make his way up to his room, while his audience in the dining room stared at him in amazement. The monsignor swallowed a mouthful of sherry the wrong way and broke into a coughing fit. This apparently attracted the attention of my grandfather, for he swung around to survey the group below, looking at each one carefully, and then at the elegant array of buns, cakes, cookies and biscuits. He rested his eyes on my mother.

"Another shingle off the roof," he said. And he continued up the stairs to lock up the treasures in his bag in the top drawer of the St. Joseph's altar.

***

The Schulte cigar box was one of the family's most intriguing mysteries. Aunt Caroline was convinced that Papa had hundreds of thousand-dollar bills stuffed in it. Uncle Tom wasn't sure. He tended to think that Papa had stashed away gold coins there. Uncle Mickey agreed, although he felt Papa might have loaded it with gold bars. All three were aware that Papa had a bankbook, which he probably also locked in the Schulte cigar box, but they theorized that the real treasure was not in the Jersey City United Savings and Trust Bank, but in the little tin box.

"Papa doesn't really trust banks," Uncle Tom would say. "He just keeps a small amount there so he can get free calendars and lollypops."

Mother had her theories about Papa's cache but felt guilty when she thought of them. She realized her family's great curiosity was generated by the feeling that instant wealth lay inside Papa's little tin box, and although he was a constant source of embarrassment to her, she would rather put up with the disgrace than see him dead so that the old cigar box could finally be opened.

No one had ever seen Papa go through the whole squirreling operation from start to finish—that is, from the time he carried his treasure up the stairs, carefully concealed underneath his jumper, until he emerged triumphantly from the room with the only evidence of the transaction showing in his eyes. However, almost all of us, including Mama, had seen part of the ritual on those days when Papa had been careless and left his door ajar. Comparing notes, my uncles, my aunt, mother, father, grandmother and I put together the following scenario:

The Blessed Virgin's altar had two doors which opened out like a cupboard. Papa would unlock these, exposing a set of four drawers, all locked. In the second one from the top was the Schulte cigar box, which Papa also kept locked with a pair of heavy chains and two padlocks. Counting the bedroom door, five separate unlocking procedures were necessary before Papa could make his deposit. Uncle Tom was the one who observed the two chains around the box. He didn't get a chance to see any of the contents, because just as Papa opened the box the vigil candle on the altar suddenly flickered out.

***

The Schulte cigar box had a companion: the Schulte alarm clock. However, Papa called it a watch and carried it around as such in the huge front pocket of his Vicks-soaked jumper. It was a wedding present from my mother—not from his wedding, of course, but *hers*. Papa didn't get around to giving Mother anything when she was married. He apparently thought his willingness to move in with my parents was present enough. Still, Mom thought the occasion warranted some sort of gift-giving between them, so she gave him a dull brown octagonal alarm clock,

Schulte's special of the week. He never said thanks or mumbled that he liked it, but his actions seemed to indicate that he did because from morning till night he carried it about, from the day of my mother's wedding to the evening of his death when the doctor in the emergency room discovered it in the pocket near his heart, ticking away noisily after the latter had stopped.

Despite the thousands of times he pulled it out of his jumper to check the hour, he only dropped it once and, as usual, he blamed his mishap on Mama.

"If ye hadn't been so damned slow moving out of the bedroom, Woman, me watch wouldn't have dropped."

"But I didn't drop it, Papa."

"Ye did, too. Ye hit me hand as I was putting it in me pocket."

"Is it broken, Papa?"

He put it to his ear and heard the familiar ticking, so Mama got off the hook that time. It never stopped running. Running was the essence of that clock. But it became capricious, playing the racehorse today and the wagon horse tomorrow. For a long time Papa did not know what time it was and had to go back to listening to the birds.

Mother's Friday night Bingo indirectly repaired Papa's clock. He discovered that by folding a 25-cent door prize ticket three times and then placing the pasteboard under the side near eight o'clock for two hours every evening it kept perfect time in his pocket the next day. Of course, if Papa wanted to check the time while he was recharging his clock, he had to tilt his head a little. But that was a small inconvenience for the restoration of his precious watch. He had the same folded-over Bingo ticket with him on the day of the railroad accident.

The early-morning boys from McDermott's Pub talked about Papa's clock for years, but never to his face. Somehow it just didn't seem proper to poke fun at a man who had Holy Communion on his tongue less than ten minutes ago. Right after mass Papa pointed Mama in the direction of home and ambled over to McDermott's, the only saloon in town permitted to operate within a minute's walk of a Catholic church. Papa would wash the Host down with three quick Jamesons, his limit for the day ever since he reached eighty. There were times he thought he really ought to stop at two since they were double shots, but the third one was always on the house, so what could he do? On those days when he started to see the leprechauns, he by passed the Vicks-bath and took a long walk instead, in search of Oscar Feld, the Hungarian rag-picker.

***

In the early days of their relationship Papa and Feld tolerated each other because, despite their mutual distrust, they sensed mutual profit. But the longer they dealt with each other, the more acrimonious they became. If Feld offered Papa six cents for a bag of rags, Papa would insist on seven. Feld would finally agree to pay seven cents if Papa would sell his tinfoil for a nickel a pound. They finally reached an agreement after Papa inched Feld's last offer to five and a half cents, much to the relief of Mother watching from the living room window and embarrassed by the angry shouting—Feld in Hungarian, Papa in Gaelic—in front of the neighbors.

Tinfoil, the issue that brought the two businessmen together, eventually caused their separation. But it took a long time for Feld to uncover Papa's scheme. There is some question as to whether he ever did discover it by himself, but Uncle Tom, who, according to my father's theory, snitched to Feld, denied vigorously that he gave away Papa's secret.

In the late afternoon Papa, and often my brother Jack and I under coercion, would scour the streets and garbage cans for junk that he could sell to Feld. His biggest objective was old cigarette packages because the insides of them contained a thin sheet of tinfoil. Just before supper he would go to his little workshop in the cellar, separate the tinfoil from the tissue attached to it and roll the foil into a ball for Feld. However, he always soaked the inside of the ball in water and covered it with dry foil to deceive his Hungarian adversary. It barely added a half-ounce to the weight of an eight-pound ball, giving Papa illicit profit of less than one-quarter of a cent per ball, but it was enough to put a twinkle in Papa's shrewd eyes.

Papa's most magnificent coup came in the wake of a violent storm that uprooted trees and knocked over telephone poles. He got $1.89 from Feld for a quarter of a mile of wiring that my brother and I found for him on Virginia Avenue. But Uncle Tom, a balloon-buster from birth, knew how to hit my grandfather where it hurt.

"Papa, the kids told me Feld gave you nearly two bucks for that old telephone wire."

"And whose business is it what I get from that old tinker?"

"Don't you know that wire belongs to the telephone company?"

Papa looked him in the eye curiously. He hadn't expected a question like that. "Tellyphone company or blatherskite company, I care not who *used* to own it. They lost it in the wind."

"Come on, Papa, you go to confession every week, don't you?"

"I do that." He was becoming more apprehensive. Tom, in his opinion, could every day come up with a dozen new ways for causing trouble.

"Well, you'll have to tell Father O'Donnell that you stole the wire. And he'll make you give restitution."

"What the bloody hell is that?"

"It means you'll have to give the money you got from Feld to the phone company."

Papa was beaten. If he couldn't keep it, there was no point in stealing it. He gave my mother the $1.89 and told her to see that the phone company got it. Obviously he didn't trust Uncle Tom with the money.

The restitution business was a bit unsettling and for a while he considered leaving the half-ounce of water out of the tinfoil. However, he wrestled with the angels for only a few nights over that one. Feld always insisted on using the rag wagon's scale for the weighing and Papa rationalized that he needed the little water edge just to break even. But when Feld found out about it he wouldn't come up Boyd Avenue any more, and Papa had to hunt for blocks to track him down. And Feld always insisted on opening up the balls of tinfoil to check for water before he made a deal.

***

The evenings brought out the best in Papa. He would sit on his favorite chair in the corner facing the huge radio that bullied all the other furniture in the room, listening to the relaxing sounds of Mama and Mother scraping pots and pans in the kitchen. Out would come his octagonal alarm clock for its fix with the Bingo ticket. My brother, Jack, and I, though ordered to bed, would sneak down to sit on the bottom steps of the stairs to see the action. We particularly liked to watch Papa sniff snuff, which he made from my father's used cigar stubs, carefully cooking them in water for five minutes or so before jabbing them up each nostril. Then he would turn to either my father, Uncle Tom, or Uncle Mickey, who were sharing the living room with him, and ask one of them to read him the "Deaths."

Since my grandfather could neither read nor write, his link with the daily newspaper was limited to what my uncles read to him. He wasn't interested in the weather and thought the news of the world and of the town was "a bunch of blarney," but he could sit attentively while being read the whole obituary page. Papa in his octogenarian and nonagenarian years had a professional stake in learning which of his colleagues had failed to outlive him and why.

Uncle Tom usually volunteered because he liked to make up a few "Deaths" and entice Papa into thinking he knew the fictitious dead by adding bits of realism, such as identifying them with the docks where Papa used to work.

"Knute Bjornsterne, 63, of Jersey City, died at the Medical Center last night of injuries he sustained when he was accidentally picked up by a grappling hook on Pier 16 Monday and tossed into the Hudson River," Uncle Tom improvised. "Did you know him, Papa?"

The name didn't sound familiar to Papa, but he didn't like to admit that he didn't know longshoremen even 30 years his junior. Besides, it sounded a little like a tinker he used to know.

"Bayornsta—Shure, I know that blatherskite. He could never hold his liquor, that one. Serves him right."

If Mama came in from the dishes in the middle of the obituaries, Uncle Tom usually added a few maudlin touches, describing the deaths of little orphans, devout priests, and saintly old women. He enjoyed the double sensation of seeing Mama cry and Papa snicker at the same time.

"Woman, in the name of God in Heaven will ye quit yer slobbering? I can't hear half the names. And Tom, ye don't have to read so bloody fast. I don't want to be missing any."

Some evenings when the obituaries and Uncle Tom's imagination were slim, Uncle Mickey would get a rise out of Papa by asking Mama to tell the story of the bottle of soda pop. Papa would snort and sniff heavily with his snuff and bellow out, "Had ye nothing to do but waste yer toime blathering about something that happened sivinty years ago and wasn't true in the first place?"

Mama, however, encouraged by her audience, would tell it any way.

"Well, it was back in County Galway, y'know, and I was seventeen years old and was Papa's intended. I ast him one night wouldn't he buy me a sarsaparilla soda pop like I seen Patrick Bannon buying Kathy

Kavanaugh, and he sez to me that a penny was a bloody lot of money for a jar of soda."

Papa would stamp his feet and threaten to go to bed, but Uncle Mickey would supply the transition.

"And so when Papa came over the next night to take you for a walk, you were with that fellow—what's his name, Mama?"

"Ah, shure it was Timmy Muldoon—sooch a handsome young lad," supplied Mama, accurately bridging seven decades.

"And this Muldoon fellow bought you a soda pop and Papa found out about it and became awfully jealous, isn't that right, Mama?"

"And Papa wanted to punch him in the eye, didn't he Mama?" Uncle Tom chimed in.

"Oh he was destroyed all right," Mama agreed, shaking her head reminiscently. "Totally destroyed."

Papa pounded the nearby table, almost upsetting his clock. "And he was the biggest blatherskite this side of the River Suck."

Mama smiled. "And the next night Papa came over early. With cherry pop."

***

Papa confused the radio with the telephone, both recent innovations during his last years. If he were near the phone when it rang, he would pick it up to stop it from ringing, but he only listened; he would no more speak to a phone than my uncles would to a radio. Conversely when the radio was on, he carried on a conversation with it. In those days there was a popular radio program called "The Goldbergs." Papa thought they were the Goldbergs who ran the little candy store on Bergen Avenue. Every time he visited the store he chided them for not answering him when he was talking to them on the radio the previous evening.

Papa also had it in for Uncle Don, the radio age's precursor to Captain Kangaroo, for not paying attention to his remarks, but he liked the man somewhat because he was constantly telling little children about their bad habits: in those days it was biting their nails and not eating their spinach. Major Bowles Amateur Hour was his favorite. Whenever an off-key singer was given the gong in the middle of a song and sent off stage in disgrace and embarrassment, Papa's face would break out into the closest approximation of a smile that I ever observed on him. He didn't seem to notice that the Major was not responding to his approval of the poor singer's rejection, so great was Papa's satisfaction at the humiliating sound of the gong.

"Bang it again, Major," Papa would call out enthusiastically. "Bang it again."

The show was boring to Papa only when the contestants were good. On these occasions he would leave for bed long before Bowles reminded his audience of the wheel of fortune.

"Round and round it goes," he would say, "and where it stops nobody knows."

That was usually Pap's signal to reach for his faithful clock and make his way to bed, not caring whether Mama followed him or not. He wound the clock in synchronization with his movements up the stairs to the room of the four altars.

One night Uncle Tom stopped Papa in half-flight. He had read a long list of "Deaths" and Major Bowles had gonged three contestants, so he thought Papa might be in a good mood.

"Hey, Pop," my uncle called out as my grandfather turned his eyes from his Schulte to Uncle Tom below, "what time is it?"

Papa squinted carefully at the octagonal relic. It was dark near the top of the stairs and his ancient eyes had trouble seeing the digits. Finally he located the two hands, but instead of announcing the hour he stared down at my uncle.

"And what's the matter with yer own clock?"

He turned his back and shuffled up the stairs.

"Can you imagine?" Uncle Tom smiled, winking at Uncle Mickey. "He's so cheap he won't even give you the right time."

***

It wasn't a brand new car, or even a good-looking used one. Uncle Mickey said it might have been one of the first Packards ever made. But it was Uncle Tom's first car, and it was the first time the whole family was going to go any place together, except for occasional trips between Jersey City and Hoboken on the Jackson trolley. He was going to take us all to Manasquan, New Jersey, and we were to have the whole day on the beach with our own pails and shovels. And we were going to stick our feet into the Atlantic Ocean.

My brother Jack and I were the most excited, but Uncle Tom and Uncle Mickey were laughing a lot for early in the morning, and Mother and Mama seemed to be having fun putting the lettuce and tomato sandwiches in white wax paper, the ham and cheese in the tan wrappers that the Dugan's bread came in, and the apples, oranges, and bananas in old bakery bags. My father, who had not ridden in many cars, had his doubts about us all fitting in, but Uncle Tom told him there was plenty of room in a Packard.

As you can see, that takes care of everyone but Papa. He said he would never go in any machine driven by Uncle Tom. Besides, he pointed out, he had a busy day ahead of him. He knew where there were loads of tin cans, and he was going there right after mass and McDermott's before the other tinkers got their hands on them. Mother had tried to persuade him to come, arguing that the salt water would be good for his arthritis, but Papa, as always, insisted on having his own way. She was a little upset about leaving him alone, but my father and Uncle Mickey both convinced her that there would be more room in the Packard, and that with Papa home Uncle Tom would keep his mind on the road.

It was a blue-sky day with an ocean to match. Outside of a little sunburn which Mama eased by putting slices of raw potatoes on my legs during the ride home, it was one of the most delightful days of my childhood. When Uncle Tom pulled up to the house at ten o'clock that night, there was a policeman standing out front. He said Papa was dead. He had been hit by a freight train while wandering around the railroad tracks looking for old tin cans.

The first thing that came to my mind was my bedroom where Papa visited every morning. I wondered how it would smell without Vicks and how long it would take before that telltale aroma lost itself in the old walls. Then I remembered one particular time he came to my room to see me when I was sick. It was a strange visit, because Papa rarely ventured from routine. I sat in bed propped up by two pillows with six adventures of *The Rover Boys* on each side of me for comfort, when he burst into the room.

"Why aren't ye in school, lad?"

"I'm sick, Papa."

He stared at me in disgust. "You're a blatherskite."

"Honest, Papa, I can hardly talk. Can't you tell I have a sore throat?"

He couldn't read, but he knew the difference from dull-looking textbooks and the colorful jackets of *The Rover_Boys*. "Why aren't ye studying yer schoolbooks thin? What's all this blarney?"

He left, slamming the door behind him to show his displeasure. For some stupid reason I felt guilty, even though I had a fever of 102. He returned in about five minutes, carrying a dirty old brown bag. He tossed it on my bed.

"Here, ye little tinker. Eat these and get back to school."

In the bag were ragged chunks of white rock candy that he had probably been hoarding for years. They were a little dirty on the outside, but that didn't bother me. Even as a little kid I realized that I was the recipient of one of the few things Papa had ever willingly given away in his life. They looked liked the jagged little chips we would beg the iceman for when his wagon rolled down our street, but they tasted warm and soothing as the surprise itself and the next day the scratches in my throat had melted away.

When I thought of Papa's spontaneous gift, I felt sorry for this old man suddenly placed on a stretcher and taken to the hospital with all of his family miles away. Papa had been in the hospital only once before in his life. He had the habit of trying to get the wax out of his ears with a tiny straight pin. Once he plunged it in too far and my parents had to call the emergency squad. As you can guess, my mother was a nervous wreck all the way to the hospital in the ambulance. Papa seemed unfazed, but perhaps slightly annoyéd by all the fuss. They had to use a powerful magnet to suck the pin out.

"Let this be a lesson to you, Pop," the interne said. "Never put anything in your ear smaller than your elbow."

Papa looked him in the eye with scorn.

"Right, Pop? Nothing smaller than your elbow."

Papa got off the examining table and placed his hand on his sore ear. "The next toime," he said, "I'll use a bigger pin."

***

The day after the funeral, Samuel Katz, the lawyer, called my father. Papa had left $876,807.42, his jumpers and five pairs of Coward's shoes in his will. Of this amount $876,307.42 went to Our Lady of Perpetual Chastity, $100. each to my mother, Uncle Tom, Uncle Mickey, Aunt Caroline, and Mama, and the jumpers and five pair of Coward's shoes to the Society of St. Vincent de Paul. Katz admitted that this might be a shock to the family whom Papa had lived with all these years, but he pointed out that Papa had told him repeatedly that he wanted to see the church put on a new wing so that Father O'Donnell might attract more worshippers to the six o'clock mass. Of course, the family was free to dispute the will in court, he said. After all, Katz insisted, he was just relaying the wishes of the deceased.

My father thought the family should contest the will on the grounds of ecclesiastical lunacy. It was all right for Papa to leave his fortune to the Church, he argued, but how about the church that had been Papa's home all these years? Mother and Mama had certainly done their penance living with Papa, he said, and were entitled to a little sanctifying grace. Uncle Tom wasn't sure; he thought it might be blood money. Mother didn't like the idea of going to court against the Roman Catholic Church, her umbilical cord with life. Aunt Caroline, widow of the man who had once fetched milk from the fire escape behind Papa's "tylet" while on his way to becoming a millionaire by inventing a rum-flavored dental floss, was furious to see all that money slipping through her fingers. She felt that any man who would give almost all of his money to the church and practically nothing to his loving family must undoubtedly have been senile. She urged the family to push the outrage right to the Supreme Court, if necessary.

Judge Pean heard testimony from Father O'Donnell, who said Papa was a good man who went to mass and communion every day of his life and therefore had full control of his wits.

"He gave to Our Lady of Perpetual Chastity because our church was his life," Father O'Donnell said. "Nothing else mattered to him as much. The record shows that."

Jack McDermott of McDermott's Pub across the way was another good witness for the defense. He told Judge Pean that on the very day Papa died he had a profound conversation with the deceased shortly after "the saintly ould man had come down the center aisle of Our Lady of Perpetual Chastity's, his hands clasped in prayer and the Sacred Host on his tongue." (McDermott did not bother to add that during the interim he had described as "shortly after" Papa had washed down the Holy Wafer with three Jamesons and one short beer.)

"Shure, there was no problem with the auld man. You can tell that by the things he said to me the morning of that tragic day. He told me he loved his family and, of course, all of mankind, but he had a particular soft spot for Our Lady of Perpetual Chastity and all the grand priests and nuns there. That's why he left them his fortune. Shure, there can be no doubt about it."

McDermott said it with a straight face and even a hint of a tear in the corner of his left eye. He knew better, of course, but he also knew Father O'Donnell could have his liquor license removed with the snap of his fingers, McDermott's Pub being the only saloon in Jersey City within one block of a church. Sometimes life's necessities overwhelm life's truths, he reasoned.

Judge Pean's address to the court was brief:

"There is no doubt that Michael Mulligan had full possession of his faculties, even at his advanced age, for the record shows that he was a devout church-goer. Although it seems evident that he loved his family very much, the court must decide on the weight of the evidence, which shows that he had an even stronger love for Our Lady of Perpetual Chastity, to whom be bequeathed most of his fortune. It is regretful, however, that he did not deem it fitting to leave more than $100 each to his wife and four children. This is indeed a most painful case."

There was plenty of drinking that night. Even Mama took a few nips of the Jameson that somehow had not found its way into Papa's will. Uncle Tom was leading the family into a chorus of "For he's a jolly good fellow" when the doorbell rang and Aunt Caroline, resplendent in mink and anger, appeared.

"The tin box!" she screamed. "Did anyone check the tin box?"

Before Uncle Tom could sigh "No," Aunt Caroline and her chauffeur were up the stairs. Mama had been sleeping on the couch in the living room since Papa had died, so her bedroom door was locked.

"Break it down!" she ordered the chauffeur.

Mother demurred. "B-but..."

No time for keys, the door came splintering down, shattered with two stout blows from Wilbur, the 240-pound chauffeur. I was amazed how much less gloomy the room looked without a door. Light from the skylight flickered in and I saw my grandfather in silvery Vicks in the splendor of rays from a full moon. Uncle Tom joined Caroline at the Blessed Virgin's altar.

"Rip it open," she ordered.

With his bare hands Wilbur broke the lock. Uncle Mickey joined the group with a crowbar. Out came the second drawer, exposing the long-sought-after Schulte cigar box.

The chauffeur struggled with the chain.

"Get a hacksaw, Wilbur," ordered my aunt.

My father produced the weapon a minute later and Wilbur and Uncle Tom sawed open first one, then another, padlock. It seemed as if five sets of hands reached the top of the old cigar box simultaneously to rip it open and resolve its mystery forever.

To their amazement they discovered four chocolate lollypops from The United Savings and Trust Bank of Jersey City, a ball of string, six piece of rock candy, and two empty Vicks jars. +++++

ONE MORE FOR THE ROAD

Taughmaconnell is a tiny rural community in western Ireland a few miles from the River Suck, which separates County Galway from County Roscommon. Taughmaconnell people are for the most part farmers. During the planting season, the summer, and the harvest, they are rarely to be seen in what might generously be called the little hamlet in which they live; but if one traveled across the fields to their farms, almost anyone in the community could be discovered atop a tractor or behind a team of horses, plowing the soil.

Almost anyone is the correct terminology because there were always a few of the townsfolk in the center of Taughmaconnell, where all the action was. And the hub of the hamlet could be described in four words: Martin Joe Finneran's Pub. Although the Guinness and the John Jameson flowed easily from six in the morning until close to midnight when a weary Martin Joe finally turned off the tap, the heaviest drinking was done when the day's chores were over and the farmers came in from the fields to spin a few tales, sing a cluster of songs, and dampen their dry, parched throats.

And so life rolled on effortlessly in Taughmaconnell, and especially in Martin Joe Finneran's. For years. For decades. For what seemed like a blissful eternity, until one day Martin Joe became so ill he had to close down his pub.

"Nothing serious," old Doc O'Brien told the publican. "But ye are going to have to take it a little aisy from now on. After all, ye are 84 years old."

Martin Joe paid little heed. How Doc O'Brien had figured out his age was more than he could understand. Martin Joe didn't know for sure, but he always thought he was 86. So he returned to business as usual, and would have gone another decade or so without interruption had he not had a bad fall and broken a leg while preparing to tap a keg of Guinness. This time he closed the pub for a week and when he opened it again, he cut the hours, telling his customers that henceforth he would not open at six any more, preferring to stay in bed and rest. He opened at noon.

But as time went by, his leg began to bother him on damp, rainy days. And in Taughmaconnell, as is the case with all of Ireland, there is no shortage of damp, dank days. On his ninetieth birthday he thought of closing the pub entirely, but neighbors and friends persuaded him to keep it open, if only for a couple of hours a night.

"We can get by on two hours of drinking, especially in the planting season," Jackie Flynn told him. "We need to be getting up especially early in the spring, so if ye could open from eight to ten at night, we'd have enough time to get our drinking done."

"And besides we heard all the same stories a dozen or more times," Dermod McDermott pointed out. "Shure, and if we know we only have two hours, we'd be tempted to spit our tales out faster than a jackrabbit in heat."

"Right, and the Guinness always tastes the sweetest when a man fasts from it all day," Denny O'Reilly pointed out.

And so Martin Joe Finneran, game leg and all, awoke from his afternoon nap each day in time to wash up, sprinkle fresh sawdust on the floor, and open up his pub by 8 p.m. He didn't always stay until closing time, occasionally leaving that assignment to his old pal, Eugene Bannon, who filled in for him two to three nights a week.

But Bannon was a little younger than Finneran and perhaps a tad more mischievous. Therefore, it wasn't long before Bannon persuaded the publican to extend the drinking hours to eleven. The Guinness flowed freely, the ballads of the days of the troubles wafted crisply into the cool Taughmaconnell nights, and the plaintive wail of Wilbur Gannon's flute echoed as far off as the eastern shores of the River Suck. It was a grand time and the folk of Taughmaconnell remember it well.

Then one night while Martin Joe Finneran, nonagenarian with a purpose, was singing the last chorus of *Come back, Paddy Reilly, to Ballyjamesduff*, he keeled over into a plate of baked spuds, at the same time upsetting a tumbler of John Jameson's Irish Whiskey.

"He'll be all right," Eugene Bannon assured the patrons of the pub after leaving his old pal in the hospital. "He has a little brain damage. They don't know if it's from banging his head on the plate of spuds tonight or whether he has had brain damage since he was born. Anyway, he told me to give everyone here a drink on the house."

And drink they did, every night for a week. But when word came that Martin Joe had been sent to a nursing home, Bannon closed the place and brought the key to his old friend.

***

For a man active all his life, whether bending his arms and legs on his farm during the day, or bending his elbow at his pub during the night, life at the Saints-Be-Praised Nursing Home was pretty tame for Martin Joe. His only relief from the tedium of the strict discipline of the Sisters of the Precious Blood was occasional conversations with Timmy McBride and Kevin Sweeney, two fellow nonagenarians, about the Easter Monday Uprising and their days with the IRA, but Mother Mary Theresa, the head nun, usually broke up their talks with a reminder that "All this reminiscing about the bloody days of yore is not the Christian thing to do."

After a hundred days of solitude, he ventured down to the end of the hall of the nursing home for the first time. Maybe he had gone stir-crazy, or maybe he saw what he wanted to see. At any rate he began disappearing from his bed around eight o'clock every night after that.

Though rigid in the daytime when most of the staff was working, the operation at the Saints-Be-Praised Nursing Home was rather loose at night, so at first Finneran's nocturnal disappearances went unnoticed. In fact if Mother Mary Theresa had not chanced to saunter down the hall one evening to see if she had lost her rosaries under one of the cushions of a lounge chair that afternoon while she was praying for the repose of the lost souls in Purgatory, Martin Joe's peregrinations might possibly have never been discovered. At first she could not believe what she was seeing.

"Mr. Finneran, what in the name of the good Lord in heaven do ye think ye are doing?"

Martin Joe considered that a question he did not have to answer, because he was not thinking about what he was doing at all. He had done this so many times that he could do it without a bit of thinking. For there at the end of the hall were two lounge chairs, covered by a long wooden door to form something that looked like a table. In this case, however, it was used as a bar, and sitting on the door were three-half-filled tumblers, a bottle of John Jameson's Irish Whiskey and a nicely aged pot of poteen, brewed by Finneran himself ten years ago. Standing behind the upturned door and facing down the hall was Martin Joe. To his left and obscured in the shadows were his two nonagenarian companions, Timmy McBride and Kevin Sweeney.

"Do ye not hear me, Mr. Finneran?" Mother Mary Theresa repeated.

"That I do, Mother Mary," the publican replied. "Tell me now, what will ye have to drink?"

"Where did ye get that door, Mr. Finneran?"

That question seemed to flabbergast Martin Joe. "Over there," he finally said, and as he pointed Mother Mary noticed McBride and Sweeney.

"Oh sweet Jesus! You've broken down the toilet door and turned this foine nursing home into a public house."

"Ah, how can ye say that, Mother Mary—with the three of us having only two bottles between us?"

Mother Mary Theresa wasn't in the mood to debate. She put the police whistle which she had hanging from her neck to her mouth and issued an ear-splitting blast. Sister Bridget of the Sacred Name of Jesus and Sister Ignatius of the Immaculate Conception came running.

"Sister Bridget, give me a hand with this door. If we left it up to these rascals, a body wouldn't have a speck of privacy. And Sister Ignatius, take these two bottles of the devil's brew and pour them down the toilet."

Martin Joe's slightly embalmed eyes came to life. "Shure an' ye can't drown me ten-year-old poteen in the tylet. Ye are a Sister of God. If ever there was one, that's a mortal sin."

But Sister Ignatius, obedient servant of the church that she was, uncorked the two bottles and let them swirl down the toilet simultaneously.

"Shure an' ye are putting a curse on this place," McBride wailed.

Paying no heed, Sister Ignatius waved the bottle of John Jameson's Irish Whiskey at Mother Mary. "This would make a foine candle-holder for Our Lady's altar, don't ye think?"

"Only if ye scrub it out well, Sister. With lye and bleach. And thin I'll have Father O'Malley bless it. And don't throw away the jar. We can use it for a pee-pot."

It was an ignominious ending to the few pleasant evenings Martin Joe had spent at the Saints-Be-Praised Nursing Home. Mother Mary told the board of directors that Finneran was a bad influence on the other patients. Hearing this, Martin Joe readily agreed and was given his release. He returned to his pub and resumed his 8 p.m. openings to the delight of the thirsty folk of Taughmaconnell.

And so once again the Irish whiskey flowed nicely down the gullets of the farmers and their families between 8 and 10 p.m. Martin Joe had an occasional pain in his leg, but he was able to snuff it out with a double shot of poteen. One of the farmers' wives baked him a cake for his 94th birthday. He cut himself a generous slice, toasted his friends and neighbors with one last pot of poteen that he had squirreled away for special occasions, and began a rousing rendition of *The Boys from County Cork.*

> *Ye will find in hist'ry pages heroes of great fame,*
> *The deeds they done, the battles won, and how they got their name*
> *The men who brought the glory to the Orange, White and Green*
> *Were the lads who fought the Englishmen in 1916.*
> *Some of them came from Kerry, some from the County Claire*
> *From Dublin, Wicklow, Donegal, and the boys from ould Kildare*
> *Some from a land beyond the sea—from Boston and New York*
> *All jined to fight the tyrants with the boys from County Cork.*

"Grandeur," called out Jackie Flynn to give Martin Joe encouragement as he paused to wet his lips with poteen before beginning the second verse.

> *Cork gave us McSweeney, a hero brave who died*
> *Dublin gave us Dwyer—*

But the folk in Martin Joe Finneran's Pub in Taughmaconnell were never more to hear the near-indefatigable publican finish his account of the contributions of Dwyer, McBride and the other heroes of 1916. He paused for one last look at the admiring faces that surrounded him, then closed his eyes and died, still standing in his place.

*****

There was no funeral home in Taughmaconnell or anywhere in the area, but Barney Fitzpatrick who ran a pub in Ballinsloe, about 15 miles away, was a part-time undertaker on the side. He brought the body of Martin Joe to his pub, treated the dead man to a derby and his second-best suit and laid him out on the bar. The word of Finneran's demise spread rapidly, and before the shank of the evening had expired, hundreds of neighbors, friends, and drinking pals converged on Fitzpatrick's Pub on bicycle, pony and trap, and even automobile.

The next morning Father O'Malley, who had blessed the John Jameson Irish Whiskey bottle, stopped by to bless the soul of Martin Joe. They brought him to the village church for a simple mass, and then to a little plot of land behind Finneran's Pub for his final resting place. At least forty men and women hopped out of their carts and cars with picks and shovels to dig the grave in shifts of eight at a time. Each group worked vigorously for ten minutes and then gave way to the next line of diggers. Through it all there was a respectful silence. It was the deepest quiet anyone remembered in the presence of Martin Joe. When the hole was deep enough, Eugene Bannon and Dermod McDermott laid two two-by-fours across the grave and six men placed the casket upon it. Then they fastened a rope to the coffin and the men held it tight as the two-by-fours were removed and the body was lowered into the earth. Once again the shovelers went to work, this time covering the casket.

Just as Eugene Bannon was placing a bouquet of roses atop the grave, Mother Mary Theresa came running up, carrying a small box.

"I have something for Mr. Finneran," she called out, gasping for breath.

She opened the box and produced the empty jar of poteen she had taken from Martin Joe when he was in the Saints-Be-Praised Nursing Home.

"Shure we had a grand time with it," Mother Mary said. "We had used it as a pee-pot, but Sister Bridget washed it out good with lye and bleach. And Father O'Malley blessed it. It will be a foine place to put some of them roses."

Bannon considered it an appropriate marker for his old friend, one last jar for the road—though he hoped that wherever Martin Joe was, he wouldn't be thinking of all the ten-year-old poteen that went down the toilet.

Barney Fitzpatrick revealed that long ago he and Martin Joe had made a pact that the one who outlived the other would be the host for the mourners at his pub. At least three hundred folks from Taughmaconnell and its environs showed up, agreeing it was a fine arrangement—for no matter what happened, there was bound to be a grand wake.+++++

II.
From a Child's Point of View

Thou shall not cover they neighbor's wife. Mrs. Vandenberg lived next door. It would take an elephant blanket to cover her.
— A Little Adultery in the Fifth Grade

THE BUTTERFLY RIDE

We could usually count on Knobby coming around shortly after the first heavy snow. When the old maple on our front lawn looked like a huge vanilla ice cream cone ready to melt, Mom would peer out the living room window, as if gauging the amount of snow that had fallen, and announce to anyone within hearing distance that she wouldn't be surprised to hear Knobby knocking on the pantry door within the hour. Then she would start shelling peas and cutting up carrots, potatoes and celery for lamb stew because she knew that's what he liked.

By the time little billows of white steam began escaping from Mom's big gray pot, smoking up the kitchen windows and filling the room with the tangy aroma of meat and vegetables, Knobby would be at the side door, snow drifting down his old brown fedora.

"Miz Cook, looks like the alley needs a cleaning, eh?"

"Why, Knobby, how good to see you again. I'm making lamb stew."

Knobby tipped his hat.

"My favorite, Miz Cook. Can I come through to get the shovel?"

"Please come right in, Knobby. It's in the basement. Same place. When you are through, the stew will be ready. And Mama's baking Irish soda bread."

Knobby would carefully wipe his feet and enter. By that time I had my heavy leather coat and galoshes on. I liked shoveling snow with Knobby. He saw me dressed in my winter work clothes and waved at me.

"Mickey, you want to help?" he would say. "I could use a Bucko on that long alley."

"But if your feet get wet, Mickey, come in at once and change your socks," Mom would say. "Don't stay out there too long."

"I'll take care of the Bucko," Knobby would reassure her. "He's a fine partner. And that's a fact."

***

The Gainsways lived next door and there were less than four feet between the houses. All the windows on the east side of the living room, dining room, and kitchen were dark because of the Gainsways' house. We both had large dwellings, or so it seemed in those days, so the alley between the two houses was long and narrow. There was no place to dump the snow, so Knobby had to carry it either to the front yard by the maple tree or to the back, depending upon where he was shoveling. He wouldn't let me carry the heavy snow through the alley until we got near one of the ends.

"Your job, Bucko, is to get it loose and pile it up," he would say. "Then I'll lug it to the yard."

We had to clear the alley because that was the passageway for the barrels of ashes that Mom and I wheeled out every Tuesday and Friday for Max, the garbage man. Our old furnace in the basement produced ashes half the size of the coal we fed it.

As I think back on it now, it had all the ingredients of a monotonous job. Scrunching my shovel through the snow to make little piles for Knobby's big fat one. Or later on, as we made our way to the front of the house, carrying the snow out myself and tossing it in front of the old maple. Knobby seldom said much as we worked—maybe a "Thata boy" or "You got the arms of a coal digger, Bucko." But somehow it wasn't boring. Maybe it was the clear winter air, so cold that I could make smoke, just by talking. Maybe it was the brilliance of the clean snow, lighting up the dark alley. It was probably both these factors, but I think now it was having Knobby with me, smiling or humming an old song about ice-fishing in Alaska as he worked. And even then I knew I liked it because I was getting hungry for the stew and Irish soda bread and the stories Knobby would tell me as we ate together in the little pantry off the kitchen.

When we had the alley cleared, Knobby would scrape his shovel across the last scraps of snow like a surgeon making sure that the incision was carefully sewn.

"Your mother won't have any trouble navigating this alley, Bucko. Except for a few little strips here and there, you would never have knowed it snowed. Right?"

And then he would usually take out his corncob pipe and a fill it with some stuff he kept in a little white bag in the top pocket of his blue gingham shirt.

"Yeh, Bucko, you have strong hands on the shovel. You would do fine in Pennsylvania."

"Why?"

"Because that's where all the coal mines are. That's where they need the help."

"Help?"

"Yep. That's what everybody needs. Although folks don't want to admit it."

"I don't getcha, Knobby."

And when I said this he would laugh. And laugh. Till this day I don't know what was so funny about a crack like that. But somehow it pleased Knobby. It didn't take much to make Knobby happy.

***

Mom told me that Knobby had been coming around since I was an infant, but the first time I really took notice of him was when I was six years old and he invited me to help him shovel the alley. Mom set out three bowls of stew—one for Knobby, one for my grandmother whom everybody called Mama, and one for me. I was surprised when Knobby stuck his Irish soda bread into the stew.

"You'll get it all wet," I warned.

Knobby laughed that easy laugh of his, making his eyes water as mine did when I cried.

"That's what ya call dunking, my Bucko. Brings out the best in the stew. All the rich flavor settles in the bread."

"Can I dunk, Mom?" I called out to my mother who was mixing batter for raisin cake.

"I suppose, Mickey."

"Are you going to stay with us for awhile, Knobby? You can sleep in my room."

Knobby broke the bread at the end where the soup had softened it and dropped it into his mouth. Then he began to smash it into little pieces with his gums. He didn't have any teeth.

"That's a grand invitation, old pal, but I've got to move on."

"Where are you going, Knobby?"

"Mind ye now, let the man eat," Mama scolded.

"Oh, that's all right, ma'm," he said. "Old Knobby doesn't have any secrets. Bucko, I'm chasing the path of the North Star."

"Where's that?"

He pointed to the kitchen window.

"There she glides now. Right over the backyard fence."

I looked at the top of the fence but couldn't see any star.

"Are you going to take a train?"

"I might. Depends upon whether it's going my way."

"But where is the North Star going?"

My mother put the pan in the oven and called out to me.

"Now isn't that a silly question, Mickey?" she said. "You must think before you talk. You'll never get promoted if you don't think."

"Do you think a lot, Knobby?" I asked.

He didn't answer right away. I figured he was afraid of getting yelled at by my mother for not thinking first.

"Aye, Bucko. I probably do."

"What do you think about?"

Mom lit the oven with a long sulfur match, which sent out a scent like firecrackers, and walked over to have some stew with us. I figured she wanted to hear what Knobby thought about too.

"This morning I was thinking about how fine it would be if I could get a butterfly to give me a ride."

"That's silly," I said.

"You may be right, Bucko, but imagine what fun you'd have, if you could do it. You could fly upside down, between the wires of fences and you could watch the bees making honey."

"What else do you think of?"

"What would happen if a llama could pitch horse-shoes."

"What's a llama, Knobby?"

***

As I got older I organized my questions better and began to uncover some of Knobby's story. He was a hobo, he said, which was different from a tramp because he worked for food.

"Like shoveling alleys?" I asked.

He nodded his head and gummed his Irish soda bread.

"What about when it's not snowing?"

"Well, I might mend umbrellas. Or sharpen knives. Or milk cows."

"Don't you ever want to make money?"

"Why should I?"

That puzzled me. Everyone I knew as old as Knobby and, of course, much younger than he, worked for money. I told him so.

"I guess that's what they like to do."

"Why don't you?"

"I don't need it."

"Why?"

"I've got the North Star."

***

Other winters I'd get him to tell me stories about Alaska where he learned the song about fishing in the ice, the Gaspe Peninsula where he said it got so cold that the ocean froze and he was able to walk on it, or the Lebanon Forest in Tennessee where the cedar trees smelled as sweet as home-made taffy. He would ride freight cars all over the United States or Mexico or Canada, stopping off when he was hungry to look for work.

"But suppose you couldn't find a job?" I asked. "Supposing the people weren't nice and didn't—"

He laughed again.

"Didn't trust me, Bucko?"

"Yes."

"Oh, I never just knock on a door and ask if the roof needs fixing. I always look for the secret sign first."

"What secret sign?"

He looked at me solemnly. His eyes were pale watery blue, and even though they were old, at times like that they looked brand new to me.

"The hobo's secret sign."

"Where would it be?"

"It could be anywhere. Depending upon what was there. Sometimes on the bark of a tree. Sometimes in a petunia garden. Sometimes underneath a robin's nest."

"And what is the secret sign?"

He laughed.

"C'mon, my Bucko, if I told you it wouldn't be a secret, would it?"

Knobby must have seen the hurt look in my eye.

"Tell you what," he said, "when I come back next winter, I'll show you what it looks like."

My mother came over to the pantry table with Mama's big red teapot.

"You'll have another cup before you go, Knobby, won't you?"

"I will that, ma'm. Yours is the finest tea in southern Vermont."

"You'll be saying the same thing when you get to Weston, if that's where you're going."

I looked at Knobby, wondering if he would make any commitment other than the North Star, but he didn't answer.

"Whatcha doing, Knobby?" I asked, when he didn't say anything for a long time.

He took a sip of the tea and smiled at me.

"Oh, thinking, my Bucko. Just thinking."

***

The following year we had our first big snow the Monday after Thanksgiving. They let us out an hour early from school. I was hoping that by the time I got home the snow would stop so Knobby would be there knocking on the pantry door. It lasted until about an hour before dark. I sat by the living room window that faced the big maple on the front lawn and waited for him.

"Don't you think you better get started on your homework, Mickey?" my mother asked. "You know how tired you get after supper."

"B-but—"

"I don't think he's coming tonight."

"But he always comes after the first big snow."

"I know, but—"

"You don't think this is a big enough one?"

"Well, I'd call it a medium-sized one."

"Then I'll start my homework. We should have a really big one before Christmas.

And we did. Barely before. On Christmas Eve the heavens opened up and we had a blizzard. It was the biggest storm I could remember and I was positive that one like this would bring Knobby to our house. I had been thinking of lots of questions to ask him over the year. So many that even the hobo's secret mark was nowhere near the top of my list. I'd been practicing thinking ever since he mentioned it and found that like throwing snowballs, the more you did it, the better you got at it. Around four o'clock in the afternoon the skies cleared. The Gainsway girls came out their front door, carrying Christmas presents. I threw a snowball at Diane, the youngest girl and the prettiest. She turned around and laughed.

"Ha, ha. You missed, Mickey."

I sat on the front porch staring at the maple tree. He would be coming up the street any minute. I was positive. This had been a genuine blizzard. We would be shoveling snow long after it became dark. But Mom and my grandmother would have the lamb stew and Irish sofa bread ready. I had so many questions. That's what happens when you start to think, I reminded myself.

Mama came out to get me.

"Your mother says you'll be catching your death of cold sitting here," she said.

"But I'm waiting for Knobby."

"You can wait inside. Your mother wants to talk to you."

***

I guess I'll never forget the expression in my mother's eyes as she told me Knobby was dead. Had died three months ago near Wolfville, New Hampshire. Drowned in a place called Lake Winnipesauke. I had never heard of it before. My mother knew his real name. Clarence E. Latchford. No wonder he just wanted to be known as Knobby. A little boy had fallen off an old wharf and Knobby had dived in to save him. But Knobby couldn't swim. The kid drowned too. When I couldn't sleep that sad Christmas Eve I thought of Knobby and the kid, wondering what he was like. Wondering if Knobby had been able to save him, what kind of questions the kid would have asked. Probably some of them had to be about the color of the lake water from underneath. Or what it would be like to ride a lake trout and never get water up your nose. +++++

UNCLE MORTY AND MISERY, THE JEWISH CAT

I'd been praying for Uncle Morty for years, even though I hadn't the slightest idea who he was.

Uncle Morty got on my list when I was about five. As the years went by he found himself a more or less permanent spot between Uncle Val, who was gassed in World War I, and Auntie Cotter, my grandmother's twin sister, who died at birth.

It was my mother's idea. Every night at bedtime she would have me get down on my knees and say two *Our Fathers* and three *Hail Marys*—the *Our Fathers* were a little longer—and then pray for all her special people. There was Marshall Foch, Supreme Commander of all Allied Forces on the Western Front, Cousin Alice the nun, who died in a leper colony, and Waldo Smilowitz, whose background Mother never did explain to me.

I was allowed to add a few of my own. The first one I put on the list was Knute Rockne, Notre Dame's football coach who died in an airplane crash in 1931. I was seven at the time and his death was devastating to me.

"When you say your prayers tonight, Dear, put Mr. Rockne at the top of your list, because he just died," my mother consoled me.

It worked, sort of. The Notre Dame football team wasn't the same next season, but the death of my hero was assuaged by that fact that I was putting in a good word for him with God every night.

My grandmother, who was *very* Catholic, was a little leery about my praying for a Protestant because although Rockne was the coach of the "Fighting Irish" he was a Lutheran, and of course was not born in Kilkenny, but in Norway. However, she stopped grousing after my mother reminded her that I had Al Smith on my list for three years and he wasn't even dead. Mr. Smith, the first Catholic ever to run for President of the United States on a major ticket, had been defeated, so I guess I was praying for a comeback, although all I said in my prayers to God was to "please help the soul of Al Smith."

I got Uncle Morty through Mrs. Antapara.

Every morning after my brother and I left for school, my mother would go up to see Mrs. Antapara who lived three houses away. Till this day I don't know what my mother did there, and I don't know what Mrs. Antapara did, but they did it every weekday morning for three years until Mrs. Antapara, and Mr. Antapara too, moved to Rochester, New York. But a few years before she moved she had managed to get my mother to work Uncle Morty onto my list.

As I said, I didn't know who Uncle Morty was. I don't until this day. Even my *mother* didn't know who Uncle Morty was. All she knew was that (1) he was Mrs. Antapara's Uncle Morty, (2) he lived most of his life in Yazoo City, Mississippi, and (3) that he was dead.

"Tonight I want you to add Mrs. Antapara's Uncle Morty to your list, Dear," was all my mother had said. And that simple sentence was worth hundreds and hundreds of mentions in my prayers for years to come. He was on the top of the list right after he died. Generally after that I usually worked him into the middle and down towards the end.

Although my mother gave me the most names, she wasn't the only one who contributed to my list. My grandmother, Mr. Tannhauser the ice man whose wife, Sophie, died thirty years ago before I was born, Sister Joseph Leo the principal of our school, and even Mrs. Ferber who operated the candy store around the corner, had representatives on it. My grandmother was a little lenient with Mrs. Ferber, whose cat *Misery* died somewhere between Knute Rockne and Uncle Morty. My mother thought she might make a stink about Mrs. Ferber because of her religion, but my Uncle Joe told her that Grandma figured praying for a Jewish cat wasn't the same as praying for a Jew. Uncle Joe himself made my list the following year.

As you can imagine the older I got the more my knees hurt at bedtime, not only because my mother increased the *Hail Marys* to seven—she had a special devotion to the Blessed Virgin and to that number which she played every day at Mrs. Ferber's—but obviously because my list was growing. But I kept saying my prayers every night because it was a venial sin not to. I was tempted to leave a few names out now and then when I was particularly sleepy, but the constant repetition of the names imbedded them so deeply into my psyche that I would have had a guilt trip if I had eliminated even one of them. My mother hinted that if I did, that might be the very night that Uncle Val, the guy who was gassed, or Auntie Cotter who lived only one day, might need a special break from God.

I can imagine my telling this story today to a bunch of kids in the South Bronx or even to the boys down Dohoney's Pool Room in Jersey City, but things were different then. Those were the days that my best educated guess as to where babies came from was from a woman's boobies—I knew that word then and had to tell Father O'Donnell in confession that I used to say it in the dark of my room once in awhile—because those soft little hills seemed to be the one place where a woman could store a kid. Besides, I never saw a man with boobies.

By about the sixth grade when I was eleven, and long division and the causes of the Civil War were keeping me up later than the multiplication tables and *Black Beauty* had in my salad days, my mother told me that it was O.K. to pray for all the people on my list in bed instead of on my knees. With the easier life, I started leaving off a few, always trying to give myself a little justification before I dropped one. Marshall Foch went when I discovered in Sister Grace Catherine's history class that he was an advocate of offensive warfare that cost the French many lives. I dropped Al Smith temporarily, silently agreeing to pick him up again when he kicked the bucket, as we used to say in those days. When Sister Frances Maria told me that all little babies went straight to heaven, as long as they were baptized, I was able to get rid of Auntie Cotter, my grandmother's twin sister who died at the age of one day. And with the sophistication of my growing years I decided I had better either eliminate Waldo Smilowitz or stop saying his name out loud since my father slept in the next bedroom.

My high school education really made life a lot easier for me at bedtime. In *Biology I* when I learned how scientists lump all living things into divisions, I thought I'd do the same thing with the dead people on my list. I stopped saying individual names like Uncle Joe, Aunt Alice, Knute Rockne and so forth, and prayed for them by divisions. First I'd ask God to take care of all my baseball and football heroes, then my relatives, and finally the politicians my mother, father, and grandmother liked. I considered grouping all the rest—people I'd never met like Mrs. Sophie Tannhauser the iceman's wife and Mrs. Antapara's Uncle Morty whom I'd been carrying for years—into a special category called *People*

And Animals I've Heard Of, but I abandoned the idea when my Latin teacher started giving us vocabulary tests the first thing in the morning. A guy's brain can hold just so much. With my new system I could get to sleep early because I could whip through my prayers in a few minutes. As I grew into maturity I decided to also dispense with the *Our Fathers and Hail*

Marys, making bedtime a breeze.

When I joined the Army I more or less did away with even my generic list. It wasn't until I landed in France in 1944, the year Al Smith died, by the way, that I thought about all the people I didn't know that I used to pray for when I was growing up. I was standing in front of the CQ's tent, looking at the long casualty list posted there when the names of Sophie Tannhauser, Uncle Morty, and *Misery*, the Jewish cat, popped into my head.+++++

A LITTLE ADULTERY IN THE FIFTH GRADE

We were supposed to get Sister Grace Catherine in the fifth grade, but the Mother Superior told us that she had volunteered to work at a leper colony in the South Pacific. Her choice wasn't too good for our egos, but some of the kids said they heard Sister Grace married a guy named Seymour Goldstein and was either thrown out of the church or decided to become a Jew.

Mother Superior said her replacement was a new nun, Sister Mary Eucharia. We didn't notice anything strange for the first ten minutes of her class, but when she went to the blackboard to diagram a sentence with an objective complement in it and her frantic jabbing at the board sent the yellow chalk flying at the ceiling we experienced a class *déjà vu*. She had been our first grade teacher, Miss Sullivan, and had joined the convent to come back to haunt us.

We had a new kid in our class that year, Kathy Korkrane, a transfer from St. Paul of the Cross in Jersey City. She looked a little older than us, so we thought she might have been left back in St. Paul's and had moved to Hoboken to avoid the disgrace of repeating the fifth grade on her own turf. Besides, she was kind of weird. She wormed her way into the boys' football games and didn't mind getting tackled and knocked down in the street. There aren't many parks in Hoboken, so we played right on Jefferson between the parked cars. At any rate Sister Eucharia was suspicious of her and put her in the first row, right across from me.

It was music time and Sister Eucharia was teaching the Gregorian Chant. She was bonkers over the Gregorian Chant and the Music period almost always extended over and cut into Poetry, a policy that left most of us with mixed feelings.

While Sister Eucharia was scribbling the notes of a complicated chant on the blackboard, splinters of chalk spraying the air like tracer bullets and her long black veils swishing and swirling like bats in the moonlight, Kathy Korkrane told me about her Immaculate Conception ring.

"Wanna see my new ring?" she whispered across the aisle.

I ignored her. My father had promised me a Yogi Berra catcher's mitt if I came up with 25 holy pictures by the end of September and I wasn't going to get in trouble for talking, especially during the Gregorian Chant.

But Kathy persisted. This time she raised her voice slightly, thinking I hadn't heard her.

"It's an Immaculate Conception ring."

"Yeh," I whispered, keeping my eyes riveted on Sister Eucharia and her flying veils.

"Well, look at it then."

I gave a quick glance to my right. The ring was on her left hand and her left hand was resting on her left knee.

"Feel the ring. It's real silver."

Fortunately Sister Eucharia had begun singing as she jotted the notes on the board, because otherwise she would have heard Kathy who had elevated her whisper an octave.

I ignored Kathy, which was a mistake.

"Feel my Immaculate Conception ring," she said fiercely, threatening to raise her voice even more.

I let my right hand drift across the aisle. Kathy grabbed it as a dog snaps up a fly and, before I knew it, my hand was on Kathy's Immaculate Conception ring and on Kathy's hand. Suddenly Kathy pulled her hand slightly under her Our Lady of Perpetual Chastity's blue skirt and my hand, attached as it was to hers, landed at the end of her black stocking.

In the middle of a high c Sister Eucharia suddenly swung around to face the class, her veils fluttering heavenward like Canadian geese, her eyes focused first on the class in general and then on me in particular with my hand underneath Kathy Korkrane's skirt.

"Master Finneran!" she screamed. "What are you doing?"

"I'm just feeling Kathy Korkrane's Immaculate Conception ring," I explained.

Sister Eucharia told her I had to see her after school. As you can imagine, I was a nervous wreck. Although at that time I did not know all the ins and outs of Immaculate Conception rings and girls like Kathy Korkrane, I had a sneaking suspicion that this was a more serious problem than the one I had when I couldn't get the hang of making 4's in the first grade. I almost wished that Sister Eucharia was a fake nun again. Somehow she might have been a little easier to deal with as Miss Sullivan.

"Louis, do you know that the Sisters of this school have high hopes for you?" she began.

I didn't know. I really didn't and I told her. Besides I didn't know what kind of hopes they were.

"In every class you have been in, your grades have been in the 90's— Sister Rita's, Sister Frances—"

"Well," I answered, "that's because my mother makes me stay home after school memorizing the number of bushels of potatoes Idaho grows each year, the three conditions for a mortal sin, and stuff like that."

"Last June when you brought your fourth grade autograph book around for pupils and teachers to sign, do you remember what Sister Joseph Leo wrote in your book? Tell me, Louis."

That was a tough question. It was a 150-page book, but I did remember Tommy Vogt's.

If in heaven we do not meet,
I hope that you can stand the heat.

Oh, God! Sister Joseph Leo's was on the next page. I remember because it was pink. She had written:

I hope that the good Lord Jesus Christ in His
Infinite Wisdom will take you into His bosom.

It was kind of scary. At first I thought she was expecting me to croak. But a principal of a Catholic school wouldn't wish that on a little kid. After awhile I just forgot about it. One other thought raced across my mind. I was only nine in the fourth grade and I didn't know too much about bosoms, but even at that early age I was a little more interested in the bosoms of girls than the bosom of Jesus. I forced my mind to stop thinking of bosoms. If Sister Eucharia had special powers like God and the Saints who knew all our inner thoughts, I would be a dead duck—especially with this Immaculate Conception ring business still outstanding.

"All the Sisters here were so proud of you, Louis," she said sadly.

"Well, I did cop my share of holy pictures."

"It is more than that. Sister Joseph and the other Sisters thought an even more wonderful gift was in store for you. That's what she was thinking when she signed your autograph book."

Great as I was with European capitals and oats and barley supplies, I was pretty weak at drawing the inference in those days. But Sister Eucharia was laying on heavy hints. I suddenly got it. Omigod, I thought, the Sisters want me to become a priest when I grow up.

"God has given you special gifts," she said. "Some day He may be calling on you to use these gifts in His name."

The Sisters had apparently connected the potato crops in Idaho with a vocation to the priesthood.

"Christ!"

I said it softly, sort of under my breath, and I think Sister Eucharia thought it was some kind of a prayer.

"Do you realize how disappointed your mother and father would be if I told them about this?"

"Yes, Sister."

"For your sake I shall remain silent, but you shall have to tell it in confession to Father O'Donnell this Saturday."

"In confession?" I asked fearfully.

"Of course," she said, swirling one of her veils significantly. "You have committed a mortal sin."

"I have?"

"Master Finneran, you are aware of the Ten Commandments, are you not?"

I have to confess that today I'm a little shaky on which is Number 7 and which is Number 8—those two commandments about coveting. When I was a kid I thought they meant *covering* and I couldn't make any sense out of them at all. Thou shalt not cover thy neighbor's goods— what if he forgot to put them in the ice box? Thou shalt not cover thy neighbor's wife. Mrs. Vandenberg lived next store; it would take an elephant's blanket to cover her. I used to tell myself that God must have been having a bad day when he included covering Mrs. Vandenberg among the Ten Commandments.

But back in my days with Sister Eucharia I could race through the Ten Commandments as rapidly as the 12-times table and I had lots of gold stars to prove it.

"Well, Louis ?"

"I know them, Sister."

"When you placed your hand on Kathy Korkrane's er—"

"Immaculate Conception ring," I prompted.

"When you had your hand on her ring, which commandment did you break?"

Let me pause for a moment for you folks who may not have had the extensive Catholic education that I had. And, of course, for the rest of you—Protestants, Jews, agnostics and others who weren't going to heaven, the Sisters told us, because you weren't baptized in the Catholic faith. Sister Eucharia and I finally agreed that the commandment that I broke was the sixth: *Thou shalt not commit adultery*, even more confusing than covering goods and wives, but Sister said it definitely included little boys who went around feeling Immaculate Conception rings. Later on when I got a better understanding of adultery I realized what the Church was getting at. *Adultery* was basically the catch-all word for what we kids called *dirty*. Now they couldn't have a bunch of commandments have a bunch of commandments like "Thou shalt not look up girls' dresses"; "Thou shalt not think of naked women"; "Thou shalt not goose." Moses had limited space on the tablets. So, for the Catholics, adultery covers all the things that little kids want to do most and can't.

"Now don't forget confession with Father O'Donnell Saturday, Louis."

Telling Father O'Donnell what I did would be worse than what facing Sister Eucharia had been. After all, she had at least *seen* me do it. He probably wouldn't believe my story of how my hand got all the way across the aisle to Kathy's...Suddenly I got an idea. All those hours of memorizing was finally going to come in handy.

"Sister, I don't hafta tell if it's a venial sin, do I?"

"Doing what you did to Kathy Korkrane was no venial sin, Master Finneran."

"But a mortal sin has to have three conditions, Sister: 1. a serious matter; 2. sufficient reflection; and 3. full consent of the will. Did I really have all three?"

Sister Eucharia picked up her black shawl and twisted it around her head. She didn't say a word to me until she had her books, music sheets and pitch pipe safely packed in her leather book bag.

"What you did, Master Finneran, was serious in the eyes of God. As for the other two conditions, my back was to the class for two minutes. Next Saturday, march off to Father O'Donnell."

That's where they had you. I memorized the conditions for a mortal sin, but I didn't know what they meant.

All this happened on a Tuesday. By the end of the week I was thinking of switching to Father Witkowski, because Tommy Vogt said he didn't yell as much. I was thinking of toning it down a bit by saying that I had accidentally bumped into Kathy Korkrane in the hallway at recess, but I was afraid that in some mystical way Sister Eucharia had connections with the priests. Besides, I had only Tommy's word on Father Witowski. Bumping in the hall might be something like covering Mrs. Vandenberg.

Father O'Donnell was extremely deaf and almost always made you say your sins again. Then he would repeat what you just said so that even the old ladies far away at the St. Joseph's altar on the other side of the church would know all the bad things you had been doing all week long. Yet, despite my promise to Sister Eucharia, I just could not bring myself to going there the first thing Saturday afternoon. I waited until five o'clock when confessions were just about over and Father O'Donnell might have even decided to call it quits early. Luck was against me, however. Father Witkowski had already left, but Father O'Donnell was there, yelling out the sins—his favorites were "Oh, my God!" and "You did WHAT!"—for all the ladies in the Rosary Society by the St. Joseph's altar to hear.

I knelt down to "examine my conscience." The Sisters told us that we always had to spend 15 to 20 minutes thinking about our sins. Now I'm not saying that I was a perfect kid, even with all the holy pictures. I did a few things that I'm not exactly proud of. And some of them I did week after week. But 15 to 20 minutes! I was only ten years old. How many opportunities does a kid as young as me get to commit a pack of sins, what with the Sisters watching me morning and early afternoons, my mother late afternoons, and my mother, father, grandmother and Uncle Tom at night?

But none of us kids would go in and confess just one or two sins. It was embarrassing to admit that was all we could come up with. So I took the examining-of-conscience business seriously.

A sure-fire sin was missing your morning prayers. You don't think that's a sin, eh? The Sisters maintained it was. And so was missing the night prayers. They were both easy to do because when I woke up I was usually too punchy to think about praying, and when I went to bed, my head filled with wheat, grain, oats and barley figures, I was too tired to pray. So I usually confessed that I missed my morning prayers five times and my evening prayers seven times.

You might be wondering about my listing the number of times. Well, that's another thing the Sisters taught us. I couldn't just say I told a lie or gave my brother a sneak punch; I had to tell how many *times* I did it. Looking back, I think the Sisters' rule gave me the incentive to commit a few more sins. Supposing I couldn't remember whether I dipped Grace Latchford's pigtails in my inkwell once or twice? Well, I just about had to do it again so I wouldn't be lying to Father O'Donnell.

Even though the Sisters told us to keep an accurate account of our sins, I had a tough time wondering why God needed all that information just to give the priest the OK to give a guy absolution. I used to picture him up in the sky with a gigantic adding machine saying, "Louis missed morning prayers five times, talked back to his mother once, lost his temper three times..." Then the huge adding machine would make a few clicks, bells would ring, and the exact number of my transgressions—a neat word I learned from the Sisters; much smoother than sins—would be duly recorded for posterity. I asked Sister Cecelia Bernard about it once and she fudged the same way she did when I wanted to know why only Catholics could go to Heaven since the other kids didn't know about our rules, and how could they arrange to be born Catholics anyway? She said at least they didn't go to Hell. God was too nice for that, she told me, so he sent them to a place called Limbo—no heat or devils, just smells like Limburger cheese.

I gave it the whole 20 minutes examining my conscience on the slim possibility that by that time Father O'Donnell might get bored because he had no more customers and might leave. When I finally got off my knees, my hands shaking and my lips trembling, I saw the light go out in his confessional. The door was open. He could be leaving. I started to run out of Our Lady of Perpetual Chastity's like a kid stealing an apple from Portabachi's Produce.

"Hey, where are you going, young fellow?"

"H-home, Father."

"Don't you want to go to confession? Have you examined your conscience?

(Do you see the spot you're in when you're dealing with a priest? I couldn't lie and say, "I'm still working on it, Father" because, according to the Sisters, the priests know everything, "even your most secret thoughts." And then when he finally got me in confession, I would have to tell him that I had lied to him. I tried a different tact.)

"Yes, I have examined my conscience, Father, but it is getting late now and I don't want you to miss your supper."

He raised his right arm so that it was level with his shoulder and pointed to the confessional. In his long black skirt and purple stole, he was a cross between one of my holy pictures cards of St. Paul on horseback and Christopher Columbus at the bow of the *Santa Maria*.

"Get in the box, Louis."

Louis! That did it. It was bad enough to have to go to confession, but it was worse when the priest recognized you. When I was able to sneak into the box in the dark I would always drop my voice an octave so he wouldn't recognize me, no easy accomplishment because Father O'Donnell knew me well. He came around every month to read our report cards and make nasty little remarks about our weaknesses. Mine was Deportment, which hovered between 60 and 75, depending on the nun. For some reason they didn't include Deportment in the general average when they were figuring out who was going to get the honor pin at the end of the year. I guess my knowledge of this made me a little reckless.

"Bless me, Father, for I have sinned. It is one week since my last confession and these are my sins."

"Go on, Louis."

(See what I mean?)

"I missed my morning prayers five times, my evening prayers seven times, I punched my little brother in the back twice, I said 'Shit' to my mother (under my breath) once, I lost my temper two times, I told 11 lies, I talked in church once, I moved my marble with my foot three times in ringsy games, and I committed adultery once. I beg pardon of God and of you, my earthly father."

There was a slight pause during which I came close to wetting my pants. This is the part of the confession where he really dished it out.

"All right, Louis, for your penance say three Hail Marys and three Our Fathers. Now make a good *Act of Contrition*. Oh my God, Who art—"

I couldn't believe my good luck; he mustn't have heard. I bypassed the little insult of his starting off a prayer that I knew my heart since I was six and raced through the *Act of Contrition* before he changed his mind. I had just got up to—

"...*but most of all because I offend Thee, my God, who art all good and deserving of*—" when Father O'Donnell suddenly bellowed out:

"Wait a minute! What was that last sin?"

"Y-you mean saying 'Shit' to my mother?"

"No, no, not that one," he shouted. "The other one."

By this time the old ladies by the St. Joseph's altar were tuning up their ears, but it really wasn't necessary. There were about two dozen people in the church at that time and I'm positive every one of them heard all. I got so nervous I found myself screaming back at him. The two of us created this weird stichomythia:

"WHAT other one?"

"The last one. What was the LAST sin you confessed?"

"I-I committed adultery."

"You WHAT?"

"I committed adultery."

"You can't commit adultery. How old are you?"

"I'm ten years old."

"Well then, you can't commit adultery."

"But I did, Father."

"It's impossible, I'm telling you."

"It was easy, father."

"H-how did you do it, then?"

"I felt Kathy Korkrane's Immaculate Conception ring."

There was a pause, this time a long one. I could hear considerable shuffling of feet around the St. Joseph's altar. Here I was, the winner of three consecutive honor pins, becoming a *cause célèbre* among the ladies of the Rosary Society at the age of ten. Probably at no other moment in my life has my name been on the lips of so many women at the same time.

"You cannot commit adultery by feeling a girl's Immaculate Conception ring. Where the devil did you ever get such an idea?"

"Sister Mary Eucharia said so."

"Sister Mary—oh, Peggy Sullivan. So Sister Mary Eucharia thinks you're an adulterer, eh Louis?"

"She didn't call me that, but she said I had committed adultery. I guess I should have told you that the ring was on Kathy's finger and Kathy's hand was a little way under her Lady of Perpetual Chastity dress when I touched it."

"All right, all right, Louis. That's enough. I'm going to have to change your penance. Better make that *five* Hail Marys and *ten* Our Fathers. And keep your hands off little girls' rings. Now make a good Act of Contrition. Oh, my God I'm heartily sorry for..."

The eavesdroppers had enough decency to leave the church before I made my way to the St. Joseph's altar to say my penance. I said *ten* Hail Marys, taking it on myself to add to my penance because as a near-adulterer I thought I had been let off too easy by Father O'Donnell. Little did I know then that Kathy Korkrane was to become pregnant by the seventh grade. Too many football games with the boys, I suppose.

I genuflected in front of the middle altar and started down the aisle The lights of his confessional were still on. As I tip-toed past his box I could hear him laughing softly to himself. It made me think that there was something gone wrong with him. +++++

BOTTOMS UP AND STRAWBERRIES DOWN

I pretended to be asleep. In that way I wouldn't have to answer any questions, and at the same time I could hear all the things they were saying about me.

"Well, Agnes, when I heard the news from Mr. Bailey the milkman, I just couldn't believe it. Joram always seemed like such a sensible little boy. Extremely polite—he never passed me by without tipping his cap and saying, 'Hello, Mrs. Crosby, how are you this fine day?' Good gracious, he was extremely well mannered. You had every reason to be proud of him, my Dear."

"I know. I must have told myself the same thing a thousand times: Joram is a good, sensible little boy. How could he do this to me?"

That last voice was my mother's. She was talking to Mrs. Crosby who lived three doors down the street from us, right next to the empty lot where we played marbles and ring-a-leave-io.

"Now, now, Mrs. Gately, you mustn't blame yourself. You certainly did everything that was humanly possibly to bring young Joram up to be a loving, God-fearing young Catholic. But all is not lost yet. Remember the Lord works in mysterious ways, his wonders to perform."

"I know. I know, Father. I must keep praying. That's all I can do."

"And I shall pray for you and your mother. And young Joram, of course. Tell me, how is he now? They told me downstairs that he was starting to regain consciousness."

"I just looked in on him a minute or so ago, Father. I think he fell back to sleep again. Maybe if we wait a little bit, he will—"

Well, they will have a long wait. I am determined to lie still with my eyes shut tight for days if I have to. I'd do anything to get them away from that door and get them away from me. The Lord works in mysterious ways! Bull! I'm not trying to deny what I did, and I'm willing to accept the consequences of my actions. But it's not as simple and cut and dried as Father Ballinger says. It's much more than that, because I really have always been fond of my grandmother. If I had it to do over again, I think I would still probably do it. Of course, I might take another approach. I'd never take the chance of getting involved in all this scandal again. Now that I have had time to think about it carefully, I have to admit that I may have been a bit impetuous. There has to be a better way. Well, next time...

***

My grandmother had always been my best pal. When I was really little and decided to help my mother and father out by painting the cellar, it was my grandmother—she's Nana to just about everybody, including me—who stood up for me. I thought the basement would look good in green, but after I got through with the furnace and the coal bin, I became bored with green and decided to paint some of it red. But there wasn't enough red in the can to paint a whole wall, so I did the rest in yellow until that ran out. I covered up the spots that were unpainted with a little black that I found underneath the woodpile. It was kind of gooey, so I spilled some on the cellar floor. That's how I got caught: when I went upstairs to get a few Fig Newtons, I must have tracked some of it over my mother's red Oriental rug. That's when she told me that I was going to have to go to the "Worser Home," a name I inadvertently coined for the family after Father pointed it out to me from a moving train, and I concluded it must be for little boys "worser than me."

It was a maudlin scene. Mother was packing my bags with snide little observations such as, "There's no sense in my packing your Donald Duck or coloring books—they don't let little boys have any toys in the Worser Home. Every time she rejected one of my little playthings, I would wail and she would look at me without an iota of compassion and remark haughtily, "You should have thought of that before you decided to become a Michelangelo." I didn't know what the dickens she was talking about; all I knew was that everything I held dear in life—my room, my marbles and my bright orange Little Orphan' Annie Ovaltine mug—were being separated from me forever.

But here was where Nana came to the rescue. She put her arms around me and hugged me with all her might. Then she cut me a fat piece of her steaming hot raisin cake, fresh from the oven, and wiped my tears away with the hem of her dress. I was distracted from my fate by the sweet warmth of the cake, but when I had finished it and two glasses of milk, the sound of Mother rattling my dresser drawers upstairs turned on the faucets in my eyes again.

"Come here, Joram," Nana said cheerfully. "Let's see how much you grew since yesterday."

She stood up and pulled me close to her white and blue flowered apron, sticking a safety pin by the spot where the top of my head reached a white petunia.

"My, My! You must have grown almost a quarter-inch since yesterday. Soon you'll be big enough to build your own house."

I sensed that she might have been exaggerating to make me feel better, but Nana insisted I was really sprouting upwards. She allowed me to draw a comparison between yesterday's pin and today's for proof. When Mother came down the stairs with two little suitcases and I started crying again, Nana stood in front of me to protect me from eviction.

"Agnes, this child is not leaving this house. If he does, then I'm going with him."

Mother knew at that point that she didn't have a chance. She would have to come up with some explanation for my claims to squatter's rights to appease Father.

Days later when the fuss had quieted down, Nana gently advised me to stay away from the paint cans in the cellar for awhile.

"Folks today don't understand the young people," she told me, "so you'll have to be abide by them for awhile until I get a little more money saved up and then I'll take you away with me to play with the leprechauns and we'll eat pumpkin pie and drink chocolate milk all day long."

That's the kind of woman Nana was. So obviously I would never have done anything to hurt her. It would be a little like killing your dog or pulling petals from a rose.

***

Nana went to mass and Holy Communion at 6:30 every morning at the church of Our Lady of Perpetual Chastity on Washington Street. Then every Saturday she went to confession. When I was old enough to go to confession myself, I was really puzzled over this. What could Nana possibly do that she would have to tell Father Ballinger? I never saw her angry, she never lied—except maybe when she was measuring me—and Nana never said any bad word words worse than, "That man is a caution," referring to my father. Yet she stayed in the confession box ten to twelve minutes every Saturday. I timed her on my Mickey Mouse watch.

When I was little I used to think that Nana was good because she went to church so much. But when I grew three pins on her apron and started to mature, I began to think that Nana's goodness may have come from inside her and the masses and Holy Communions were just extra little bonuses she was picking up along the way. But Nana didn't think the way I did. Nana wasn't at all convinced that she was good and felt that she needed every one of those Holy Communions to get into Heaven. And if there was one thing I was positive of, it was this: Nana really wanted to go to Heaven. Well, considering the alternatives, it was a pretty decent goal, I suppose.

The one thing the nuns drummed into our heads was that no matter how good you are, if you commit a mortal sin all the good you have ever done is wiped off your slate. Sister Catherine Eucharia had a way of dramatizing it.

"Just imagine. You have been a good boy all your life. Then one day you indulge in an immodest thought (I wasn't sure what that was at first, but I suspected it had something to do with wondering what was underneath little girls' dresses). Then there is a bad thunder storm. Lightning hits you and you die. You go straight to Hell and all the good things you have ever done in life don't count one single bit."

I always thought of that as rank injustice. But Sister Eucharia insisted that these were the rules that God had made up. He gave us all an out, she said, by letting us go to confession. After we told our sins to a priest, and didn't hold a single thing back, we would get credit for all the good stuff we had done until we committed another mortal sin. Even with confession, you still had to fry a little in Purgatory for committing the sins in the first place, but you would never go to Hell if you died right after making a good confession, she told us.

***

The church of Our Lady of Perpetual Chastity is located at one of the busiest intersections of Washington Street, so when I first started going to confession, I had to go with Mother because they didn't have a policeman to cross us on Saturday afternoons. It was a pain because I was sure that Mother was timing me when I was in the box with Father Ballinger. Not that I was ever there very long. When I first started going,

I had to make up a few sins be-cause I didn't want him to think I was a goody-goody two-shoes.

But when I began to become more of a kid of the world, I began adding a few interesting sins to my collection. It was then that I started going to confession with Nana. This was infinitely better. She would never pull a stopwatch on a guy in the box or ever say anything about the degrading business of having to tell your sins to an old man in a long black skirt.

Oh, Nana would talk on her way to church, and especially on her way back home. She would tell me how she liked the smell of the yellow candles in their little red jars in front of the St. Joseph's altar, the littlest one in the church, by the way. And she seemed fascinated by the streams of light that filtered through the huge blue and yellow stained glass window of the Annunciation of the Archangel Gabriel to Our Lady, over the main altar, around five o'clock on an April afternoon, just about the time we were leaving church.

Nana was in there saying her penance and staring at the late afternoon sun that was lighting up the folded, lily-white hands of the Virgin Mary, when I finally thought of a way to repay Nana for all her years of kindness.

I had often shuddered at the thought that Sister Eucharia had instilled in my head—that if a person died in between confessions with a mortal sin on his soul, he was doomed to Hell. I wasn't worried so much for myself, because now that I was approaching my fifth pin on the apron and becoming considerably more worldly, I thought it was almost impossible to go through life without committing a few thousand mortal sins. I would just have to take my chances on getting to confession when I needed to.

No, I was thinking of Nana. Here was this thoroughly decent woman, who by all rules of fairness should get a spot in Heaven right up there with St. Peter and St. Theresa of the Holy Flower. But what if one day, by some curious stroke of bad luck, she should commit a mortal sin and die before she has a chance to check in with Father Ballinger? It was a long-shot, I had to agree. But Sister Eucharia had also told us that anything was possible. So why take chances? Nana was the best friend I had ever had. It would be horrible if, after all the raisin cakes and lemon meringue pies, she should one day screw up and wind up shoveling coal. It wasn't an easy decision, but it was something that just had to be done.

I hid behind one of the huge stone pillars near the cornerstone of the church. Nana came out and started calling for me. She wandered near the curb, thinking I might have strayed onto Washington Street with its heavy weekend traffic.

"Joram, where are you?" she called out.

I could see that she was worried about me. I hated for it to end this way, her warm, kind voice lost in the din of all that traffic.

"Joram! Are you all right?"

She bent down to get a better view of the street. Her weary rear end was exposed to me. This was a perfect opportunity. I braced myself against the cold stone wall of the church of Our Lady of Perpetual Chastity and stuck my left foot against its huge stucco pillar to get a good running start. A huge Mack truck loaded with fresh strawberries and purple grapes was barreling down the Washington Street. Now was my chance! I lowered my head and charged at my grandmother's behind. Father Ballinger had just cleared her soul. No danger of a slip-up now. She would get the first fast express train right up to Heaven. I ran as hard as I could and butted her behind with all my might, like a regular nanny goat. My grandmother went flying through the air in the path of the Mack truck with the strawberries. My momentum was so powerful that I also kept going after my head made contact with Nana's bottom. The last thing I can remember was the strawberries and grapes whirling through the air like crimson and lavender snow, the awful sound of the screeching of brakes and the sick smell of burning rubber.

When I woke up in the emergency room at St. Mary's Hospital I heard Miss Wilburham, who is a head nurse there and a parishioner at Our Lady of Perpetual Chastity's, telling the X-ray technician that Father Ballinger saw the whole thing. There was nobody in line at his confessional, so he had decided to come out for a smoke. I didn't even get Nana. They said a lot about abrasions, contusions, and possible fractures, but there's no question that she's going to live.

The same goes for me, I heard Miss Wilburham saying, after she got through telling the X-ray technician what a demented little boy I was. Come to think of it, I suppose from my point of view that it was a good thing that Nana and I didn't get killed. Murdering your grandmother is no doubt a mortal sin, especially since the church seems to be loaded down with purists like Sister Catherine Eucharia and Father Ballinger.

Of course, Nana has to watch her step now so that she doesn't blow it all by going awry, like getting a crush on Mr. Bailey the milkman, an act which in some circles might be considered a mortal sin. I rather doubt it, though. Mr. Bailey has a crooked nose and a funny moustache and he usually smells of garlic. It's strange. I never thought of Nana ever doing anything with a man until that Mack truck hit me. I guess when Nana measures me again I'll be another pin higher.

I think Mother and Mrs. Crosby are convinced I'm asleep. I heard them say they were going downstairs to visit my grandmother to see how her broken arm is coming along. Hmmm. I wonder if Nana can still make raisin cake with one arm. +++++

III.
Remembrances of World War II

Far off in the distance, a dog began to howl. It was a long and plaintive cry of a lonely animal wailing at the moon on a cold December night
—A Dollar and Six Cents

A DOLLAR AND SIX CENTS

Walker shivered as he patrolled the wooden deck of the old prison tower. It was a cold and windy December night with a hint of snow in the air. He was tempted to go inside where it was warm, but he was afraid the heat would make him sleepy. If he fell asleep on guard duty, he would be thrown into the compound with the prisoners, where his friend Bobby Blake now lay under a pup tent.

Bobby had allowed a prisoner to escape while on a work detail because he could not bring himself around to shooting him when he scaled a fence and made his way to freedom in the Lebanon Forest of western Tennessee. Blake had protested to the C.O. that he had fired a warning shot from his carbine, but found it difficult to shoot the prisoner because he was an American soldier like himself. The Army's response was to commit Blake to the stockade for negligence of duty. His new companions did not appreciate his humanity towards the man who escaped. On his first night in the stockade one of them urinated in his canteen cup while another tried to rape him. Walker shivered as he thought about what happened to his friend. Company C had a mean C.O. If he didn't want to wind up in the stockade as well, Walker knew he had to fight off sleep at any cost.

Everything seemed quiet below. He turned on his powerful searchlight and let it wander over the pup tents and the walk leading up to his tower. He wasn't checking on the prisoners, but on the O.D., who had a habit of sneaking up on the guards to make sure they were alert.

This was not what Walker had expected when he enlisted in the Army. He had high ideals then. Although only 18, he was going to join in the ultimate invasion of France and march to Germany to help rid the world of Adolf Hitler. But here he was high above a stockade in the freezing hills of Tennessee guarding prisoners, not POW's but American G.I.'s. His first sergeant had told them that some of these guys were meaner than Nazi storm troopers, that they were men who had been criminals in civilian life and were just following their natural bent in the service. Some of them were in the compound for murder, atrocious assault, robbery, and rape. But Walker knew that Bobby Blake was there because he would not shoot another human being, no matter what the Army decreed.

This prison duty for Company C was a brief assignment, Sgt. Crane had said. They had just finished Tennessee maneuvers and were awaiting assignment overseas. Since they would only be guarding the stockade for two weeks, they might as well do everything they could to keep the C.O. happy, Crane argued. The men of Company C generally agreed. They were well aware that the C.O. was a martinet and had a strong distaste for American prisoners.

"They're the scum of the earth," the C.O. said. "We can't take them overseas with us. It's too bad we can't just line all of them against the wall and blast them away with a few rounds of a .30 caliber machine gun."

Walker's squad leader, Sgt. Mountcastle would just shake his head sadly every time he heard the C.O. sound off like that. In civilian life Mounty, as the guys in the squad called him, used to sing country songs and play the guitar for a small radio station in North Carolina.

"The C.O.'s looniness is going to appeal to one of the locos in our outfit, Walker. Just you wait and see."

And Mountcastle was right. Jerry Danforth, one of the G.I.s who shared the six-cot tent with Walker and Sgt. Mountcastle, was mesmerized by the C.O. Whenever he called the battalion out to issue orders, Danforth was one of the first G.I.'s on the company street.

He had asked to have McCaw, one of the stockade's most recalcitrant prisoners, assigned to him. McCaw had been charged with theft from an officer and had denied it, claiming he had been in Nashville on a pass at the time; however, he had not been believed and had been sent to the stockade, where he had been for the past two weeks. He had built up a reputation for being sullen and slow to follow commands when he was on work details.

"I'll attach my bayonet to my Enfield, and if he doesn't move when I order him to, I know how to use it," Danforth told the C.O., who was quick to grant the request.

The first day McCaw had balked as usual and Danforth had slashed him in the arm with his bayonet, sending him to the field hospital. He had been hospitalized for two days, but was expected to be back on a work detail today, Walker recalled, realizing that Danforth would probably be marching his prisoner around the stockade fence by 7 a.m., an hour before Walker was finally relieved.

Walker looked at the sky. Dawn was slipping through. As the early winter light began bathing the compound, McCaw appeared at the stockade gate with another prisoner, a heavyset man who had gone AWOL in the middle of maneuvers. Waiting on the other side was Danforth. He must have somehow received permission to march them off before the prisoners' work day started. He could hear Danforth bellowing to McCaw:

"Listen, you friggin' nothing. You do what I say, when I say it, and as soon as I say it, or I'm going to make you think that little slash on your arm was a kiss. Now, MOVE, you rotten little son of a bitch. MOVE!"

McCaw stared at Danforth defiantly, but he followed a few steps behind the other heavyset prisoner and left the compound. When McCaw had gone about 50 yards from the gate, he turned around and stared at Danforth.

"Damnit, I told you to MOVE IT."

McCaw remained motionless as if he had not heard a word his guard had said.

Danforth took the Enfield from his shoulder, switched off the safety, held the rifle in the *present arms* position for a moment and then pointed it directly at the prisoner. McCaw stared into the barrel of the old World War I rifle, known for its accuracy at long range, but did not flinch.

"Move. Goddamn it, or I'll blow your brains out."

The early morning light was beginning to fill up the sky. Although Walker could make out the silhouettes of Danforth and McCaw, he reached for his field glasses to get a better look. He saw McCaw glaring at Danforth, unfazed by the rifle he held a few feet from his head. The silence throughout the compound at the beginning of the work day was eerie. It was as if everyone within earshot was listening in on this early morning confrontation.

Crack!

Danforth flicked the bolt, ejecting the spent cartridge, and closed it again. In the still winter air the noise of the rifle shot seemed magnified by a dozen loudspeakers. McCaw was still standing. Danforth must have fired over his head, Walker mused. At that close range, the bullet would have ripped a hole right through him. Doesn't he know he's dealing with a madman? Why the hell doesn't he—?

Crack

McCaw staggered and fell to the ground. Sgt. Crane, who had left his tent at the sound of the first shot, rushed to the area where McCaw lay. He knelt down over the body for almost a minute before rising. The heavyset prisoner stood a few feet behind them trembling and mumbling to himself, as if he were praying.

"Is he dead?" Walker shouted from the tower. "Is he dead, Sergeant?"

Sgt. Crane looked up at Walker in the tower for a moment and then solemnly moved his head up and down. Soldiers in the area came running to the scene. A few feet to the left of the dead body Danforth calmly began to clean his old Enfield, as if nothing of any significance had happened.

***

Word of the shooting spread quickly. Sgt. Mountcastle, who had been assigned to stockade guard duty in peace time, knew the routine. He explained it to Walker as the two of them were sitting on their cots writing letters at the end of their long and fitful day.

"They'll transfer Danforth tomorrow. Tonight will be the last night he'll be sleeping in this tent with us, which is fine by me. He'll be found guilty of the shooting by the Army and fined $1.06—$1. for court costs and six cents for the cartridge. This will protect him from a civilian suit by McCaw's family after the war is over. I don't understand how the law regulating this mumbo-jumbo works, but the C.O. says it's all nice and legal, and Danforth doesn't have a thing to worry about."

"Except living with his conscience," Walker pointed out.

Mounty shrugged. "I don't think it's as hard for him as it is for most folks. You ought to know, Walker. You weren't far away from him in your tower when he shot the man dead without batting an eye, right?"

Walker nodded. It had been awful to watch a human being fall suddenly to his death and be powerless to stop it. All day long he had been second-guessing himself, wondering if it would have made any difference if he had had the presence of mind to fire a few rounds from the tower machine gun over Danforth's head. Mounty told him it would not have mattered.

"In the first place, it happened so quickly there was no way you could get to your machine gun. But even if you had, I doubt that it would have stopped Danforth. That guy is weird, Walker. My guess is that even if you fired a round over his head he would still have shot McCaw and then would have given you the finger. He had made up his mind to kill somebody, and nothing was going to stop him."

"I guess," Walker mumbled, still not reassured.

Danforth walked into the tent, his Enfield slung over his shoulder. Neither Mounty nor Walker looked up. Zimmerman, Knox, and O'Donnell, the other three G.I.'s sharing the tent, were already asleep. Danforth surveyed his tent mates and, without speaking, began to unlace his leggings. He was a short man in his early thirties, but his thin, balding hair and G.I. glasses made him look considerably older. He threw his leggings under his cot and started cleaning his rifle again.

Walker was tempted to ask him if he was trying to wipe the death out of it, but he didn't feel like becoming involved. He knew that if he said anything at all, he would get a response, for Danforth seemed to be looking for an excuse to talk.

The three of them sat in silence on their cots for several minutes. Realizing that no one was going to speak unless he did, Danforth broke the silence.

"Well, I'm leaving in the morning, guys. The C.O. said something about Wyoming."

Walker pulled off his leggings and started untying the laces in his shoes. Sgt. Mountcastle cleared his throat and picked up his guitar.

"Our thoughts are the idle wave caps on the deep that never breaks," he sang softly, his eyes turned towards Walker, but seemingly far away. "It is only in contemplation that the mystery speaks to us."

It was a song Walker had heard him sing before. Mounty told him the words were written by an Irish poet on the day he was sentenced to be hanged by the British. Mountcastle had set it to music and sang it a few times on the North Carolina radio station where he worked before the war.

Walker tossed off his shoes and lay on his cot with the rest of his uniform on. It would make it easier getting up at midnight when he went on guard duty again. Danforth finally put his rifle in the rack and started to undress. Cpl. Mountcastle sang again softly "our thoughts are the idle wave caps on the deep that never breaks" and his voice faded away into the night. Then just as Walker closed his eyes, far off in the distance, a dog began to howl. It was a long and plaintive cry of a lonely animal wailing at the moon on a cold December night. +++++

CHRISTMAS IN A BARN

We were thinking of how we would spend our first Christmas in France when the word of the Ardennes Offensive broke. In the beginning it wasn't considered a counter-attack at all. The Ardennes, where the snow was nearly waist deep, seemed the most unlikely of places to try to move tanks and infantry. But as Christmas approached and the weather worsened, the Germans pressed on. The 101st Airborne division was surrounded by the Germans at Bastogne and was running out of everything from ammunition to dry socks. The heavy fog made air lifts impossible. We heard stories of the SS troopers taking American prisoners and killing them in cold blood. Belgian civilians, too. And it was so cold and damp. Many of the G.I.s we brought to the hospital had trench foot. Some guys were in such bad shape they had to have their legs amputated. We guessed our casualties had to be way up in the thousands. Later we learned that it was around 81,000, including 19,000 killed.

We got an early Christmas present. On December 23rd the weather finally cleared and American planes filled the skies, dropping supplies to those trapped in the middle of the German Bulge at Bastogne and attacking their supply lines and armored columns in the Ardennes. Every time we looked up we saw either the planes or the vapor trails they were leaving behind. It was a reassuring sight.

The next night, Christmas Eve, Farley and I heard of a midnight mass that was going to be held in an old barn not far from the field hospital that we had been attached to.

"What do you say?" he asked. "Do you want to go for old times sake?"

Since we entered the Army we only bothered with religious services every now and then, although we had two sky pilots in our outfit, whom we called Big God and Little God. It had nothing to do with their spheres of influence; we named them by size. Big God, the Protestant chaplain, had the best jokes and Little God, the priest, had the best booze, so we were democratic and generally divided our time between the two of them. Surprisingly, neither of them was around on the eve of their big day. I suspected they were with the wounded.

"That's right," I told Farley. "The last time we were at Christmas Eve mass was when we were back at St. Malachy's. I think Father Voza said it."

"So how about it? Maybe we'll can get Tex to come. Now that he's seen his first snow, maybe he'd like to have his first Holy Communion."

"But he can't receive. He's not a Catholic."

"Who's checking, Mickey? If a priest is going to risk his ass to say mass in a place like this, do you think he gives a shit if a Protestant or atheist swipes a little Catholic bread and wine?"

It was a Christmas setting that would have out-Hollywooded Hollywood. There was something for everyone from sentimentalist to cynic. The barn wasn't unlike a blown-up version of the stable St. Malachy's set up every year by the main entrance. There were even a few animals in it—*real* ones, not those fake ones made out of plaster of Paris. Some of the guys who had come down from Neufchateau and Arlon decorated a large spruce tree with anything they could find—cans of C-rations, packages of the pills we were supposed to mix with the drinking water, letters from home, and even a few hand grenades. For music there was an old-fashioned wind-up Victrola. As we walked in we heard the crooner the Krauts called *der Bingle* singing on an old Decca record.

I'm dreaming of a white Christmas
Just like the ones I used to know...

Tex came with us. Farley told him they gave out free wine at the Consecration. The three of us had had a few shots of Calvados on the way up and the booze had accentuated a sense of indifference to the institutions of the world that didn't usually surface when we were sober. I thought of the guys in the 101st trying to hang on in Bastogne while some fat businessman back in the States was writing out his Christmas envelope for his church, realizing that if he gave $100 his name would lead the list in the next issue of the parish bulletin. At this very moment a G.I. was probably being blasted into eternity by an SS Panzer tank while back home a merchant was raising one hand in the *V for Victory* sign and dropping money into his cash register with the other.

Preceded by two soldiers, who were to be his altar boys, the priest walked to the front of the barn holding his chalice close to his chest. He was an old guy, maybe seventy or more. Thin, almost completely bald and wearing rimless glasses. For a moment I thought he was a German. That would have been the ultimate irony. Farley had told me that some German soldiers, who spoke English fluently, had been dropped behind our lines and were causing havoc up north.

But this guy couldn't speak English. He spoke to us for a moment in his own language. It sounded like Russian to me, but Farley told me it was Polish. Now what the hell was a Polish priest doing here south of Bastogne on Christmas Eve?

In nomine Patris, et Filii, et Spiritus Sanctus. Amen.
Ad deum qui laetificat iuventutem meum.

The guy was Polish, but his words were as clear to me as if he were saying, "How are things, Mickey?" I had heard that Latin of the mass for so long that it was as much a part of me as English. It was an odd feeling. Somewhere among the troops surrounding Bastogne a German priest might be saying these same old Latin words and carrying on the same ritual. Generals were talking about troop movements and sky pilots were talking about the Christ child. And all the while men, women, children, and soldiers were dying at Bastogne.

I thought of the afternoons we played with Eddie Bannon's toy movie projector. It had been fun to roll back the film and see how the characters looked running backwards. If all these guys, Germans and Americans both, could see what and who they were dying for, would they still want to do it? If they could roll the film of their lives forward and see the women they would marry, the children they would have, and the job they would go to every day, would they think that what they were doing right now was worth the sacrifice? If they could, would they roll the film back and skip the war? Was Hitler, democracy, and all the other high-sounding phrases worth what they were going through?

Kyrie Elison.
Chryste Elison

And yet that Polish priest, whoever he was, fascinated me. What the hell was he doing in this old stable spouting out the ancient Latin when he probably could be in a soft bed somewhere sipping vodka? I guess he was used to it. Consecrating the Host, blessing the congregation. I think it was James Joyce who quoted the Jesuits as saying, "Give me the child for the first six years and you can have him for the rest of his life." Somebody had apparently gotten to this Polish priest when he was young. Intellectually I had discarded the ravings of Sister Eucharia and Father Chagree, but I couldn't drive out of my mind the ideas they had screwed into it. Otherwise why was I in this stable in the first place?

Orate frates.

Tex seemed to be having a good time. I knew he had been eying the few nurses in the stable, but I think he was also intrigued by all the standing, kneeling, and genuflecting.

"Y'all hev lots of action in this heah Mass," he said.

I looked over at Farley, the guy who couldn't understand why the Pope wouldn't sell his gold dome to help the poor. Somehow he had gotten hold of a pair of rosaries and was fingering them. *Farley?* Had that Jesuit dictum applied to him, too? Or was he just trying to impress the nurses with his piety?

A staff sergeant approached the Victrola and flipped the record. Bing Crosby's voice, soft and easy, defied the scratches in the old record and floated casually to the chestnut beams of the old stable. Most of us had heard him sing it before. The familiar song and the familiar Latin words, spoken by a man who knew no English, transformed this old barn by the Luxembourg border to scenes of back home.

Silent night, Holy Night
All is calm, all is bright

"Do you know that's originally a German song," Farley whispered. "I think they called it *Stille Nacht, Helige Nacht*"

"Like *Lili Marlene*," I said.

"Well, in a way."

Ite, Missa est.
Deo Gratias.

We always got a kick out of that bit of liturgy. "Go, the mass is ended," followed by what we construed to be a cry of happy relief: "Thanks be to God."

In the distance we could hear the rumbling of long-range guns. Christmas or no Christmas, the war was going on. And while the Christ Child was being born again, some poor bastard was dying for the first time. I looked over at Tex. He was fascinated by the gyrations of the priest and congregation.

Sleep in heavenly peee-eace,
Slee-ep in heavenly peace.

The priest raised his hand to bless us.

In nomine Patris, et Filii et Spiritus Sanctus. Amen.

He shook hands with each of the soldiers who had helped him serve the mass. As we were leaving he called out to us:
"*Joyeux Noel.* And hoo-ray for Baby Ruth!"

***

We walked back in silence over the frozen ground. Although we knew that Christmas was just another day in wartime, we had to admit to ourselves that this one had a flavor that none of our other Christmases had ever had. Maybe it was the absence of all the statues. It always gave me the creeps to look at a piece of marble with round squares where eyes ought to be. Maybe the smells were better. No incense, but some good solid horse manure. And no collection basket either. Just an old priest whose English was limited to the name of a legendary baseball player, but who communicated with us all the same.+++++

SHINE, MISTER?

I thought for sure that when I got off the train at the Southside Station I would run into somebody I knew, but the place was deserted. I supposed it was because it was mid-afternoon and relatively few people traveled at that time of day. In fact, I was the only passenger who had disembarked from the train. The newspaper stand was closed and shuttered, and so was the ticket office. Although it was three and half years since I had been in this station, it looked about the same. It was true that the red paint had faded and some of it was starting to peel. The women in the cigarette and soap advertisements were wearing longer skirts, and the posters for the Broadway shows were different. When I left here for Fort Dix at the beginning of the war the big hits were Thornton Wilder's *The Skin of Our Teeth* with Tallulah Bankhead and Fredric March and *Star and Garter* with Gypsy Rose Lee. Now the top shows seemed to be Tennessee Williams' *The Glass Menagerie* and Rodgers and Hammerstein's *Oklahoma*.

Still, back in 1942 there was usually some activity at the station, even on quiet November afternoons like this. There were generally some people here—the news vendor, station master, and a few passengers. I realized that if I craved a welcoming committee I could have called a few people before I left camp. But I rather liked the idea of re-discovering Bergentown all by myself. My discharge had come through faster than I had expected, so everyone would be surprised to see me a day or two ahead of time. I was contemplating the loneliness of the depot when I was startled by a human voice.

"Shine, Mister?"

That was another of the missing ingredients of the Southside Station! There were usually five or six little kids hawking shoeshines.

"I make 'em shine like mirrors. How about it, Mister?"

"Oh? Why, sure. The works."

He was about nine. A skinny little kid with freckles, a checkered cap a size or so too big for him and brown pants with a patch over the knee.

"There used to be lots of kids around here giving shines. Where are they?"

The kid stopped brushing and pointed to the inside of the station.

"They're robbing our business."

"Who are?"

"Them."

He pointed again. I couldn't see what he meant.

"Them there machines."

"Oh, I see. How much does the machine charge?

"A dime. Same as me. But I rub harder."

He demonstrated with a fancy flourish of his two brushes.

"And besides," the kid said, "can a machine spit?"

"I would think not."

He tapped my shoe to indicate it was time to change feet.

"The cheapskates figger they don't hafta give no tip to a machine, but they ain't got nobody to talk to either, right?

"Oh, absolutely."

For the first time he took his eyes off my shoes and looked up at me.

"Say, you're a soldjer, ain'tcha?"

"Yes. Until—"

"Who'ja kill?"

It was a question I hadn't anticipated.

"Why, nobody."

He slowed his brushes down to half-speed. I could tell this kid was used to disappointments. He spat on my shoe and gave it a few half-hearted swipes with his rag. Then he started putting his brushes into his box. I gave him a quarter.

"Nobody," the kid said half-aloud and, I suspect, with a little bit of sympathy mixed with his disgust. As I walked down the steps he called after me.

"That's O.K., Mister. They'll probably be anudder war soon. Maybe ya ken plug someone the next time." +++++

A FRENCH VILLAGE BY THE SEA

Memories, like sudden summer rain, were constantly surprising Marty Murphy. Sometimes he thought he had a pocketful of Proust's *petites madeleines*. Almost everything he tasted, saw, heard, smelled, or touched brought him back to his past. But of all the memories that his senses evoked the one most frequent and most poignant was Etretat.

He had spent a few days in Etretat during World War II shortly after his outfit left their LCIs for the beaches of Normandy. He was only 19 at the time, hardly schooled enough to know that this beautiful village on the English Channel had been the inspiration for writers like Guy DeMaupassant and Victor Hugo and the French impressionists, Monet, Delacroix, and Courbet. But even in his youth Murphy was able to appreciate the superb beauty of Etretat's coast with châteaux high up on the hills overlooking the sea. And, of course, he observed the spectacular rocks jutting out into the channel that Monet had made famous in several of his paintings.

Hoboken, New Jersey, was a long way from Etretat, France, both in miles and majesty. Every time Murphy looked out at the polluted Hudson River, his mind turned quickly to the wind-swept beaches of Normandy. When he stared at the endless brownstones on Hudson Street, his imagination turned them into sun-stroked chateaux on the hills of Etretat. Even when he was watching television with his wife, Helen, he was reminded of his experiences in Normandy because Tom Brokaw and other news commentators kept referring to the World War II servicemen and women as "The Greatest Generation."

Then one morning while they were on vacation Helen suggested a change of pace for breakfast.

"What do you say, Marty—would you like some French toast?"

"That does it!" he shouted, jumping up from the kitchen table.

"Does what, Marty?"

"Does—does it take long to get a passport?"

Helen smiled. She and Marty had been married a long time and she often knew what he was thinking almost before he himself was aware of it. He had told her about Etretat many times. And their living room walls were enlivened with Monet's seascapes.

"There's a small shop on Washington Street that takes passport photos," she said. "If we hurry we can get there before they close for lunch."

***

The bus arrived at Etretat by nightfall. Since Marty and Helen were traveling light with backpacks, they decided to walk along the beach and see if they could find an inn overlooking the English Channel so that when they awoke in the morning they would be able to gaze out into the sea. It did not take long before they found just what they were looking for: *La Roche*, a handsome chateau on the beachfront. The proprietor, Monsieur Bardell, spoke a little English and Marty spoke a little French. They each managed to understand about a third of what the other was saying, but Marty's main objective—to obtain a room overlooking the English Channel—was in that two-thirds area where communications failed. Marty was busy consulting his French-English dictionary when Madame Bardell, the proprietor's statuesque young wife, came to the rescue.

"I overheard you as I was coming down the stairs," she said in fluent English. "You are in luck. We have just the type of chamber you are looking for—a penthouse suite on the top floor. It gives you a fine view of the sea."

Monsieur Bardell waved his hands enthusiastically. He seemed to get the gist of what his wife was saying.

"I think he understands your English better than my husband's French," Helen said.

Madame Bardell smiled. "Oh, it is not my English he comprehends; it is my hand signals. When I studied English in Oslo, I was surprised that there were no flourishes to go along with the dramatic nouns and spirited verbs. Let me show you to your chamber."

After Madame Bardell left, Marty and Helen sat down in their balcony and stared out at the sea, now peaceful and calm, that was once the scene of one of the greatest invasions and bloodiest battles in history. After a few minutes, Marty interrupted their reverie.

"There's a café across the lane," he said. "Let's eat before we unpack. Then we can go down and walk along the road that parallels the channel. My outfit occupied a few of the chateaux after we landed. I would like to see if I can find any of them."

Helen agreed. The long ride had made her hungry.

***

The wine was from Bordeaux, but the fish was caught off the coast of Le Havre, Denise their buxom waitress, told them in melodic French. The Murphys could not remember when they had such a delightful meal. They were on their second after-dinner calvados when Marty felt a tap on his shoulder.

"*C'est bon, monsieur?*"

When he wheeled around he saw a smiling Monsieur Bardell, the proprietor of La *Roche*. Marty thought for a moment of how to respond. He knew from his time in France during the war that the natives liked it when Americans made an attempt to speak to them in French.

"*C'est délicieux,*" said Marty, trying to enunciate carefully. "*Très délicieux.*"

Monsieur Bardell smiled again. He explained in great detail how the fishing boats left early in the morning from Le Havre, how the chef of their restaurant was on the docks to greet the ships and select the best of the catch, how his staff prepared special sauces and salads all afternoon, and how much of a perfectionist the restaurant owner was. Monsieur Bardell spoke so rapidly that Marty could only catch an occasional word, but he did not want him to think he did not understand him, so he nodded his head and said *Oui. Je comprends* from time to time to appear to be a rapt listener.

The Murphys invited Monsieur Bardell to join them for a calvados. He did, but then insisted on buying the next one. And so it went for an hour or more. After the third round the waitress left the bottle on the table.

***

It wasn't really the late hour and it wasn't the calvados, although the alcohol was certainly a contributory factor. When Marty and Helen tried to reconstruct it in their minds later, they attributed it to the similarity of *collation* and *collaborateur* to the untrained ear.

"Almost two years in France and I couldn't get it right," Marty had lamented. "And I had two more years in college too."

Earlier on it had been a delightful evening. Monsieur Bardell spoke very rapidly, assuming that since Marty knew some French he therefore understood most of what he was saying. When the Murphys seemed a little lost, the proprietor of *La Roche* used hand signals or drew vivid pen and ink sketches on the tablecloth. He told them that he was the unofficial historian of Etretat, collating data from a variety of sources in the village.

"*Et vous, monsieur?*" he asked of Marty.

Marty reached back into his memory and by producing a few key French words was able to explain to Monsieur Bardell that he had landed on the beaches of Normandy in 1944 after climbing down a rope ladder from a troop ship into an LCI. This brought the subject to World War II and the sad days when Etretat was in the hands of the Germans.

And that was when Marty tried to say in French that he and Helen had never dreamed they would be staying in an inn operated by a collator of the rich history of Etretat. But that's not the way it came out.

"*Comment? Pour qui me prenez-vous? Un collaborateur!*"

With that Monsieur Bardell rose to his feet angrily. Raising the near-empty bottle of calvados high over his head, he brought it down on the table with such force that the glass ricocheted in several directions, barely missing Helen's flailing arms. Hardly noticing the debris that he had created, Monsieur Bardell stomped out of the café muttering "*Un collaborateur. Vraiment!*"

The buxom waitress, who had watched the whole scene unfold, apologized for Monsieur Bardell as she handed them a package with the two pieces of chocolate cake they had not eaten when they started drinking the calvados.

"Monsieur Bardell is very sensitive to the nasty rumor in the village, circulated by a competitor, that during the war he was a collaborator. It is not true and he gets infuriated every time anyone alludes to it. Of course, the calvados didn't help either. Ironically, the truth is that he was a member of the resistance movement."

"It was a mistake." Marty said. "I confused the nouns. I meant to say *collator.*"

The waitress smiled. "It is understandable. *Collaborateur* and *collateur* *have similar sounds.* But don't worry about Monsieur Bardell. He has a bad memory, especially when he is drinking calvados. Tomorrow he will have forgotten the whole incident."

"You speak English very well, Denise," Helen said, putting on her coat.

The waitress smiled, displaying nicely capped teeth. "I should. I was born in Brooklyn."

As the Murphys left the café, they felt something whizzing by their heads. From their second floor balcony overlooking the sea Monsieur Bardell was rubbing his hands together in glee. The innkeeper may have a short memory as Denise had said, Marty reflected, but it wasn't that short: he had just flung their backpacks into the street. Things had suddenly gone awry. Here it was two o'clock in the morning and the Murphys were in the beautiful coastal village of Etretat without lodging.

***

At first they thought that despite the hour it would be easy enough to find another place to stay, but after walking the coastline and venturing into the side roads and country lanes, they discovered only four inns and each one was closed and locked for the night. They kept hoping they would find someone to ask where they might find shelter, but the roads were deserted. It appeared that all of Etretat went to sleep by 2 a.m. Helen suggested they go back to the café where they had dinner and see if Denise the waitress from Brooklyn was still up and could help them, but when they arrived that restaurant too was shuttered for the night.

"Well, we will just have to sleep on the beach until the inns open in the morning," Marty said. "It's a good thing we brought sweaters. We can use them for blankets."

They walked to the beach and, using their backpacks for pillows, stretched out within view of the famous rocks of Etretat. For the first few minutes it was restful as they listened to the steady rhythms of the sea.

"Here I am resting on a beach in Normandy," Helen said. "It is as if I were in a time capsule and were with you during the invasion of France."

"Except I eventually wound up in one of those beautiful chateaux on the hill," Marty grumbled. "Well, maybe we can get a few hours sleep if the wind dies down a little."

***

Despite the gusty winds, they soon managed to fall asleep huddled in each other's arms. But shortly after they dozed off the rains came, not a little drizzle but a heavy downpour.

"What will we do now?" Helen asked, shivering.

"There's no shelter nearby. By the time we run around looking for one it could stop raining. We might as well stay where we are and hope it lets up."

Helen had no better plan, so she snuggled closer to her husband, pulling her sweater over her head. They lay there for a few minutes, getting thoroughly soaked. Suddenly Helen sat up.

"D-did you hear that, Marty?"

"Hear what?"

But she did not have to reply. From the direction of the channel a pack of wild dogs came charging across the beach. Even in the misty light Marty could see they were huge dogs, probably shepherd mixes. The Murphys grabbed their backpacks and raced for the road. The dogs followed, barking and howling. Despite their heavy, water-soaked clothes and backpacks, Marty and Helen were running faster than they had ever run in their lives. Nevertheless the dogs were gaining on them.

"What'll we do, Marty? They're catching up with us."

"Quick, give me that bag with the chocolate cake."

Helen slowed down and reached into her pack. "But it's all soggy."

"Doesn't matter. Wild dogs aren't fussy,"

Marty pulled the two slices from the bag and swung his left arm back like a southpaw throwing a fast ball. Helen tried to stop him but succeeded only in slowing down the speed of the flying cake. The dogs changed direction and ran for the food. Minutes later, drenched to the skin, the Murphys stopped to get their breath on a road leading away from the sea. Marty looked at his wife curiously.

"Why did you try to stop me, Helen? I almost didn't get the cake out of my hand."

"Marty, that was chocolate cake."

"So?"

"Chocolate is not good for dogs."

Despite the icy wind and rain beating down on him, Marty had to laugh.

"Better a little sick stomach from chocolate than a case of dog gout from eating the prettiest legs in France," he said, ringing the water out of his sweater.

The rain began to fall harder, so rapidly that the Murphys could barely see more than a few feet in front of them. Not knowing what to do, they kept following the road that was winding its way away from the sea in the hope that they might find shelter somewhere. But all they could see was the blinding rain and all they could hear was the wind howling across the rooftops. It seemed that all the citizens of Etretat were nestled in their beds, oblivious to the raging storm outside.

When they turned a bend in the road, Helen gave a shout.

"Look, Marty, a light!"

Marty strained his eyes and stared into the distance. Through the blur of the rain he could make out a blue light. When they came closer they saw that it hung from a white pole which carried a sign with the single word *Gendarmerie*.

"We're in luck," Marty said. "This is a police station of sorts."

"It doesn't look like a police station, Marty. It must be somebody's house. Did you ever see a police station surrounded by a white picket fence?"

"But the sign—"

Marty tugged on the handle of the gate. It was locked. He looked behind the *Gendarmerie* sign and discovered a large copper bell with a rope dangling from it.

"Maybe this is a one-*gendarme* town and he lives here," Marty said. "The bell is probably for a night time emergency,"

"But if he's in that cottage, he's probably fast asleep."

"Of course he's asleep. It's past two o'clock in the morning."

"But do you think we should wake him up? The bell is for an emergency."

"This *is* an emergency, Helen. We're drowning in this freezing rain."

Marty grabbed the rope and gave it a tug, albeit a timid tug.

They waited a few minutes. There was no response.

"We had better forget it, Marty. He's sound asleep."

"He may be asleep, but he's got a night bell. I'll give it a good ring this time."

Marty pulled vigorously on the rope, letting it ring for a minute or two. It clanged loudly over the sound of the wind and the rain.

"I-I think we had better go, Marty. The *gendarme* is going to be boiling mad when he sees that two Americans woke him up in the middle of the night. Remember what Monsieur Bardell did to us."

Before Marty could reply, the Murphys saw a light go on inside the cottage. Almost as soon as it went on, it went off.

"We had better go while we can, Dear."

Marty hesitated. He was about to move on when he saw a figure exiting the cottage door and making his way down the slate path to the gate, He was hatless and wearing a blue terrycloth bathrobe and matching slippers.

"*Bon soir, monsieur,*" Marty began. "*Parlez-vous anglais?*"

The man in the blue bathrobe shook his head. "*Parlez-vous français?*" he asked.

"*Un petit peu.*"

Reaching deep into his memory, Marty tried to explain in French the predicament he and Helen found themselves in. The *gendarme* listened patiently while the rain flowed down his face in little rivulets, at the same time soaking his blue terrycloth bathrobe and matching slippers. Helen thought this was a good sign. If he was willing to get drenched to hear our story, he will surely want to get out of the rain himself soon and will most certainly invite us into his quaint little cottage. As soon as Marty finished his spiel in broken French, the *gendarme* let loose with a rapid-fire monologue. Marty strained his ears to catch words and phrases that he understood. When the officer stopped speaking, Helen turned to her husband.

"What was he saying?"

"I didn't catch too much of it, but I did hear him say *Je suis très désolé.*"

"What does that mean?"

"I'm very sorry."

"You're sorry about what?"

"*I'm* not saying *I'm* sorry. *He's* saying I am sorry. That's what *Je suis très désolé.*" means. He's telling us he can't help us."

"What a pity. He has such a cute little cottage. I'd break down and cry to see if I could make him sympathetic, but he would never see my tears with all this rain. Say, Marty, tell him you were here during the war and you brought me back for sentimental reasons."

Searching for words that could translate military terms like *Landing Craft Infantry*, Marty tried to explain that it had been the war and sheer chance that had brought him to this lovely Normandy town in the first place, causing him to return this time with his wife so she could see the beauty of this little village. And now here they were without a place to stay.

The *gendarme* seemed to get the drift of Marty's story and in the middle of it he reached out to shake his hand. But when Marty had finished and waited for a reply, the man in the drenched terrycloth bathroom merely repeated:

"Je suis très désolé.."

He turned on his heel and waved, saying *Bon soir* as he made his way to the cottage door. Marty and Helen looked at each other forlornly, watching their last hope of shelter fade away down the rain-splattered slate path. The *gendarme* closed the door and turned on his hallway light. The Murphys stared at it, expecting it to go out at any second, but it stayed lit.

"I supposed he is having a little late-night snack while we stand here shivering in the rain," Marty growled.

Suddenly the door swung open and the gendarme, now in a dry white bathrobe, came running down the path. He was holding a blue umbrella.

While the Murphys looked on in surprise, he handed them the umbrella and let loose with a torrent of French, punctuated from time to time with à *droit* and à *gauche*. When he paused for a moment to wipe his head with the sleeve of his bathrobe, Helen turned to her husband to ask what the *gendarme* was saying.

"I think he said there is an empty house about two kilometers from here. He kept telling me to take a right, then a left, then a right so fast that I couldn't keep up with him. Give me a paperback from your bag and I'll ask him to tell me again so I can write the directions down on the inside cover."

Once again the *gendarme* began to wave his arms about furiously between flourishes of à *droit* and à *gauche* while Marty wrote furiously, trying to get it all down. After the officer had described the *ancien maison*,

Marty handed him the book to see if he had jotted down the directions correctly.

"*Très bien,*" the *gendarme* said. He flicked the cover over and glanced at the title. It was Camus's *La Chute.* This discovery seemed to please him immensely. He handed the umbrella to Helen and shook hands with Marty.

"*Bon soir et bonne chance.*"

And with that he saluted and turned rapidly on his heels. Helen wasn't sure, but she thought she heard him whistling as he splashed his way down the winding slate path to the cottage door.

***

As they were trying to made sure they had each à *droit* and à *gauche* right every time they turned from one road to another, at the same time struggling to keep the umbrella from blowing away in the fierce wind, Helen asked Marty if he knew why the gendarme had a change of heart.

"I couldn't get all the French, but I think what happened was that when he returned to the cottage, his wife reminded him that her father had been a member of the *FFI,* the French Underground in World War II."

"So since you were here as an infantryman, she felt the least her husband could do was provide some sort of shelter, is that it?"

"I suppose so. And you saw how his eyes lit up when he looked at the cover of *La Chute?*"

"Right. Camus was the editor of *Combat,* the French underground paper during World War II. I just bought *La Chute* yesterday. See, it pays to go to book stores."

But Marty wasn't listening. He was staring at an old two-story house that looked like it might have once been a barn. He tried the door. It was unlocked.

"This must be it, Helen. Looks like we finally have a place to stay."

They entered a center hallway, illuminated by a tiny night light. It led to a large empty room which held a pleasant surprise for them: a working radiator. They could barely make it out in the dim light from the hallway, but they could hear the welcome sound it made letting out steam. Marty and Helen peeled off their clothes and rummaged through their packs, where they found underwear that was miraculously dry.

Helen gathered up the wet clothes and brought them to the radiator. They nestled close together, enjoying the warmth of each other and the nearby radiator, and soon were sound asleep.

***

Suddenly Helen awoke with a start.

"Did you hear that, Marty?"

Her husband made a feeble effort to open his eyes.

"Hear what?"

"Shhh. There, do you hear it?"

They both sat up and rested their backs against the wall. There was no mistaking the noise. It was heavy footsteps coming down the stairs near the far corner of the room. Helen huddled next to Marty, who reached in his backpack for his flashlight to use as a weapon. The footsteps came closer.

In the dim light they were able to make out the figure of a man in his socks and underwear. He went straight for the radiator and muttered something in French, which Marty guessed was probably a curse. While the Murphys watched in awe, the half-naked figure picked up their clothes and dropped them on the floor. Then he bent down, apparently to examine them with a small flashlight. The light enabled the Murphys to make out that this was an elderly man wearing white underpants with images of Mickey and Minnie Mouse on the seat. He grunted once or twice and then exclaimed *Voila*! He replaced the Murphys' clothes on the radiator and made his way back to the stairs, carrying a shirt and trousers.

"Did he steal your trousers, Marty?" Helen whispered after the sound of footsteps began to fade up the stairs.

"No. It looked like he was carrying a pair of white pants. Mine are brown. I guess we covered up his things when we put our stuff on the radiator. He must have thought someone swiped his clothes."

Helen felt a little nervous lying half-naked on the floor of a strange house occupied by an old man in Mickey Mouse shorts, but she was tired and Marty was already asleep again, so she cuddled close to him and shut her eyes. They did not hear or see a thing until the first light of dawn filtered through the window over their heads. The rain had stopped and a bright sunny morning awaited them.

***

Comfortable in dry clothes, they took one last look at their strange sleeping place, half expecting the old man in the Mickey Mouse shorts to do a reprise by the radiator. But they made their exit without a sign of their upstairs sleeping mate.

"What next, Marty? Shall we move on to Paris where they have more hotels?"

"I'd like to stay a few days in Etretat and see if I can find the châteaux I stayed in during the war. Those inns that were closed last night should be open this morning."

They spent the next hour walking through the village and its outskirts, retracing their steps over several of the places they had passed the previous night. Helen marveled at the quaint beauty of the little Normandy village and the rugged coastline where Monet had spent so many days painting the rocks he made famous. Marty pointed out that he had read that one time the artist was so intent in catching on his easel the various changes of light on the rocks as the day wore on that he had almost drowned when the tide changed.

"He was that involved in his work?" Helen asked.

"Yes. And the tide changes rapidly here in the channel."

The more they saw of Etretat, the more they wanted to stay there, but every inn they tried was filled to capacity. Tired and frustrated, they made their way to the bus stop and rested on a roadside bench. The bus for Rouen was due in fifteen minutes.

"I hate to leave this beautiful village," Helen sighed. "If the floor wasn't so hard, I'd be tempted to go back to the old house where we slept last night."

"I don't think the old guy in the Mickey Mouse underwear would appreciate it. Besides, we would be overstaying our welcome if we tried it again. What's that coming down the road? Do you think the bus is early?"

But it wasn't the bus for Rouen. It was a police vehicle. The Murphys recognized the man behind the wheel as the *gendarme* of the blue terrycloth bathrobe of the night before.

"*Venez ici, s'il vous plaît,*" he said, gesturing them into his vehicle.

Marty started to ask him why, but the *gendarme* guided him gently, but firmly, into the police car.

"Is he arresting us?" Helen whispered nervously.

"Why are you whispering? He doesn't speak English."

"Maybe he understands more than he lets on. I can't fathom this. He was so nice last night to lend us his umbrella. Do you think it's the umbrella? We left it at the house."

"That doesn't make sense, Helen. Besides, he probably checked the house and picked it up. I wonder if he thinks we stole something. Let me try asking him again."

Marty tried *je ne comprends rien* and a few of his stock comments for his inability to understand what was going on, but the *gendarme* either did not hear him because of the noise his vehicle was making, did not understand what he was saying, or chose not to answer. Marty gave up and sat back just as the police car came to a halt in front of *La Roche*. The gendarme sprung out of his vehicle to open the door for Helen. He was smiling. Standing by the garden gate of the old inn was Madame Bardell.

"*Bonjour*, Mr. and Mrs. Murphy. Would you come in, please. *Et Charles, aussi, s'il vous plaît.*"

The *gendarme* followed the Murphys and Madame Bardell into the inn.

"D-do you think your husband wants to see us—after what happened last night?" Helen asked.

"He is quite embarrassed," Madame Bardell replied. "You see, Charles here stopped by this morning to explain what happened to you last night and told Marcel, in no uncertain terms how he had mistreated a former soldier who had taken part in the invasion of Normandy. My husband did not remember much of what happened last night, except that he thought you had called him a collaborator. But once he heard the whole story, he felt awful. I suppose I did not ease his conscience any when I reminded him that my uncle had been a member of the *FFI*. We both want you to be our guests tonight in the penthouse. Here comes Marcel now."

Monsieur Bardell entered the living room and embraced both the Murphys, first Helen and then Marty.

"*Je suis très désolé,*" he said over and over.

With that he left and returned seconds later with a tray bearing a bottle of calvados, five brandy glasses, and a corkscrew.

"*À votre santé!*" Monsieur Bardell exclaimed, raising his glass.

The Murphys, Charles the *gendarme*, and Madame Bardell clinked glasses with each other and the innkeeper. The brandy went down smoothly, as smooth as the sea gliding over the famous rocks of Etretat, Marty thought. Monsieur Bardell filled the glasses again, but this time the Murphys politely refused. Might as well quit while they were ahead. Visions of the pack of wild dogs and the teeming rain were still fresh in their memory banks. +++++

IV.

On the Satirical Side

Satire is a sort of glass, wherein beholders do generally discover everybody's face but their own.

—Jonathan Swift

DADS' DAY

Cast thy bread upon the waters
For thou will find it after many days.

—Ecclesiastes 11:1

Once upon a time, way back around 2006, there was a Prince of Business named Vernon Schaffner. He wasn't a real prince, of course, at least not like the princes in fairy tales; some of his enemies said he wasn't a real fairy, either. But there was no doubt that he was called Prince.

He got that name from an editorial writer on the *Wall Street Journal*. When Mr. Schaffner saw the editorial, he had his pilot fly him to the newspaper office at once. The writer was a little frightened when he saw the Schaffner entourage coming down the hallway of the editorial office, but all Mr. Schaffner wanted to do was present the writer with a check for $50,000 because he liked the name. The writer, honorable journalist that he was, accepted it under the proviso that he could donate it to his favorite charity. The Prince smiled amiably; he was a man of the world.

Almost from that point on he was referred to as Prince Schaffner. You see, he didn't have any title, not having gone to graduate school, studied medicine or law, or run for public office. He was too busy making money with his disintegrating aerial diapers, better known by the trade name of DAD.

It was really a simple invention. He got the idea from a toy boomerang his parents had given him when he was a kid. Boomerangs go up, then come down. All he had to do was eliminate the second part. With DAD, one didn't even have to dispose of diapers any more. Schaffner's diapers were treated with a special chemical, making it possible for Father to simply hold the soiled diaper over his head in a stiff wind and it would dissolve right in front of his eyes. Convenient, and not at all messy unless Father (or Mother, for that matter) grabbed the diaper in the middle rather than at the edges, as the instructions on the box advised. But even in extreme cases like that, the damage was usually limited to the inside of the fingernails.

Of course, a package of DAD wasn't cheap, but that didn't hinder its marketability. The rich and middle class gobbled them up, and many of the poor postponed payments on their cars and VCR's to keep their homes stocked with DAD. The American people liked convenience and there was nothing more convenient than getting rid of excrement by simply waving it at the sun. Rumor had it that Prince Schaffner was instrumental in having legislation passed that permitted the poverty-stricken to purchase DAD with food stamps. In some cases it meant cutting down on potato chips and hot dogs; thus in an indirect way it educated the impoverished on the value of eliminating saturated fats from their diet.

As you must have guessed Prince Schaffner's success with DAD soon led to even better things. After all, once he had established the principle of merely sticking something into the air and watching it disappear, you can imagine how the Prince revolutionized the waste disposal industry. Here in the twenty-first century the word garbage has become almost as obsolete as *23-skiddoo*, *hula hoop*, and *poetry*. It wasn't long before the Prince applied his patented chemical process—more closely guarded than the secret for *Coca Cola*—to just about anything that could be held up in the air. For sentimental, and perhaps marketing, reasons he retained the name DAD for his new disappearing solution, which he sold by the tube, spray can, and in some cases gallon jug. Deposit bottle and cans became a thing of the past. All one had to do was drop a dab of DAD formula on a object, open a window, and stick it out. How fast people began getting rid of plastic containers, old newspapers, magazines, boxes, paper bags, broken toys, outdated telephone books, and, obviously, garbage cans!

It was wonderful on the Christmas and Thanksgiving holidays. No more hours of clean-up in the kitchen for Mother. As soon as dinner was over Father usually summoned the whole family outdoors with the dirty paper plates and turkey bones. A little squirt of DAD all around. Hands up in the air. Poof! All Mother had to do was put away the leftovers.

It wasn't an unfamiliar sight to see men, women, and children in front of their houses holding up their old radios, cassettes, waffle irons, and TV sets. Once in awhile you might have spotted two or three men struggling to lift up an old washing machine or refrigerator. It usually took a little longer than your simple toaster or microwave oven, but with a bit of patience and three or four guys with linebacker physiques and mentalities, a family could get rid of a freezer, baby grand piano, or Honda Civic in a matter of minutes.

Commodes came back into fashion again. This time disposable, of course, and in high fashion colors and stripes. Obviously there was no need to go through all that trouble of flushing toilets any more. It certainly was fortuitous since the water supply was low, what with so many reservoirs and wells drying up. Generally speaking, it was not the best idea to stick your commode in the air early in the morning, the most popular housecleaning time in the western hemisphere. The disintegration was still as rapid as ever, but with a few trillion commodes aimed into the air at precisely the same time, the atmosphere for those who still had partial use of their olfactory nerves was a tad stifling.

Oh yes, the Prince was international. His DAD was the electric light bulb of his generation. What a job they did in Venice. Let's face it, even the most chauvinistic Venetians admitted their city had been a walking sewer since the Renaissance. And still the tourists kept coming. With DAD the smell had abated somewhat. The Prince devised a machine that was a cross between an armored tank and the street sweepers that towns used before double and triple-deck parking tiers were installed on most of the streets of the world. When it was late at night and the tourists had spent all their money, the city fathers turned the machine on and aimed its gun at the center of St. Marc's Square. It sucked up all the pigeon droppings in less than a minute. Then they would pour a half-gallon of DAD into the cannon and shoot it off into the night. Voila! Early morning tourists could stroll along St. Marc's Square in their bare feet.

What a medley in the skies on some days! Empty vodka bottles from Russia, old teabags from England, cartridge shells from Israel, and throwaway cameras from Japan. A journalist on the now defunct New York *Times* dubbed the phenomenon "the United Nations of the heavens." Yes, every country in the world was represented by some type of airborne garbage.

Of course, the airlines didn't like this very much. Visibility was zero more often, not only from the smog and pollution, but from high-flying debris. Special radar had to be designed just to avoid an occasional mid-air collision with an old dishwasher or Corvette that had taken too long to dissolve. The excrement that lingered on before becoming part of the atmosphere wasn't as dangerous as it was messy. An early-morning encounter with a trillion pounds of slowly dissolving waste could be upsetting for businessmen on the shuttle flights. That's why they discontinued the practice of serving a light breakfast on the executive specials.

Like everything else, there were debates on the use of DAD. The old chestnut about "the greenhouse effect" didn't get very far since most people had already become used to wearing oxygen masks nine or ten hours a day anyway. Besides, the department stores that had invested trillions in designer masks were foremost among the lobbyists for DAD. The airlines would have squawked more about clogged engines, glop on the windshields, and a few dozen fatal crashes a week, but their cargo planes were making a fortune freighting DAD, a truly American product when you come to think of it, to the seventh world countries, who paid for their supplies from funds they acquired from 100-year loans. Incidentally, the nice thing about a plane loaded with DAD going down was that as soon as it crashed, the DAD was released and the giant airplane, cargo and crew, soon became a part of the never-never-land of space, a new version of the good old reliable self-destruct of bygone years.

There was a story, which might be apocryphal, that in the latter part of the twentieth century a garbage barge left New York and sailed pretty nearly around the world looking for a country that would accept its load. Back in the Prince's time that would never have happened. His men would have just poured two gallons on top of the barge and it would soon be sailing around among the stars.

The trouble with checking out the barge story and others like it was that ever since they started applying DAD to the libraries to make more space for parking lots, jetports, shopping malls, and condominiums, there just weren't that many books around. But we do know that there were lots of oil spills and nuclear waste back in the twentieth century because there were some in the twenty-first until Prince Schaffner gave us DAD.

***

Word came slowly and inconspicuously. It began as one of those tiny items that the *New Yorker* magazine sometimes carried to fill up the space at the end of the page when the re-run of a John Updike story didn't stretch out to its usual ten pages. It read:

BEANS IN THE WINDY CITY

Mrs. Maureen. O'Leary from Chicago told police
that she had been attacked by a can of *Bile Beans*
while she was strolling along the shores of Lake
Michigan yesterday evening. She was booked for
questioning, but was later released in her own
recognizance.

The following week a man in Etretat, France, reported that his
German shepherd had been laid low by a set of pink hair curlers that
dropped from the sky. Then the next day came a story out of the Gaspe
Peninsula in Canada of a truck driver who narrowly escaped getting
hit by a sewing machine. By the end of the week a woman in Athens,
Georgia, was smacked on the back of the neck by a bag of fish heads, an
old ammunition box dropped at the feet of a monsignor in front of Sacre
Coeur in Paris, and a Mack truck landed on the Grand Ole Opry House
in Nashville, Tennessee.

And still they kept coming—beer cans, old tires, half-eaten
spaghetti dinners, outdoor plastic furniture, prune pits, transistors,
hypodermic needles, the works. All one had to do was look up in the air
and something was raining down, from lingerie to lawn mowers, from
radios to wrenches. The wonder was the casualties were relatively small,
when you consider all the stuff that was flying around up there. To be
sure there was considerable property damage. The world grieved when it
learned that 17 freight cars loaded with truck parts, old generators, and
shredding machines leveled the Pentagon on the same day that a carton
of assorted trash including slot machines, No-Nonsense pantyhose,
poisoned grapes, and black shoe polish exploded in front of 10 Downing
Street.

But there were occasional bits of good news. A considerable amount
of living waste landed on the Sahara Desert, causing scientists to
speculate that it might fertilize the hot barren sands. Although most of
the libraries that sailed back to earth had half their books missing, all
of the works of Danielle Steele, Stephen King, and Richard M. Nixon
landed unscathed. On another happy note librarians reported that most
of the missing books were by obscure, little-read writers—Swift, Camus,
Dickinson, and Rabelais were among the names they recalled—so the
loss was minimal.

Meanwhile the Prince was naturally upset by the sudden turn of events. DAD had made him the richest man in the world, but his fortune was quickly dissipating. The day a dump truck loaded with used condoms splattered all over the Vatican DAD dropped 1,000 points on the stock market. At first he had his people re-applying DAD to the returning objects and sending them up again, but they came down once more within the hour, and even sooner if they had mid-air collisions with the steady rain of furniture and appliances that were descending every minute.

Even though Prince Schaffner was a businessman, he was not without imagination. From his penthouse office in Rockefeller Center he looked up at the heavens through the debris and began to discern a pattern in the skies: his boomerang had discovered its missing part. Everything DAD had sent up was returning in the reverse order that it had been launched. That left only the diapers. Oh my God, he ejaculated, the diapers! The Prince looked at his watch. There wasn't a moment to lose. He summoned his pilot and raced for the roof where his helicopter was waiting. He would fly to Bayonne. Everyone was safe in Bayonne.

The pilot and the Prince raced across the roof like frightened rats. But it was too late. The diapers, soft and fleecy, soft and soggy, had already begun to fall on the Twin Towers, on the Empire State, on Rockefeller Center. The Prince looked up and closed his mouth just in time. His soul swooned slowly as he heard the diapers falling faintly on the streets of New York and faintly falling through the universe on all the dead down below. +++++

WHAT HAVE YOU DONE WITH DOCTOR BLOOMINGDALE?

So there was Parker, the only man in a room full of pregnant women—at least a dozen of them with bellies the size of beach balls—when this woman with a pearl-handled umbrella and a hat with a purple ostrich feather burst through the door like John Wayne entering the Last Chance Saloon.

She didn't have any six-shooters, but she wielded a mean yellow umbrella. Parker looked on with interest. He badly needed something to break the monotony of sitting in the waiting room of an obstetrician's office.

"When I made the appointment they told me I would not have to wait," the umbrella lady shouted to the expectant mothers. "They never said there would be a room full of people with wax in their ears."

The women had been perusing magazines or staring into space the way people do in doctors' offices, but at the militant sound of the intruder, they turned in her direction.

"Lady, if you want to get your ears unplugged, you've come to the wrong place," one of them said with a smile.

"Yes, we're here for a different kind of unplugging," another added.

For the first time the umbrella lady looked at the dozen heaving bellies.

"I'm ninety-two years old and my eyesight isn't what it used to be. Are all of you having—?"

The secretary slid her glass petition open.

"May I help you?"

The umbrella lady spun around. Her eyes sought the direction of the voice that had called out to her.

"What have you done with Doctor Bloomingdale?"

"I beg your pardon?"

"Dr. Bloomingdale B-l-o-o-m-i-n—-"

"There is no Dr. Bloomingdale here. Are you sure you have the right office?"

"Sure I'm sure. I have been coming here for 25 years and Doctor Bloomingdale always took care of my ears."

"But there is no ear doctor here. This is an obstet—"

"What happened to him? I didn't see his name on the door."

A nurse, who had been on the phone, appeared at the partition.

"When was the last time you were here to see Doctor Bloomingdale?" she asked.

"Six months ago. I got a call yesterday to come for my semi-annual check-up. It's about time too. The wax build-up in my ears is horrible."

"Dr. Bloomingdale moved from here four months ago. His office is in Cedar Falls now. You'll have to go—"

"How am I going to get to Cedar Falls? My taxi just left. He told me he was taking a fare to New York and he's the only cab in town. I can't walk to Cedar Falls. I'm ninety-two years old. Get Doctor Bloomingdale on the phone and tell him to come and get me. He shouldn't have moved without telling me."

The nurse fought back a smile. She did not want to be rude to the elderly woman, but the thought of a doctor dropping everything and driving to pick up a patient struck her funny bone. It was nice to meet someone who was out of touch with the contemporary medical world.

"I'll call his office to tell him you were unaware that he moved. Who shall I say is—?"

"Mrs. Gertrude Wintergreen. Tell him that this is a fine way to treat a patient who has been coming to him for years."

***

Parker watched curiously as the little drama in the obstetrician's office played out. When Mrs. Wintergreen was told that Dr. Bloomingdale was with a patient and would call her back, she settled herself down in the middle of the room and addressed the dozen pregnant women and Parker as a college professor might lecture his class.

"This ear problem of mine is hereditary," she began. "My older sister has the same trouble, only she just has it in her left ear."

"How old is your older sister?" a short heavy-set woman asked.

"Ninety-five, but she looks a lot older. I keep telling her she has to take better care of herself. So you're going to have a baby?"

"All of us are," the heavy-set woman said.

"Except me," Parker chimed in.

Mrs. Wintergreen stared him straight in the eye. "And why not?"

"I couldn't pass the physical," Parker quipped.

"Well, you did a smart thing."

"How?"

"By being a man. That's the trouble with women today—they are always having babies. It's no wonder that you see so many beautiful trees being cut down to build tasteless houses and make paper diapers, or whatever you call them."

The secretary leaned over the counter. In her role in charge of the files in an obstetrician's office she had heard only praise for babies. This was a new twist.

"You never had any children, Mrs. Wintergreen?" she asked.

"Of course I had children. Five of them."

"Then why—?"

"Why did I have them?"

The secretary realized she had to be tactful. "I mean, since you had five children, you must love little—"

Mrs. Wintergreen let her eyes circle the room. She spoke, almost confidentially.

"When I was young—and that was nearly a hundred years ago—we did not have all the contraptions women have today."

A young woman in fashionable eyeglasses, who appeared to be hours away from adding a new citizen to the state, moved to the edge of her chair so she could have a good look at Mrs. Wintergreen.

"But surely, even if you had birth control resources, you would still want to have children, wouldn't you?"

Mrs. Wintergreen fanned the air with her umbrella like the conductor of a Wagnerian opera.

"And who are you, may I ask?"

"Peggy Cochrane. Mrs. Margaret Cochrane."

"Well, Mrs. Cochrane, if I had it to do all over, I would swallow a bottle of birth control pills and have my tubes tied in sailors' knots."

"But think of your children. And you must have grandchildren as well."

"At last count I had twelve grandchildren and three great-grandchildren. And who knows what's going on right now?"

Even though they assumed that because of her age Mrs. Wintergreen would have had many offspring, the women were still surprised by the number. Mrs. Cochrane felt called upon to say a word in defense of the unborn, just-born, and works in progress.

"Why, with your children, grandchildren, and great-grandchildren, you have accounted for five...twelve...and three more. That's twenty offspring. Just think of it, Mrs. Wintergreen."

"Yes, I know. I've got enough there for two baseball teams and a couple of pinch-hitters."

"That's quite an accomplishment, Mrs.Winter- green," the heavy-set woman said.

"Yes, people like me are polluting the planet."

Three of the women gasped. Mrs. Cochrane looked down the rim of her expensive spectacles and, in an age reversal, eyed the elderly woman as a kindergarten teacher regards a recalcitrant child.

"Mrs. Wintergreen! You are talking about your own children. Certainly you are not wishing them out of existence!"

"Who said anything about that? They are here now and I wish them well. But if I knew then what I know now—"

"Oh come now, Mrs. Wintergreen. I'll bet you love your children just as much as we mothers here are going to love our little ones when they are born."

Mrs. Wintergreen grunted and turned to the secretaries to see if Doctor Bloomingdale had called. One of them shook her head. Parker left his chair and walked over to her.

"Was it very expensive having five children, Mrs. Wintergreen?" he asked.

"Money was not the problem. My husband had a pretty good job and those were different times. Is your wife having a baby?"

"We don't know yet. That's why we're here. But if money was not the problem, why do you wish you hadn't got involved?"

The other women had returned to their magazines, but they were regarding Mrs. Wintergreen out of the corners of their eyes. The elderly woman dropped her yellow umbrella on the floor and settled back in her chair. Parker could see that despite her age she was youthful looking. She was slim and relatively few wrinkles lined her face.

"All you have to do is look around you. The traffic is so bad I had to give up driving. And when you are stuck in a traffic jam you can see all the trees coming down to build houses and schools for the new babies being born. It's not the children's fault; they didn't ask to be born. And the parents, like these women here, try their best to make good kids out of their children. But once they are old enough to go to school, they are lost. They pay more attention to their peers than their parents, and most of them don't learn much in school anyway. The towns raise taxes to pay for the schools and some of the old folks can't pay the taxes, so they lose their homes. And most of the time they are old, beautiful homes. Not these plastic things that are going up by the numbers. Don't get me started; it's a mess."

Parker hesitated. "May I ask you a personal question?"

Mrs. Wintergreen smiled for the first time. "Personal? What's personal at my age? Fire away."

"Was it just the effect on the environment that made you feel this way?"

"Do you mean did I love my children?"

"Well, yes."

"I have lived a long time and I am still not sure what love is. When the children were small I got a kick out of them. When they started to grow up they became more interested in their friends than my husband and me. That's understandable. And their own children are the same way. Every now and then one of my daughters calls me to complain about the way my grandchildren are behaving."

"And what do you say to her?"

"I tell her it must be the water. More arsenic in it than usual."

"And she believes you?"

Mrs. Wintergreen eyed Parker curiously. "You say there's a chance that you may become a father?"

"Yes."

"First time?"

"We've only been married three months."

Mrs. Wintergreen sighed. "We live in dangerous times. Nurse, any word from Doctor Bloomingdale?"

"I'll try him again, if you like."

"Please do."

Mrs. Wintergreen sat back in her chair. A young woman appeared at the door leading to the doctor's office. She had been crying. Parker got up and ran to her side. The two entered the office, closing the door behind them. Seconds later the door opened again and the nurse entered the waiting room. She approached Mrs. Wintergreen.

"Dr. Bloomingdale's office called. He said he was sorry about the mix-up and he would be happy to see you, if you can come to his office in the next half-hour. After that he has an emergency operation."

"Is he going to pick me up?" His secretary said he was with a patient," the nurse lied tactfully.

"Well, how about his secretary?"

The nurse thought quickly. "Her license was suspended. I would take you there myself, if your appointment was a little later, but the doctor needs me now."

Mrs. Wintergreen picked up her umbrella and used it to prop herself up. "I think they have a taxi in Cedar Falls, but who knows where it is now? And besides by the time I got hold of him, he could never get here and back to Cedar Falls in a half hour. Would you call Doctor Bloomingdale's office and tell them I cannot make it."

Parker stepped into the waiting room. "I can take you to Cedar Falls, Mrs. Wintergreen. My wife is going to be with the doctor a little longer."

"Is she all right?" Mrs. Cochrane asked.

"Well, she is not pregnant," Parker said. "She is disappointed, but the doctor is talking to her."

Mrs. Wintergreen waved good-bye with her umbrella to the personages in the waiting room and office. Parker held the door open for her and led her to his station wagon.

"Well, this is very nice of you," she said, settling herself down in the passenger seat. "I suddenly have a feeling that this is going to be my lucky day after all."

Parker started the engine. He wondered if any of

Her children or her grandchildren had ever taken her to a doctor's office.

"Not only my lucky day," Mrs. Wintergreen smiled, "but maybe yours as well."

And she gave him a big broad wink. +++++

LAYOVER IN HALIFAX AIRPORT

You're from New England and you've never heard of an airport in Wembley, Vermont? Look, mate, I never said there was one. All I said was that I was flying there.

Let me explain. I've never been much for priests, nuns, Hari Krishnas, Seventh Day Adventists, rabbis, Jehovah's Witnesses, ministers, Buddhist monks, those who have gained full enlightenment and those who haven't. I've even been a little suspicious of Boy Scout leaders—y'know, full-grown men in khaki shorts and long brown socks, playing around with ropes and tomahawks with little tykes. Perhaps I'm a bigot, but all those men and women—mostly men—dressed up in ladies' underwear, waving wands and crosses, telling us what God has in mind and what God wants us to do, have always made me a mite suspicious. Especially when their rantings and ravings are followed by the passing of the collection basket. You've probably observed the scene: the minister-priest-rabbi stands at the door on a blimey May day, shakes hands with every bloody member of the congregation, and drives off in a Mercedes-Benz.

That being said, I hope you will believe what one who has been called an agnostic, an atheist, and an abiogenist is about to tell you. Believe me, this whole business has put a few questions in my head about who is running things and how.

I had better start off by telling you that I've been taking my holidays in the States for years now—Wembley, Vermont, a decent British name now, wouldn't you say? Nice little town. General store, summer theatre, antique shops and oodles of Yankee hills. Delightful for the jogger and outdoor aficionado. They also have a priory there. I didn't even know what that was until about my fourth or fifth trip to Wembley.

It was in the early fall, probably the time of year Wembley is most crowded. The brokers and buyers from New York City who rarely see grass, let alone leaves turning gold, red, russet, and brown, were jamming the roads to New England to get a glimpse of Nature getting undressed. Among the crowds of people was a blonde woman named Julia. She had square eyes in a round face, a short chin and a long nose, but Julia had a way of getting your attention and making you want to do the things *she* was interested in.

"Have you ever been to the Wembley Priory?" she asked me over a tea and cupcake at the General Store.

"Is that the church up the hill?"

"Well, they have a chapel there, but the Priory is lots of things—a farm, recreation hall, picnic tables, trails through the woods. I'm on my way up to see Brother Thaddeus. I'll give you a lift."

Do you see what I mean? As if I had already told her I had intended to go there. Before I knew what was happening, she was driving me up the winding dirt road to the Priory in her Kharman Ghia convertible. She parked by the entrance of the grounds in front of a huge wooden cross as tall as a willow with nothing on it but a few wandering maple leaves. We walked to the picnic area where one of the priests, monks or brothers—it was hard to tell them apart because they all wore the same uniform—was plucking away *That's what friends are for* to a crowd of 50 or 60 visitors, who were singing and clapping hands. We sat on the grass and one of the monks handed us paper cups like the kind you'd find by water bottles in old-fashioned offices on Queen Victoria Street.

"They make their own wine," Julia pointed out. "Isn't it good?"

I had to admit it was better than tolerable. The second cup was even more remarkable. By the third I was humming along with the crowd. I couldn't make out the words, but the gist of it was that a little love goes a long way. I took a quick look at Julia and then decided to amble off to the table for another drink.

The guitarist was Brother Thaddeus. He introduced himself to the latecomers and told us he would like us to listen to the Abbot, Father Aloysius, for a few minutes. I knew there had to be a hitch to this somewhere.

Now here's where it got a bit out of hand, so I don't blame you if you meander over to pick up the paper. They have them in French and English here, so you have your choice. That might be more to your liking. You'd prefer I'd continue? Thank you, mate. Y'know, I would have flown the coop myself if I didn't need a ride down the mountain from Julia—that and the fact that they had opened four more bottles of wine. Father Aloysius started out with the same old bloody routine about how important it is to have faith and love, but suddenly he interrupted himself to tell us we only use 7% of our brains.

I woke up at this. I never heard this theory, although I know quite a few fellows who use considerably less. Then he told us without blinking an eyelash that in that unused 93% was our ability to...I mean, what's the sense of talking? He had a proper way of putting it. I took notes—got them right here in my vest pocket. Never know when you may want to document your story, I always say. These are his exact words:

"My friends, I am convinced that we have the power within ourselves to stop the creeping death that is affecting so many of our brothers and sisters. We can put an end to the pollution caused by traffic congestion, which even we in this beautiful state of Vermont are beginning to feel. Best of all, allies in Christ, we can travel more of God's gorgeous world without filling the land, sea, and air with machines. In short, ladies and gentlemen, I believe we can fly."

I'm not pulling your leg. He was talking about standing on a little hill, flapping his arms like a bloody bird, and taking off through the air. And as far as I could ascertain, he hadn't even sniffed the wine. Then he lowered his voice and became really secretive.

"Dear friends, you know the ways of the world. I am afraid we are going to have to confine our little secret to the people of Wembley. For now, I think we must limit it to this small group and my colleagues here at the Priory. If you agree to secrecy, would you please stand up."

You would have thought a commander of the royal navy had called his crew to attention. Even I stood up, not so much in agreement but because I was carried forward by the momentum like a leaf in a hurricane.

"Come back at the same time tomorrow and we shall have our first flying lesson," he said as casually as if he were inviting us to tea.

By the end of the week each of the 50 of us could fly from the Priory to the general store in less than a minute. And Father Aloysius wasn't urging speed. He said later on we could work on what he called his theory of transcendence. Once we had mastered this, Father Aloysius said, we could simply concentrate on a destination—say the Champs Elysees, for instance, and in seconds we'd be looking in the shop windows and carrying on conversations with the Parisians. No need to study French, either. Learning languages instantly was Section 18 of the unused 93% Much easier than flying, as a matter of fact.

Within three weeks almost all of Wembley's 1,103 residents, including 13 infants, could fly. After the second week Father Aloysius and the monks and brothers offered the town's visitors and itinerant merchants the opportunity to learn, providing they agreed to become residents. Only two people besides Julia and me accepted his offer. One was a retired fireman from Hoboken, New Jersey, who said "after being grounded by King Farouk"—we discovered later that this was what he called his wife—"for so many years, flying would be a real change of pace." The other person was an 83-year-old former ballet dancer with arthritis.

***

Mike Bonacchio of Fair Deal Car Insurance, who had received 54 requests for cancellations by the middle of the second week, called for a town meeting at the Priory to object to our actions. He was joined by Mayor Blatzer, who had been quite upset by the turn of events from the beginning but had given us the impression that he enjoyed flying. Looking back, I think he hung on because he suspected that the town's new activities would be good for the tourist business. He owned a crafts shop.

"Fly up to the front of the room, will you please," Brother Thaddeus asked the two men. "The acoustics are poor in here tonight."

Bonacchio and Blatzer stood still.

"Come, fly," Brother Thaddeus repeated.

"Now that I think of it," Julia whispered to me, "I never saw either of them flying. Did you?"

"Well, if you won't fly to me, I shall have to fly to you," Brother Thaddeus sighed and landed a few feet in front of the two businessmen.

The crowd started chanting to Bonacchio and Blatzer: "Come fly with us," but the two men remained adamant.

"Look," bellowed Mayor Blatzer, "I don't know how you do your little parlor tricks, but don't think you have me fooled. I'm going to report you to the FBI and CIA. You're not getting away with this."

Bonacchio left too. He said he was going to New York City to set up an office because insurance rates were much higher there. You should have seen his look of disgust when he drove past the former site of Gorden's Goodyear Tire Store. Brother Thaddeus had changed it into an art gallery by composing a haiku to a heroic ant.

There were a few others like Bonacchio and Blatzer, but they departed early too. It took us awhile to understand why they didn't believe us, because all the rest of us believed each other. When you see an 83-year-old erstwhile ballet dancer forgetting her arthritis to pirouette through the air at 75 miles an hour, you believe. Julia deciphered it: the ones who didn't believe us, didn't *see* us. Bonacchio and Blatzer never saw us floating through the air. I guess he thought Brother Thaddeus used mirrors to get from the front of the chapel to the rear.

The fourth week began with the season's first snow storm, a blizzard so fierce that the only road leading to and from town was closed. We were isolated from the rest of the state and nation for two delightful days. Brother Thaddeus called for a town meeting at the Priory. When some of us protested that the drifts were 15 feet high in places, he flew through the blizzard with a powerful bullhorn, announcing that we could fly to the meeting. By applying Unused Brain Section 8, we could avoid the wind and snow currents. "Just concentrate on the Priory and you'll be there as quickly as sound and safer than radar," he told us.

It was an important meeting because this was when we learned about Unused Sections 27 and 44, significant because they covered a few loose ends. Some of us had been afraid that the people who had left Wembley might report us to the authorities on the charge that our new outlook endangered the capitalistic system. The last thing we wanted was to be prosecuted for being unpatriotic.

***

The day after the storm we began work on Wembley's three petrol stations. It took us only one hour to dismantle them. We used thought waves, ESP, mental telepathy, and a few old prayers translated from the Greek. After we forged the grease racks into runners, we fashioned huge sleighs out of parts of the air machines, cash registers, and old auto parts. Then Brother Thaddeus led us through a short Dionysian dance, which even Julia said was in relatively good taste. We danced the stations' foundations out of existence and within twenty minutes purple, pink and white rhododendrons with blossoms as big as soccer balls reached to the sky where the Exxon, Getty, and Shell pumps had stood.

***

When the storm cleared, we got rid of the macadam on all but the main road leading through Wembley. Individual driveways no longer being necessary, most residents extended their gardens. Those with two-car garages turned these ugliest areas of their homes into greenhouses or libraries, depending upon the sun. Using the 17th section of the brain, they created a crystal clear brook in place of the road in front of their houses so that everyone in town could look out a window and see water flowing lazily in the warm months and a winding silver stream for skaters in the winter. Of course, they could fly if they didn't want to take the slower path along the ice, but most people in town decided to keep their ice skates. Gliding along the ice and looking up at the sky was a little like flying upside down.

We left room for little dirt roads along side of the stream for deliveries by horse and wagons during the mild months and horse-drawn sleighs in the winter. With the end of cars and trucks in Wembley the residents felt less guilty about using up so much energy with appliances, so they occasionally allowed themselves the luxury of a modern washing machine or freezer. It was a delightful anachronism to see a spanking new computerized Westinghouse refrigerator delivered by old Wells-Fargo wagons. Sally Richardson and Tim Conway, the town's letter carriers, delivered the mail on horseback, but when the weather was bad or they fell behind in their work—the holiday season, for instance—they simply flew from house to house. That's what you *really* call Air Mail, I'd have to say.

It was delightful for the people who were accustomed to moving about in wheelchairs. They didn't need them to fly, so by making sure they always landed on a soft comfortable spot, they could eliminate them. We donated the ten we had to a hospital in southern Vermont. The blind and bedridden fared just as well. Once they were air-borne, they didn't have to worry about any of the trappings that made their life on earth so unfulfilled.

***

As I said in the beginning, I've changed my ideas on religious groups, at least ones like the monks and brothers at the Priory. I used to think of churches as organizations that take a stand against the things we enjoy the most in life—like having a drink now and then and, y'know, a little sexual activity. Can't hurt all that much, can it, mate? Whether it's out of love or for a few bob. Well, I already told you about their home-made wine at the Priory. Good as it is, their approach to sex would make the wine taste like grape juice. As they say in the Bible, they saved the best stuff for last.

"There's absolutely nothing sinful about flying sex," Father Al told us. "When God created the pleasures of life, He also created the wherewithal within us to enjoy them."

I don't have to tell you, chum, that the good Father made jolly good sense. Even a rollicking swing and a gently-rolling hammock in their greatest glories can scarcely match the euphoria of the wind, air, and sky as lovers fly high together on St. Agnes Eve. Wouldn't you say so, chum? At any rate, the sale of beds in Wembley has dropped off considerably.

I haven't seen Julia in three days now. She told me she was flying to Australia to watch the sailboat races. The ballet dancer and Mickey the fireman fly by occasionally. They have spent the last week in the Gaspe Peninsula in Quebec researching the effects of wind currents on dancing. Father Aloysius and Brother Thaddeus are in Athens right now. They have a theory that if they concentrate on the stones of the Acropolis that the plays of Euripides and Sophocles were performed upon, they are likely to get an insight into—

I say, chum, I have the feeling that you don't believe a word I've told you. Well, have it your way. I just wanted to explain why it doesn't matter to me that Wembley, Vermont, doesn't have an airport. I have nothing against them, you understand. Matter of fact, I like to stop off in airports like this one now and then to have a chat with chaps like you who fly by machine. Could you hold my lunch box till I stand up on this bench? Thank you. Now I'll just flap my arms a bit and be off. Cheerio.

+++++

THE VIAGER AT HAPPY HOMER'S ICE CREAM HAVEN

Until he became ill, there wasn't a man in Cherryville who thought more about the children of the community than Happy Homer. His whole life seemed to be engaged in their pursuits. For example, long before other merchants started putting the faces of the town's missing children on milk containers and bread wrappers, Homer had snapshots of all five of them blown up into life-sized enlargements and installed in his large display windows, along with a promise of a $10,000 reward for any information leading to their return.

Cynics tended to pass this off as good public relations. After all, how much does it cost to have a photographer enlarge photographs, they asked? And what danger was there that Homer, already rich from his lucrative ice cream business, was really going to have to shell out ten thousand dollars? The kids had been missing a long time now. But those who had seen Homer in action, stoically brushing away chocolate ice cream spilled on him by exuberant youngsters or slipping on a strawberry yogurt casually dropped on his shiny stone floor by another and still getting up with a smile, knew it wasn't just a matter of publicity. Happy Homer had earned his name and reputation as a lover of kids the hard way—by putting up with their foibles and temperaments for a number of years while Happy Homer's Ice Cream Haven built up its reputation as a popular gathering place for the kids of Cherryville. And, of course, for their mothers and nannies.

Besides, Homer had been quick to point out, since the five missing children had been last seen in his ice cream parlor, where they had been frequent customers, he had a special obligation to do all that he could to see that they were found and returned to their frantic parents.

Thus when he was taken to the hospital with a coronary, there was a great deal of trepidation among the mothers of the community. It was as if someone had threatened to take their favorite soap off the air. They stormed the hospital, but Homer assured them they had nothing to worry about. His assistant, Whitlow, who had already become a new favorite of theirs, would continue Homer's *laissez-faire* policy and nothing would change until he was released from the hospital. Really. Not a thing.

There must have been twenty or more kids in *Happy Homer's Ice Cream Haven* that day. Most of them were talking at the same time, although screaming would be a more accurate way of describing the noises that writhed their way out their mouths and noses. Sometimes they reminded Whitlow of pigs squealing; other times it was more like errant fingernails scratching across a blackboard. It was difficult to smile in the company of so many of God's most active creatures, but through it all Whitlow tried to keep smiling for the sake of the children, the mothers, the nannies and, most of all, for the sake of Homer, whose infinite patience amazed his assistant. Whitlow realized, of course, that these were no ordinary customers. Houses in Cherryville started at $650,000, and when the mothers of this town took their little ones for ice cream at Happy Homer's, they were prepared to plunk down what the hoi polloi usually spent for dinner and wine at a restaurant that accepted all major credit cards.

Business was flourishing. None of the mothers had ever complained about Homer's penchant for raising his already high prices just about every month. As long as the mothers had a place for their kids to whoop it up, they were happy. And they always made sure to ask Whitlow about Homer's health.

"I'll have Argeroid call him at the hospital tonight to tell him what a splendid job you are doing," one of them said. "I'm sure it will cheer him up to hear his place is in such good hands."

"Oh thank you , Mrs. Brewster-Brockhausser," Whitlow replied. "I want so much to show Homer that his shop is in tip-top condition. He loves his Ice Cream Haven so dearly, you know."

"I know," Mrs. Brewster-Brockhausser said. "We all love this place. So clean, so uplifting, and so much fun for the children."

A comment like that was reassuring for Whitlow, giving him the strength to go on. He knew Mrs. Brewster-Brockhausser was as good as her word and that Homer would receive still one more excellent report on him. Ever since Homer had been taken to the hospital three weeks ago Whitlow had been running the place practically by himself. Part-time help was extremely difficult to come by. When all the kids in town are rich, who wants to work in an ice cream store?

And life as the manager of Happy Homer's was not easy for a man of Whitlow's delicate sensitivity. The kids were accustomed to having their own way, treating everyone they met as just one more servant in their lives, and bellowing like banshees when something displeased them. Their mothers saw nothing unusual in this behavior because they seemed to regard the actions of kids as Marie-Antoinette had regarded the culinary habits of all of France.

It wasn't so much the screaming *per se* that bothered Whitlow: it was the ingenious little noises the children made to surprise him as he was struggling to meet the great demand for his services in the mid-afternoons, his busiest time because this was when the little ones were freed from school.

Little Davey Klein, son of an investment broker, for instance, started a trend that lasted a week when he discovered that by standing on his chair and holding his soda glass high over his head he could provide enough momentum to explode it like a cherry bomb on Homer's stone floor. Within minutes Whitlow thought he was back in Viet Nam. The mothers, of course, made mild protestations to their Stephens and Ruthies, but their hearts weren't in their reprimands. In fact, some of them found it slightly amusing, especially if they happened to be looking in Whitlow's direction when a glass smashed against the floor while he was cutting a piece of cake or pouring a cherry vanilla malted into a soda glass.

Whitlow's fragile nerves left him with no choice but to visit Homer in the hospital and get his permission to have wall-to-wall carpeting installed, a request Homer acceded to without argument. He seemed to take pride in reflecting that his was about to be the only soda store in Cherryville with such lavish floor covering.

Thus when the expensive cleaning bills were forwarded to Homer at the hospital, he didn't bat an eye.

"Pay them," he told Whitlow on the phone, even when his manager reported the new practice of the young Cherryville elite of throwing chewing gum on the rug and stomping it in until it eradicated parts of the pattern.

"Kids gotta have fun," Homer said. "You were a kid yourself once, Whitlow. Just charge their parents a little more."

His manager sighed and hung up the phone. The following day he raised the price of ice cream cones and called in Waxin' Jackson, the floor man, to remove the gum and weave the rug. At this point, if it had been up to Whitlow he would have let the carpet look the way it was and pass off its condition to the vagaries of age. But Homer wouldn't hear of it. He knew the matrons of Cherryville wanted their afternoon rendezvous to be in a soda parlor as comfy as an opera house when they arrived, no matter what condition it was in when their offspring left it. When the kids bombarded the rug again the day after Jackson got rid of the last traces of gum, Whitlow started charging $10 for small milkshakes and $20 for large ones. The women didn't say a word. They knew a good deal when they saw it. The more their kids vented out their rage for being deposited into the human race at this particular time and place, the easier they were to handle as they made their way home, arm-weary and whimpering. Mayhem in the afternoon meant peace in the evenings when the lords of the business world came home to their palaces, parties, occasional flirtations, and/or seductions.

Harrison Temple, a former college roommate of Whitlow's, and, like him, one of the town's few bachelors, loved to come to Homer's just to see the little children go berserk. His dismal efforts to hide sadistic smiles made him a cross between the Cheshire Cat in a tree and a cabbie in a rainstorm. He found something pleasurable out of watching children becoming re-born as monsters, especially when he realized that he had absolutely no responsibility towards them. Temple had never had any plans for marriage or fatherhood, whichever might come first, but he had recently taken the precaution of having a vasectomy just in case he was ever tempted along those lines.

Temple's profession also had something to do with his pleasure in watching Cherryville's young set act out their anger and exuberance at the expense of the huge maroon rug and Whitlow's nerves. He was a dentist and was well aware that he would be soon seeing some of these very same children in his professional capacity. From time to time he had to control himself from buying a round of icky sundaes for the kids. It wasn't that he realized this would be rubbing it in: it was because his calendar was so filled that he knew he would be unable to cram any more patients into his battery of chairs for another year.

Watching his old college buddy, Whitlow, flip his wig also amused Temple, who was one of those persons who saw the vicissitudes of life as uproariously funny as long as they weren't his vicissitudes.

"I can't picture you playing King of the Kids, Whitlow," he observed one day. "In the old days when you just walked past a grammar school, you used to break out in a case of hives."

"I know, Harrison, but college teaching for twenty years was even worse. Here I was with a Ph.D. in Romantic Literature teaching remedial English to students who thought Keats was a French cheese dish and Shelley was a Jewish rock singer. At least all these kids do is scream and break things."

"Yeh, but to work in an ice cream parlor! With your background you should be able to——"

"Work for an insurance company? Depressing."

Temple eyed his friend curiously. Whitlow also had not married, mainly because he was afraid he might somehow have a kid. Now he was surrounded by them. Something was up. It was 2:15, almost an hour before the witching time when the schools released their legions to the parks, homes, and soda stores of Cherryville. Temple was the only customer in the store. It was a rare opportunity to talk to his old friend without being interrupted.

"Tell me, Whitlow, why are you doing it?"

"Doing what? Playing with——"

"You know what I mean."

"Why do I run Homer's business for him?"

"That's what I'm asking. Why are you stalling?"

Whitlow looked round the empty shop. All the dirty glasses were soaking in the sink, the man from Waxin' Jackson's had come in to clean the carpet, and his ice cream bins were filled and ready for action. Then he looked carefully at Temple. Harrison had been his friend since Prep school days. Because Whitlow's parents had died when he was a teenager, there was no other human being in the universe that he had known longer than Harrison Temple. Might as well take a chance. He looked around the room again, as well as the door. Nobody in sight.

"Can you keep a secret?"

"You know me, Whitlow. I could keep my lips sealed if I were being propositioned simultaneously by Mata Hari and Helen of Troy."

"Not if you had a condom handy. Well, O.K. I'll tell you, but if you don't keep quiet about this I'll have my ass in a sling."

Temple was beginning to get a little anxious to find out what this guy was hiding.

"Your secret is safe with me. Shoot."

Whitlow paused. He had never mentioned this to anyone before. The only ones who knew about it were Homer and he and their two lawyers. Well, he had to tell it; he had to get some advice beyond legal advice.

"Did you ever hear of the term *viager?*"

"Sounds French."

"It is. It means for life."

"Is it a prison term?"

Whitlow smiled for the first time in weeks. The comparison of his ordeal with a life's sentence in prison was more accurate than Temple realized.

"Well, it's like one. You see, I've entered into a *viager* with Homer."

"The Happy Homer who owns this joint?"

"Right."

"What kind of a deal is that?"

"Well, you know Homer had a heart attack. I've agreed to run the Ice Cream Haven for him for the rest of his life."

"Are you serious?"

"Absolutely."

Temple looked into his friend's eyes to see if there were any indications of drug addiction. That had to be it. No one in his right mind would run this place on a weekly basis. But for life—?

"He pays you, right? This is not some sort of sick sacrifice on your part?"

"No. I get paid."

"How much?"

"$220 a week."

"What! You're here seven days a week ten hours a day. You're getting less than the minimum wage. And you've got your Ph.D."

"I'm not doing this for my weekly wage, Harrison. The $220 is just to cover my basic expenses—you know, laundry, booze, and rent."

"And you can have all the ice cream you can eat," Temple said sarcastically. "Have you flipped, Whitlow? What kind of a deal is that?"

"It's a good deal. When Homer dies, I get this place. And he is in pretty bad shape. I check the hospital every day."

Temple looked at his friend curiously. Maybe he wasn't on the stuff.

"That's what the *via*—whatchamacallit is?"

"The *viager*. Right. It's an ancient French property transfer in which the *acheteur*, the purchaser, agrees to give money—in my case it's service— to the *vendeur*, the seller, generally an elderly or sick person without heirs, in exchange for property when he or she dies."

"Let me get this straight, Whitlow. You agreed to work slave wages for Homer on the condition that when he croaks he wills you the Ice Cream Haven?"

"That's it."

"How sick is he?"

"Oh, very sick."

"But he hasn't shown any sign of dying lately, has he?"

"They had him on the respirator for a whole day two weeks ago."

"How old is he?"

"Seventy-six."

Temple shook his head.

"That's not too old these days. You could be stuck in this sweatshop for years."

Whitlow paled.

"The last time I visited him in the hospital, he said he didn't feel so hot."

"Well, what did you expect him to say? If he told you he felt like going out and getting himself some nookie, you'd get the hell out of here. Don't you see what he's up to? He gets his rocks off running this place, but he can't handle it right now. So he gets you to keep it going for him for peanuts, figuring as soon as he's up to par, he's going to come back and be the smiling dandy for all the nannies and rich mamas."

"But even if he gets better, I still take over here when he dies. I saw his will."

"Even if he did kick the bucket and you got the place, what the hell would you do with it?"

"I'd sell it."

Temple heard screaming and yelling in the distance. They must have let school out a little early. He considered Whitlow's idea.

"That's the first bright thing you said all day, old buddy," he said. "So you're sweating out Homer so you can dump this place and make a killing?"

Whitlow nodded.

"Well, I guess it would be easy to unload." the dentist agreed. "Homer built up some business over the years by taking a lot of abuse from the little tots of Cherryville. His reputation is good. I suppose a lot of people wouldn't mind having all his rich customers."

"Oh, I wouldn't sell the business."

"But you just said—"

"I said I would sell this property. On the condition that the buyer tore this store down and put something else in its place."

"Like what?"

"Oh, I don't care. A condo, a gun store, a castor oil factory, a prison. Anything except a store that caters to little kids. It's my revenge."

"But you'd lose money."

"I don't think so," Whitlow smiled. "Property values are so high around here that I'd probably do even better selling the Ice Cream Haven for demolition than I would selling it for a soda store."

The phone rang.

Whitlow picked it up nervously. He hoped the caller would be brief because in a few minutes the mothers and nannies would be here. He thought of asking Temple to watch things while he was on the phone, but he suspected Harrison might yield to a lifelong temptation and turn the place over to the kids.

"Happy Homer's Ice Cream Haven," he said.

For a moment or two Whitlow just stared at the end of his fingers, as if they were apparitions.

"Bad news?" Temple asked.

"For Happy Homer. The hospital said he died a half-hour ago. About the time Waxin' Jackson was getting the last bits of chewing gum out of the rug."

***

Whitlow got the best deal from *The Greatest Dimension*, a New Age funeral home. Money was no object for *The Greatest Dimension* because they knew they had thousands of untapped customers among the wealthy ice-cream eating, scotch-drinking folks of Cherryville. Happy Homer's had a good-sized chunk of land behind the shop, so *The Greatest Dimension* gave their architect elaborate plans—an aerobic center a swimming pool, a miniature Bloomingdale's, a small chapel, a putting green, a bar with a ten-foot television screen, and even a small ice cream shop for the kiddies. Their motto was "Come to *The Greatest Dimension* when you go. Nothing really changes except you don't gain weight." Announcement of the new concept in mortuaries received rave reviews in the *Wall Street Journal*, which dubbed it a "Disneyland for the Dead."

When they tore down Happy Homer's Ice Cream Haven and starting excavating for the swimming pool, workmen discovered the bodies of the five missing children, victims of too much screaming in an ice cream parlor, according to the cynical Dr. Harrison Temple. The investigation was stymied, however, with Happy Homer himself having passed on and Whitlow out of the country, rumored to be somewhere in either Switzerland, Paraguay, or the Australian bush. +++++

THE PEOPLE'S CHOICE OF WINDY HILLS

At first I thought some one had fooled around with old film clips the way they do on *Saturday Night Live ,* but when I called the Associated Press, the reporter who answered told me it was legit. Not only had the AP carried the story, but so had Reuters, the Turner Broadcasting Network, CBS, NBC, ABC, and the BBC. He said that with so many of the affiliates of the networks and wire services likely to run the piece, before the night was out millions would undoubtedly know about it. Once Beijing got into the act, world-wide notoriety was inevitable.

"Do you hear that, O'Casey?" I asked. "You're famous. World famous."

O'Casey just glanced at me in that smug, blasé way of his. I've seen that look before when he was feeling cocky. He's always been popular with all the gang, but I have to admit that once in a while when he puts on airs, he can get to be a pain. Even my wife, Patti, who reads a lot and is interested in Irish writers, admits that O'Casey is a little stuck up. The way he was strutting around with his nose high in the air, you'd think he pulled it off all by himself.

We've talked about why we did it. Luigi Muscariello, who is a little more philosophical than the rest of us, said it was to show the indifference of society. I think Dutchy Dougherty and Barney Bettenbender did it because they suspected there was a buck in it somewhere. And Patti did it because she thought O'Casey could do at least as good a job as anyone they had before him. I suspect, however, that one of the main reasons we did it, was to see if it could be done.

You see, all of us came from Jersey City originally. You probably heard of Jersey City politics, right? Well, you don't hear much about them nowadays, but when the five of us lived there, things were really hopping. We had guys who could jam voting machines with toothpicks and screw up whole districts on Election Day. Of course, we never touched the machines where we knew we had the vote. You may have read about the election in which a district went to the Democrats 267-0, even though 43 registered Republicans swore under oath that they had voted the GOP ticket. That was way back—in the days of the ballot boxes when it was not unheard of to see the names of people long dead on the registration lists. Every ward had one or two guys whose main job was to canvass the cemeteries from time to time to add to the names of future voters for the party. Our ward leader, Louie Lombardi, used to argue that in this great nation of ours everyone had the right to vote and no one should be deprived of this privilege "Justa because he wasa dead."

We had a guy elected mayor who wasn't a resident of Jersey City. It turned out that he wasn't even a citizen of the United States. Remember that one? It made the front pages on most of the New York and New Jersey papers.

So you see we were used to that sort of stuff. When we lived there, elections were like Christmas to us because that's when we made our money. Even when they got rid of the paper ballots, we still knew how to hustle a vote. Dutchy Dougherty was able to convince the people in the district that the big boys could tell which way a person voted by the way he positioned his feet under the curtains or by special secret peep holes strategically located right over the voting machines in the barber shops and clubhouses throughout the city. Talk about Big Brother. The pols may not have had all those sophisticated spying and bugging devices they have today, but they had something better going for them: ignorance and superstition.

"I'm not telling you how to vote, Mrs. Katzenberger," Dutchy would say, "but just between you and I, them boys down in city hall know what's what. Who knows how they do it, but I hear they have those voting machines rigged in such a way that a little bell rings in the basement of the barbershop every time someone votes for a Republican."

"You don't say?" the nervous woman would answer, thinking of her son who was on the pad as a truant officer. Dutchy had no doubt about her vote.

Many of us left Jersey City around the time all the immigrants started coming in from Central America, and the Republicans began buying their votes with bottles of wine on Election Day. It's hard to believe how corrupt some people can get. A lot of these newcomers couldn't even speak English and some couldn't read or write. What business did they have in electing crooks to office? When we had voted in behalf of the dead people we at least picked men and women who usually had earned grammar school diplomas.

But part of living is adapting to change, as they say. So when our boys were thrown out of city hall, we figured we might as well get out of town too. What the heck, we told each other, with all our experience pretty soon we could run the suburbs as efficiently as we had Jersey City.

So a bunch of us moved out here to Windy Hills, New Jersey. It took a little while to get used to it. We knew there wouldn't be any apartment houses, candy stores, pool rooms, or saloons, but we never suspected they wouldn't have sidewalks. Not even mailboxes; you have to drive to the Post Office in Morrisburgh, the really big town around here, to mail a letter.

Our kids became stuck up right away. No more shooting baskets in the school yards any more. They play inside—in a gym. And when they finish up they have fancy showers with hair dryers. And these are not just for the girls either. We figured that if the pols in Jersey City had this kind of know-how they would be getting kickbacks from companies we never heard of.

Well, naturally after awhile we thought we could break up the boredom of living in Windy Hills by working for the local pols in the Democratic Party. Can you imagine our surprise when we found out there wasn't one? Right here in the U.S. of A.—right here in New Jersey, U.S.A., as a matter of fact, there was a town without a Democratic Party. Ever since the village had been incorporated in 18-something, there had never been a Democrat elected to office. Yang Sun, the owner of the only store in town, a Chinese take-out restaurant, told Dutchy that he had never heard of anyone in Windy Hills even admitting that he was a Democrat."

"I think," he said quietly. "They maybe ashamed to say 'I am Democrat.'"

When I tried to press Yang Sun to tell me why, he told me that he had a special on fried shrimp and rice. Sun wasn't the most talkative guy in the world. I knew he had relatives in China, so I figured he had a different view of democracy than I did.

Since there was no party to join, we started one ourselves. We called it the Windy Hills Regular Democratic Organization, Luigi Muscariello, standard bearer. We decided to have Bettenbender as our first candidate for mayor because his name had the snobbiness to go with the town. We made him call himself Bernard instead of Barney and we started hustling votes with flyers, buttons, bumper stickers, posters and a little doorbell-ringing.

We had a feeling when even our free beer bash didn't attract many of the hoi polloi of the town that Bettenbender might be in trouble on Election Day. Luigi and Dutchy had noticed it when they were ringing doorbells for votes, and Patti said that when she asked women to join our ladies auxiliary, three of them called her a male chauvinist. On Election Day J. Alan Baker, the Republican candidate, got 633 votes and Bettenbender wound up with 42. If you subtracted the Muscariellos, Doughertys, Bettenbenders, and Patti and me from that total, you see we didn't attract too many of our new neighbors.

On election night we had a surprise visitor at party headquarters: Mayor-elect J. Alan Baker himself.

"We were supposed to come over and congratulate you," Luigi said as he let him in, "but it is nice of you to offer your condolences."

"I am so happy to meet you," he said. "I'm sorry we didn't get to talk during the campaign."

I was going to tell him the main reason we never saw him was that he hadn't campaigned. But since he won in a landslide, I guess he knew what he was doing. Windy Hills is definitely no Jersey City.

"We have an election every year," Mayor Baker said. "I hope you will run again. Or one of your friends."

I thought that was rubbing it in a little, but I kept my mouth shut.

"No thanks," Barney said. "You beat me fair and square. I guess you've got this burgh locked up. A Democrat couldn't get elected street cleaner here. Even if you had streets."

"I wasn't thinking of the Democratic party."

"Y-you want us to be Republicans?"

"Don't look at it that way," he said. "I know they call us Republicans, but we're actually nothing. The *Party* is what you could call us, I guess. People here are so used to voting for the candidates of the Party that they don't know anything else. So whoever runs on the party line is elected."

"That means even us?" Luigi asked.

"Don't consider it personally. We all take turns being mayor for a year and it's a real drag. So if you boys wouldn't mind taking over the town for the next five years or so, we would surely appreciate it. As a matter of fact, I could step down in a month for health reasons and one of you could take my place on the party line in a special election."

Barney and Luigi were confused, but Dutchy eyes lit up.

"You mean you're willing to give up all that graft?"

"What graft?"

"The contracts, the kickbacks, the no-show jobs."

Mayor Baker smiled. He realized for the first time that, as they say, you can take the kid out of Jersey City, but you can't take Jersey City out of the kid.

"I am afraid there are very few jobs in the village and most of those are handled by $1 a year volunteers."

Dutchy wasn't sure whether all they got paid was $1. a year or whether they paid the dollar for the job. But he was disgusted. He had never heard of a governing body without graft before. He looked like a kid who had just lost his innocence.

"It's strictly an honorary position," Baker said. "No graft to speak of, but if you want to get elected without a hassle, just join the party and let me know. I'll resign and any one of you can be mayor within a month."

"*Any* one of us?" Luigi asked.

"No problem. Or a friend, if you want. No need to campaign, as you can see. Just call me up with a name and I'll make him or her the Party's candidate."

Our first reaction to Baker's offer was to turn it down. After all, what's the sense of being mayor when there is no graft? But Patti said she knew of a perfect candidate: O'Casey. And, as the fellow said, the rest is history.

All Mayor Baker did was to ask for O'Casey's first name and his place of birth. We told him it was Sean and that he was born in Jersey City. Baker didn't blink an eye. I guess he was so relieved to get out of the mayor's job that he didn't make the connection. Or maybe he was too much in the world of sparkling gyms with hair-dryers to pay much attention to Irish writers. O'Casey happened to be born in the year they were celebrating the 100th anniversary of the playwright's birth. As I said before, Patti was into Irish writers, so the name was a natural. Anyhow, that's how O'Casey got on the ballot as the only candidate in the special election for mayor of Windy Hills, N.J. Nobody challenged him. Like the good citizens they were, most of the people of Windy Hills came out to vote and O'Casey won in a landslide.

To the best of our knowledge he was the first dog ever elected mayor of a town in the U.S. of A. At least the first golden retriever. It made the front page of both *The Star-Ledger* and the Windy Hills *Gazette*. That would have been the end of it if Yang Sun hadn't clipped the story out and sent it home to his relatives in China.

It was after the government-run newspaper in Beijing re-printed it as an example of the corrupt politics of the West that the wire services began picking up O'Casey's story. The way the Chinese Communists looked at it, who are we to complain about their indifference to human rights when we elect a dog to run one of our towns?

Dutchy Dougherty wants to write to the Chinese kingpins to tell them a golden retriever running the show is nothing compared to what happened in Jersey City. Luigi Muscariello is writing them to point out that the way our world is going, things could be much worse than having a dog like O'Casey in charge. As I said, Luigi gets a little philosophical at times.+++++

PROPER ATTIRE REQUIRED

I'm not psychic or anything like that, but I knew it would be just a matter of minutes before Washburn would ask his wife to excuse him so he could come into the cocktail lounge to see Claire and me. I could tell by the quizzical look on his face as soon as he came in. Most of the regulars at *Borchiazzo's Buena Vista* figure that Claire and I are the authorities on the goings-on at the restaurant because we are here almost every night after work. The prices at the *Buena Vista* are steep and Borchiazzo serves four-day old fish which he gets from a guy with Mafia connections, but my accountant has figured a way we can write off most of our drinks and dinners on our income tax, and Claire and I always stay with the pastas. Besides, the *Buena Vista* is the only place in town with clean tablecloths—Claire says they're Irish linen—a ten-page menu, and a bar and cocktail lounge with Persian rugs and crystal chandeliers. Otherwise it's either MacDonald's, Burger King, or Fatso Freiburg's All-Night Diner. Union Village has tripled its population since the yuppies started moving in from Chicago, but we're still a small town.

I can see Washburn is anxious to get to the point. His wife, Margaret, likes the frescoes and gold-edged plates in the dining room, but she disapproves of alcoholic beverages and anyone who uses them. So you can see where Claire and I stand with her. I order Washburn a vodka collins, which Margaret can't smell, and let him ask me what I know he is dying to ask me.

"What the hell is going on, Ziggy?"

Naturally I play dumb.

"I don't get you, Washburn."

"I mean with Borchiazzo. This is the third time I've been here this week. He keeps changing the sign in the lobby. All I ever noticed before was the sign that said *Proper Attire Required*. Then Wednesday he had a trailer to it saying *Ladies Must Wear Formal Shoes*. Now tonight he's added *And Stockings*. Is Borchiazzo cracking up?"

"Well, you know how Borchiazzo is with his dress code. The men have to wear ties and jackets and the women have to wear dresses or skirts."

"He's living in another generation," Claire pointed out. "He won't let me wear slacks in here. And now he's bugging us on shoes. But pantyhose are no problem. If I have to put on heels, I might as well wear stockings."

Washburn takes a long drink of his vodka collins. He knows he has only a few minutes more before Margaret starts getting edgy.

"Yeah, I know Borchiazzo is a little off the wall in his black tux, red sash and white boutonniere, but what's with the signs all of a sudden? He's always had everybody coming to his place dressed up the way they go to church. Probably better."

Claire smiles at me. She knows what's going on in my head. Washburn feels the pressure to get back to Margaret, but he's nosy enough to want to hear the story.

"Have another quick vodka," she says. "Margaret is going to the Ladies Room. I'll get her to talk about her grandchildren and that will give Ziggy a few minutes to fill you in on Borchiazzo's signs."

When we see Claire intercept Margaret in front of the lighted portrait of the Pope at the entrance of the Ladies Room, I tap Washburn on the shoulder.

"Do you see that old lady with the sweet face sitting in the corner by the potted palm tree? Over there—the lady with the black and white dress."

"Yeah."

"That's why Borchiazzo is so busy with the signs."

"Wait a minute, Ziggy. That doesn't make sense."

"You may be right. Then I'm going to have to tell you about Knobby McCormick. Do you know him?"

"I think I've heard of him. He lives in the woods a few miles outside of town. Tall, skinny guy with an attractive wife and no children, right?"

"That's Knobby all right. Well, he and his wife came in here two weeks ago. The two of them had been pitching hay on their farm. Knobby had thrown a jacket on over his overalls. He looked like the farmer in Grant Wood's *American Gothic*. Knobby's wife, Patti, was wearing shorts. They had never been here before. I think he wore the jacket because he figured the air conditioning would make it chilly in here. When they came in, Borchiazzo was at the door."

"Wow! I can imagine what happened."

"I heard him. He acted as if Patti were Eve in the Garden of Eden about to tempt all the poor men in the *Buena Vista* into so many variations of mortal sins they would all wind up in the inner circles of Dante's *Inferno*. Patti has pretty nice legs."

"But what has this got to do with the old lady in the black and white dress over there?"

"Everything. Don't go near her."

"Why?"

"She stinks."

"But—"

"Do you notice that no one is sitting within three tables of her? That's how it's been every night this week."

"I still don't understand, Ziggy."

"Stay with me. Knobby and Patti have a few bucks, you know. Most folks in Union Village don't realize that because he and Patti stay home on their farm with their dogs and don't socialize much. I never saw him in a suit jacket before and Patti's always in shorts or slacks."

Washburn looks towards the Ladies Room. No sign of our two wives. He buys a round of drinks. I think he figured out what happened, but he is gentleman enough to let me finish the story.

"When I saw Borchiazzo ushering them out, waving his arms through the air like a ruptured duck, and staring contemptuously at their old Ford pick-up truck as they left, I figured Knobby and Patti would be sore. But they didn't show it."

"Then they ran into the old lady?"

"By the bus depot. Her name's Anna Gluck. She lives by herself over in Lamington. Used to work in the Lamington Glue Factory. No family. She gets by on a small pension and her social security. Nice old lady, but she doesn't believe in baths. I understand Knobby and Patti offered her a thousand dollars if she would come to the *Buena Vista* every night for dinner for two weeks. She was wearing a dress at the time so Borchiazzo couldn't kick her out. After his customers starting complaining about the smell, Borchiazzo tried to get rid of her through subterfuge. But when he put up that sign about *formal shoes*, Patti bought the old lady a pair of high heels. And then the next night the pantyhose. I understand she had to show her how to put them on. They mustn't have had things like that in the old lady's time. She eats a lot of curry and garlic. That's probably why she lives so long."

Margaret and Claire return from the Ladies Room. Washburn swills down the last of his vodka and leaves so he can beat his wife back to their table. But he takes a little detour by the potted palm tree where the old lady is digging into her Lobster Newburg. He takes a deep breath and smiles at me. I'm sure he believed me all along, but I suppose he wanted to take a smell for himself to appreciate the impact it had on Borchiazzo as he ushered her in each night in his black tux with the red sash and the white boutonniere. +++++

WATCH OUT FOR MRS. PRONGAY

Well, how d'ya do? They told me downstairs that I'd be getting a new roommate today. Your name is Mrs. Peterson, ain't that right? My name is Mrs. Oldmere. Not *Odd*mere, *Old*mere. Rhymes with cold beer. Ha ha, pretty good, eh? That was my late hubby's joke. Passed away in '86. Gout, elongated intestines—or was it testicles? Can't remember now. Anyhow, he was sick for three years. Always complaining too, George was, God rest his soul.

So what's the matter with you? I heard you ain't had no supper. Oh, your tooth. Three of them! My, my. Well, at least you got them. Mine came out in '91, the year I buried my mother. She had diabetes and cancer of the cubicles, I think it was. Suffered awful. I visited her in the hospital every day. St. Michael's in downtown Bergen City. You know the one with the nuns in the brown habits. Used to be black, but nothing is the same nowadays, is it? Had to take two buses to get to the hospital. It was no picnic, I'll tell you. Between you and I when the old folks get sick they start to smell. You know what I mean? You're not feeling so good? Toothaches can be awful, I know. One of them trailer-trucks rolled over my Cousin Agnes's car and she got her head wedged between the dashboard and the emergency brake. Had to cut up the car with a chain saw to get Agnes out. Broke a dozen teeth and had to have her jaws wired up. All she could eat for months was Pablum. Was complaining about her teeth until the day she died. Tarkington's Disease. November of '95. Buried her in the freezing rain. But Cousin Charlie bought us drinks at a roadhouse on the way home. Yeah, the doc did a lousy job on Agnes's teeth. When she smiled you could see the jagged edges. The dentist was a shoemaker.

Mmmm. So how are you feeling, Dearie? Aw, you'll get used to it. Everybody does. Even Mrs. Costello. She's the one who had the bed you're in right now.

You never saw nobody do so many crossword puzzles. I'm telling you she could do ten a day maybe. And never peek in the back of the book for the answers either. Yeah, she had books of them 'cause she finished all the newspaper crosswords before lunch. All day long she's figuring and figuring, writing letters in them little white squares. I never heard of anyone who knew so many words.

The funny thing is with all her words she hardly ever spoke any. Just wrote them down in the little boxes. But you could stand on your head till your drawers were up to your eyeballs and she wouldn't say a single word to you. Me and Mrs. Costello was roommates for seven years and in all that time I got maybe three sentences out of her. And teeny-weeny ones at that. Well, there's some that likes to talk and some that's likes to listen.

As you can guess, it was up to me to keep the conversation going in here. I told her about the deaths of my four uncles, my mother, father, Cousins Agnes and Millicent—'93 of a misplaced goiter—and all the hospitals where I visited my friends and relatives. You know, if I didn't know her well I'd a-sworn she wasn't paying any attention to me. But every now and then she'd wave her arm at me when I used her side of the closet or stepped on one of her crossword puzzle books.

But she liked me. I knew that. The one that drove her nuts was Mrs. Sheehan. She was here with Mrs. Costello when I was in the room down the hall without any window, staying with Mrs. Prongay. They promised me Mrs. Sheehan's spot as soon as—as soon as her time came. Poor old woman was always going through Mrs. Costello's things. Not to steal anything, you understand. She thought Mrs. Costello's bras and drawers were hers even they were about three sizes too big for her. They say she was a little disoriginated. You know, she kept forgetting which part of the closet was hers. Looked like Omar the tent-maker in Mrs. Costello's nightgown. Worst thing was when Happy Helen—that's what we called Mrs. Sheehan because she laughed a lot—confused the beds. When Mrs. Costello was in the shower it wasn't so bad because she could just wake Helen up and give her the sign to move. But when Mrs. Costello was already in bed and Happy Helen flopped right on top of her—well, that really got Mrs. Costello mad. But she still never actually said anything, as far as I know. Just wrote a little note to Mrs. Martin, the head nurse, which I happened to read when I was dusting her desk.

I wouldn't have even bothered to look at it except that I was next in line to get this room and—well, it pays to know what's going on in this world, I always say. This ain't an easy room to get into. You must have some pull, Mrs. Peterson. Mrs. Prongay, the lady who had been with me in the room without the window, thought for sure she would take Mrs. Costello's place when she passed away. She was always asking the head nurse how Mrs. Costello was feeling. But between you and I, she was asking for just one reason. Ain't it a shame how some people just think of themselves? Love and let love, I always say.

Well, there was a couple other notes on the head nurse's desk and I knew that Happy Helen must be getting worst. First she had penetrating ulcers, then contusions of the clavichord. That's when she fell down the back stairs and hurt her shoulder. She was supposed to have an operation at St. Mary's where they have the nuns with the white habits. Only thing was the doctors were a little worried that once she got on the operating table she might not be able to take the ethics. I told her I'd be saying a prayer to St. Jude for her. Y'know, St. Jude, don't you? He's the saint for the hopeless.

Naturally, she couldn't eat or nothing like that on the day she went off to St. Mary's, but Mrs. Martin said she could sit at the breakfast table with the other guests—that's what they call us, you know—while she was waiting for the ambulance. I and the rest of them said little things to her to cheer her up. Mrs. Prongay told her that the operation wouldn't hurt much because she would be all doped up, and I said that I heard that the head nurse was keeping her bed ready for her upstairs, just in case. I didn't want her to think I was eager to grab her spot or nothing like that. Especially since she was about to go under the knife. Mrs. Costello, naturally didn't say nothing, but just kept shoveling her oatmeal into her face. She was probably anxious to get back upstairs to her crossword puzzles.

But just as they were wheeling Happy Helen out, a funny thing happened. Mrs. Costello looked up from her plate and turned to Mrs. Sheehan and said:

"Now you take care of yourself, Helen. I want you to know that I'll be thinking about you and I'll miss you when you're gone."

That was it. Twenty-four words. I memorized them and counted them later. Enough for two telegrams. No one had ever heard Mrs. Costello say so much. And no big words, either. Not like the ones from her puzzles.

Well, I guess you know what happened. Helen passed away two days after the operation. October of '93. Mrs. Prongay had been packed since the day the ambulance took the poor old lady to the hospital—that's how positive she was that she was going to get her bed. Some people, I tell you! The least she could have done was waited until after Helen's funeral was over.

But as you can see, Mrs. Prongay didn't get the room. I have to admit I had my heart set on it a little bit. I told Mrs. Martin, the head nurse, that my relatives would be very happy with the nursing home if they gave me the recognition I deserved. You see, I'm not pushy like Mrs. Prongay. I just dropped a little hint here and there and...

Well, you should have saw Mrs. Prongay's face when I started moving my things in here. She screamed and cried and I-don't-know-what. Said the darkness in her room was making her sick to her stomach, claimed there were snakes in the walls behind her bed, and reminded Mrs. Martin that she was a first cousin, once removed, of a congressman of the United States of America. Boy, has that woman got gall! That's why I couldn't believe it when I saw you here. For more than two years she's been talking about the strings she can pull and what's going to happen to Mrs. Martin and the rest of us when she starts pulling them. She's one *pre*-ty tricky number. You've got to watch out for Mrs. Prongay.

Well then. You must really know somebody, Mrs. Peterson. Ain't this room grand? You just missed watching the sun go down, a great big glob of orange and gold like an oversized fried egg settling down in them there hills. And in the morning you'll see lots of cows and nanny goats on Harrigan's Farm down the road by Muskrat Pond. They skate there in the winter. When the ground's all filled up with snow the window looks like a great big Christmas card.

Mrs. Costello and me got along pretty good. The only thing that really bothered her was when someone went through her drawers and stole maybe a bra or sweater or something. Naturally she still didn't say anything when something was missing, but whenever it happened she would do more crosswords than usual that day and never—I mean never—lift her head up from the puzzles once. It wasn't easy for me living with a woman like that, I'll tell you. I used to have an aunt who never talked to anybody, but instead made funny little noises by clicking her tongue against the top of her mouth. Sounded like a horse clop-clopping along. Lordy, she drove me crazy. That was Auntie Cotter. Passed away in '88 of a dilated dingus.

People said Mrs. Costello began to go downhill after Helen died and I moved in. That makes no sense at all because when I came in here I was always talking to her to cheer her up. But I do have to admit in the last month or so she didn't look so hot and was leaving a lot of crosswords half-finished.

S'matter, you want something, Dearie? A glass of water, maybe? You've going to have to talk. I ain't no swami or nothing like that. Geez, what did the good Lord do to me?—first Mrs. Prongay with all her scheming and then two Silent Susies, you and Mrs. Costello. Oh well, everybody has to bear her cross on this earth, I always say, and I guess being roommates with old ladies who don't know how to conduct a decent conversation is what the good Lord has ast me to do in His name. Amen.

Anyway, just the other morning the cook says she's got some scrambled eggs left over and is there anybody who would like a second helping. All of the old ladies, even Mrs. Costello, raise their hands like kids in grammar school trying to get the teacher's eye. You'd think these old biddies never saw food before, the way they're shoveling down them eggs. I'm about halfway through mine and I happen to look over Mrs. Costello's way. She was the last one served, so she's just starting to gum away—she had all her teeth yanked out in '86. All of a sudden she looks up at the ceiling. Or maybe it was at the sky coming through the top of the window in the dining room. Anyway, her eyes is aiming way up in the air like a little kid watching his kite fly. Then, quick as a wink, her head comes down and lands right in the scrambled eggs. Ker-plunk! Eggs are in her eyes and nose and some pieces of yellow are stuck to her gray hair. Nobody says anything because I guess maybe they think she's getting a dizzy spell or something. I see Mrs. Prongay's eyes light up. She's thinking: "This is my big chance." I can tell just by looking at her. You've got to watch out for Mrs. Prongay.

Somebody goes for Mrs. Martin, who was in her office doing charts. When she grabs Mrs. Costello's wrist to take her pulse, I can tell by the look on her face that I got an empty bed in my room. Mrs. Costello had passed away right in her scrambled eggs without saying a word to anyone. Well, she hardly ever did when she was alive anyway.

The *Daily Record*—that's our newspaper—didn't mention anything about the scrambled eggs. It just said she died in her sleep.

Shhh, listen! Did you hear that? Shhh, there it goes again. Sounds like a cat scratching, doesn't it? I think I know what it is. You stay still in your bed while I take a peep through this keyhole. Hmmmph. Just what I thought. Do you know what that was, Mrs. Peterson? It was Mrs. Prongay snooping around outside. She's right by the stairs. I wonder if she heard what we were talking about. All right, you be still now. I'm going to open this door quietly and see what's what. I'll let you know later on.

***

Wellll, Mrs. Prongay! Don't you look nice in that blue blouse? It matches your eyes just perfect. You're going downstairs to watch the evening news on television? Well, so am I. I'll walk down with you. Maybe they will have some more news on that woman who was attacked in the Bronx. I tell you, Mrs. Prongay, there are a lot of animals out there.

Come over here by the landing where our voices won't carry. You know, I've been thinking about you lately, Mrs. Prongay. The sunset from my window tonight was simply beautiful, reflecting off Muskrat Pond. I know you get a nice view from your room too, but you're facing the East and you can sleep right through the sunrise and miss it. If I was you I'd speak to Mrs. Martin about moving into my room. I don't know why you just didn't say something after poor Mrs. Costello passed away.

Oh, I know Mrs. Peterson just moved in, but she won't be there long. She has a perforated dementation of the brain. Yes, sad case. It affects her kleptomaniac cells. She was only in my room five minutes and I caught her trying to steal my bras and underpants. Poor thing, they would never fit her anyway. You didn't see her when they brought her in, but I don't think she weighs 80 pounds. Probably all that perforation causes her to lose weight. I have a cousin with a mild case of dementation and the doctors only give her three weeks. So Mrs. Peterson isn't long for this world and you could move into the room in a few days if you play your cards right. As soon as the evening news is over, tell Mrs. Martin that the sunrise hurts your eyes. Oh, and by the way, if you mention Mrs. Peterson's perforated brain, you needn't say that I told you. We'll go down now; they're starting to look up at us. Noseybodies. Well, there she is, the woman from the Bronx. How awful! Who would ever think anyone could do that to another human being? I tell you, I just don't know what this world is coming to. +++++

V.

A Touch of the Strange

There are more things in heaven and earth, Horatio, than are dreamt of in your philosophy.

—Hamlet, Act I, iv

THE ANTEPENULTIMATE ACT

Corey's Corners is one of those small villages that you can drive through in a few minutes. A bicycle ride, of course, is more enlightening, but if you really want to get the feel of this tiny hamlet, it is best to take a stroll south down Elm Street till it reaches County Road 42. When you arrive there, you are at the heart of Corey's Corners. Across the road is the United Methodist Church, its shining white steeple pointing to the heavens and all things saintly. On this side of Elm is Bert's General Store, followed by Mimi's Bakery, Mom's Diner, and *The Antepenultimate Act*

Why I chose to stop at what proved to be an antique shop when I could have gone down the street a hundred feet or more to the River Edge Saloon is something that puzzles me still. The highway had been a little dusty—at least that's what I kept telling myself—and my most immediate need was for a nice cold one. But there was something that appealed to me about that old shop, or *shoppe*, as the proprietor called it in the sign in the window which read:

The Antepenultimate Act
Treasures of the American Past
Shoppe Established in 1891

I had arrived at Corey's Corners by sheer accident. My boss told me there was a good motel about three miles from Exit 8, but it wasn't until I had driven for fifteen minutes that I finally found a service station to ask directions. The guy pumping gas told me I had got off at Exit 3. The kids in the neighborhood had filled in the loops to made the *3* an *8*. I figured, what the hell, I'd come this far. I might as well look for a place to bed down nearby. My eyes were bleary, my head thumping, and my heart was pounding. I had been on the road all day and I was dead tired. The attendant told me if I took the next left, the road would take me into Corey's Corners. I guess the name of the village appealed to me the same way that *The Antepenultimate Act* enticed me to forego my beer for a few minutes. I had parked my car at Joe's Garage at the end of Elm Street, where it was getting an oil change and a grease job. It was four blocks away, so I knew I would not be tempted to buy anything heavy. Anything light either, for that matter. I just figured I would browse around. These kinds of places don't charge you for looking.

The first thing that caught my eye as I walked in was a kelly-green umbrella, tied by a long yellow cord to a solid oak captain's chair. Printed across the umbrella was the legend *The Capitalist's Tool.* Curious. I have not the slightest idea what capitalists and umbrellas have in common and thought that might be something I might ask the proprietor if he came nosing around, egging me on to buy something. The opportunity came quicker than I anticipated.

"You are wondering about the inscription?"

The proprietor turned out to be a proprietress, a thin woman with light brown hair tied in the back in a bun, reminiscent of the way Audrey Hepburn looked in her later years. She seemed to be in her early fifties and spoke with a British accent.

"Why, yes. Is it because capitalists are always saving their money for rainy days?"

The woman smiled. "I'm sure I don't know what it means. I should have asked the man who gave it to me."

"A friend of yours?"

"Heavens no. He was passing through our little village campaigning for the Republican nomination for president in the winter of 1996. He poked his head in my shop and handed me the umbrella saying that it would keep my powder dry. I can't remember his name, but he was a very wealthy man."

"Malcolm Forbes, the former magazine publisher?"

"Yes. That's who it was. He reminded me a little of that fellow from *Sleepy Hollow*: Ichabod Crane. I guess it was because of the awkward way he moved his arms and legs. But he seemed to be a pleasant enough person."

"Well, his umbrella makes a nice decoration for your window—that and the captain's chair."

"Thank you, but would you like to see something more interesting?"

I followed her gaze and stepped back into the shop a few feet. I turned to a display of expensive Lennox china, but the woman pointed to the umbrella.

"No, not there," she said. "Look out the front window through the silhouette of the umbrella."

I did. Directly across the road was a cemetery, its tombstones lined up neatly like soldiers in a European honor guard. The grass between the graves must have been recently cut because it looked as smooth as velvet. About thirty feet from the gate was a freshly dug grave, apparently in preparation for a funeral the next day. My normal reaction would have been to ask her if she signed the lease for her store before she looked over the neighborhood, but for some reason these words didn't come out. As far as cemeteries went, this was not a bad-looking one.

"Well, you certainly do not have to worry about anyone building a high-rise in your neighborhood," I managed to blurt out.

The woman favored me with a half smile. She had velvet-blue eyes. Quite pretty.

"Actually I think it is rather nice having a cemetery across the street, don't you agree?"

"In all honesty, it's not really my taste, but I suppose it has its advantages."

But the Audrey Hepburn-woman did not appear to be listening. Or else she was so lost in her own thoughts that she did not hear what I had said. The two of us stood there in silence for a minute or so.

"You see, there does not seem to be a way to get in there," she said.

"Well, that should be the least or your worries," I could not help but pointing out.

"Oh, I am content to look at it from here, but I do wonder how people manage to go inside. I doubt if anyone climbs that tall wrought iron fence. It must be ten feet high and it circles the entire cemetery. I never saw such a long fence. Its circumference is more than a mile."

"But wouldn't they just enter through the front gate right across the street from you?"

The Audrey Hepburn-woman shook her head solemnly.

"Oh, no. They don't enter through that gate."

"You seem quite certain."

"I am. I have never seen that gate open."

"Is it broken?"

"I am sure I do not know. But I can tell you no one has gone into the cemetery from the county road."

That didn't make sense to me. Just because she had never seen anyone pass through the gate didn't mean that it had not happened. But maybe she was right. Perhaps it was not practical for cemetery officials to use this entrance.

"Well, then there must be other gates. You say the perimeter of the cemetery is more than a mile? How many entrances are there?"

"There are six gates all told. But none of them has ever been opened. And yet I have seen many people inside that big black fence. From right here, where we are standing. And I have observed many, many funerals over the past years."

I turned from the cemetery to look at the proprietress. She was a tall woman, nearly as tall as I am. That would make her just a little under six foot. She was wearing a long black dress that trailed almost to the ground, relieved only by a tiny brass belt and matching brass earrings and choker. The dress accentuated her thinness. Ordinarily by this time I would have given her a little wave, made a quick exit, and headed *toute de suite* for the River Edge Saloon. But there was something about her easy manner that made me want to linger a little longer.

"You're saying that over the years you have noticed many people inside the fence, but you are yet to see a single one of them enter through any of the gates?"

"Exactly."

"However, there is no way you could have been in a position to see all of the gates simultaneously, isn't that correct?"

The woman paused, ostensibly to evaluate the logic of my question. There did not seem much to ponder. No one could view six gates simultaneously. Unless...Unless she was on a low flying plane. I asked her if that is what she meant, and she shook her head vigorously.

"I did not have to see each gate to be able to tell if it had been opened for members of the public. I *know* they were never opened."

I saw no need to argue with my Audrey Hepburn friend. The cold beers were waiting for me at the River Edge Saloon. Still, I thought I would I would make one last effort to see what she was driving at.

"These people that you have seen inside the fence—they were members of a funeral cortege?"

"Sometimes."

"Are you saying you saw people in there who had nothing to do with a funeral?"

"Many times."

"They were employed by the cemetery?"

"Some might have been."

I looked at the woman to see if her expression would give a clue to what she was obviously holding back from me, but she was staring straight ahead at the cemetery.

"So you are saying that some of these people you saw on the other side of the fence apparently had nothing at all to do with the cemetery, either as workers or as family members attending a burial."

"Oh, absolutely."

"Were there many of them?"

"What do you mean by *many*?"

"Well…would you say that with the exception of funerals, there ever were more than ten people in there?"

"Oh, easily. I would say there are usually two dozen people in there most of the time."

"Men and women both?"

"Yes indeed."

All of a sudden it seemed to me that my Audrey Hepburn woman had an easy way to solve her problem.

"Did you ever talk to any of these people?" I asked.

The proprietress regarded me a mite suspiciously, I thought. "Why, in heavens name, would I ever do that?"

"Well, if you spoke to them, you could ask them how they got into the cemetery."

"But I could never ask them that."

"Why not? You want to know how they got in, don't you?"

"Oh, I am interested in that, of course, because it seems a conundrum of sorts. I suppose it would be nice to know. But I would never think of asking them."

The last of the sun was sliding down over the tops of the neat line of tombstones across the street. That meant that when my Audrey Hepburn woman looked out on the cemetery, she was facing west. I was going to mention to her that this seemed fitting, but I suspected that this kind of comment might appear as banal to her as my suggestion that she speak to the people on the other side of the fence.

"You would consider it an act of impropriety?"

"To some extent. But I never considered asking them because every time I saw them they were so far away from the gate that I would have had to scream my lungs out to be heard. And that certainly would have been unseemly. Besides, not knowing how they got in has its advantages too. In our modern society there are too many questions that are served up with the answer supplied, printed upside down in small type at the bottom of the page. Life would be more interesting if one could imagine if the lovely lady in red is wearing the same color silk underwear, rather than have her whip her dress off at a moment's notice and show all."

It was not the type of reply I had anticipated, but it was consistent with her premise that some things in life ought to remain mysteries. I decided to store the case of the cemetery visitors in the rear echelon of my brain for a little while and come back to it later. Perhaps after the third beer at the River Edge Saloon. For some reason beyond my understanding I tipped my cap at the proprietress and made my way to the door.

"Well, I see it's getting dark and I have to find a room for the night. It was nice talking to you ma'm."

The Audrey Hepburn woman nodded. "You'll find the Inn at Corey's Corners a hundred yards or so to your right when you leave here. Just on the other side of the River Edge Saloon. Ask for Jed Witherspoon. You can tell him Pamela Morrison sent you. It is a cozy little inn, the rooms are reasonable, and you should have no trouble reserving one because it is off-season now. Heavens, I hope I didn't frighten you away."

"Oh, no, ma'm. Not at all. It was interesting talking to you. I hope you find the answer to your riddle. If you want to, that is."

"Thank you," she replied, walking towards the display of Lennox china. "And good evening."

Outside, I remembered I had to go back to Joe's Garage for my car. But on impulse I decided to cross the street and have a look at the gate in the cemetery. There was still enough light to be able to check the lock. I resisted the temptation to look back to see if she was watching me as I crossed the street.

It struck me that if I were caught trying to get in the gate I might be accused of being one of those weirdoes who rob graves for the jewelry buried with the deceased. Or for the corpse itself. I had heard that a cadaver brings in a good price in some science laboratories. But this was the little village of Corey's Corners. Still, you never know about these small towns. I decided to take a chance. I pulled on the gate. To my surprise, it swung open cleanly. They must have forgotten to lock it. An oversight, I guess. I was tempted to go back to the antique shop and tell Pamela Morrison that here was her big chance to take a walk around the inside of a cemetery. But as I stood there, hesitating, I saw that she had turned out her lights. This was a little surprising, because she left me with the impression that she was going to stay open for another hour or so. Too bad, because I would have liked to have asked her why she insisted the gate was locked. Well, maybe this was a fluke of some kind. I didn't feel as tired now. The cool evening air must have revived me. Or was it the tales of the cemetery that Pamela Morrison had spun? I wondered if the other gates were also open.

Once again my feet strayed away from what I thought would have been their natural destination: the River Edge Saloon. I told myself that between cemeteries and saloons, the latter was most likely to remain open the latest. I walked south along the cemetery's perimeter, searching for another gate. I found one five minutes later and pushed against it carefully. It swung open at once. Why would Pamela Morrison tell me that all the gates were locked when the first two I tried were open?

It suddenly dawned on me that Joe's Garage must be closed by now. Well, I could pick my car up in the morning, and it was not a long walk to the Inn at Corey's Corners. I doubted if I would have any trouble getting a room this time of year. Pamela Morrison had assured me that there would be plenty of rooms. Just ask for Jed Witherspoon, she said.

I decided I might as well finish circling the cemetery to check all the gates. It would take me back to *The Antepenultimate Act*, which was not far from the inn. I am a Taurus and once I get a notion in my head I am determined to see it through, no matter how crazy it is. At least that is what I thought at the time. In the back of my mind was the notion that subconsciously I may have wanted to do this little research on the gates so that I would have a reason to confront Pamela Morrison again. That's possible, I suppose, but it doesn't make much sense. I am sure that I would have rather spent the shank of the evening guzzling a few brews rather than following the perimeter of a cemetery. Besides, how can anyone know what he is thinking subconsciously? Anyway, I found four more gates. They were all open. In the distance I saw the lights of the Inn at Corey's Corners. I had almost completed my circle of the cemetery.

As I approached County Road 42, I saw the River Edge Saloon, the pub that had eluded me, or vice versa, all evening. I decided to by-pass it one more time, at least until I registered at the Inn at Corey's Corners. It occurred to me that they might think it strange that I was arriving without any baggage. But I could explain that I had left my car at Joe's Garage and had become involved in circling the cemetery. On second thought that didn't seem like the best way to introduce myself. That's the trouble with the truth nowadays: it always sounds like a pack of lies.

***

"I'm looking for Jed Witherspoon," I told the night clerk at the Inn at Corey's Corner.

The clerk, a thin, rather attractive blonde woman in her late forties, looked at me strangely.

"I'm sorry. Would you repeat the name, please."

"Witherspoon. Jed Witherspoon."

"And for what reason?"

"Reason? I just want to rent a room from him."

"I am afraid that's not possible."

"Are you all filled up? I was told you had lots of rooms."

"Oh, we do have several unbooked rooms, but—"

"Then why can't I have one?"

"Oh, but you can. I was just trying to tell you there is no Jed Witherspoon here. He—"

"That's strange. I was told to come here and ask for Jed Witherspoon and he would take care of me."

"Unfortunately, that's quite impossible."

"Why?" I asked. Her cryptic answers were beginning to get under my skin.

"Because Jed Witherspoon is dead, my dear."

"Dead? Since when?"

The woman stood up and looked at me curiously. She was quite tall. Taller than I, as a matter of fact.

"For these past ninety-seven years. Mr. Witherspoon was the founder of the Inn at Corey's Corners.

"Well, maybe it's his son I am looking for."

"Mr. Witherspoon never married. Someone told you to come here and look for him?"

"That's right. The woman from the antique shop around the corner."

"*The Antepenultimate Act?*"

"Right."

"You said a woman?"

I was beginning to feel like a witness to a crime whose story everyone pretended not to believe because they were afraid of the consequences. And yet the clerk, who had rather attractive deep violet eyes, was not really being threatening in any way. But why did she seem to doubt everything I said?

"Yes, a woman. A rather tall woman who looked a little like Audrey Hepburn. In fact she looked a little like you, but her hair was brown."

"Hmmm. Do you know her name?"

"Yes. She told me she was Pamela Morrison."

The night clerk flinched and then stared hard at me.

"She is *not* Pamela Morrison."

"She's not? But that's who she told me she was. How do you know she is not Pamela Morrison?"

The woman fixed me sternly. Perhaps even angrily.

"Because *I* am Pamela Morrison." she said.

There were plenty of rooms in the inn. In fact I think I may have been the only one staying there. The night clerk gave me Room 6 on the second floor.

"But I don't believe you will be staying here tonight," she said.

I laughed. "If you think I have my eye on that old-fashioned saloon next door, you're right. But I don't plan to stay there long. I haven't slept much in days and I am going to hit the sack early."

But after a shave and a nice warm shower, I felt rejuvenated and ready to try a few of those cold ones I had been thinking about for the last few hours. However, as I walked through the lobby, the night clerk called to me.

"You won't like The River Edge Saloon. It's not bad during the day, but at night it's jammed with the young crowd from the village. Loud hard rock. And awfully smoky. We have a nice quiet bar here in the inn.

The only things that interrupts the silence is the strains of Beethoven, Haydn, and Mozart. Just down the hall. First floor on the right."

It turned out the night clerk was the bartender too.

"I double in brass until the ski season starts and we get a regular bartender," she explained.

I ordered a dry martini on the rocks with a lemon twist.

"But before I have even one sip of this, could you tell me how in one day—within a few hours, as a matter of fact—I meet not one, but two Pamela Morrisons, one of whom you say does not exist?"

"I have no way of determining who exists and who does not, but I can tell you there is no woman working at *The Antepenultimate Act.* There never was."

I explained how the first Pamela Morrison had told me about the gates always being locked in the cemetery, as away of proving I had had a conversation with her.

"And you decided to check the gates for yourself?" she asked, smiling.

"Well, yes."

"And you found them to be open?"

I noticed the mischievous glint in her velvet-blue eyes. She looked a little like the other Pamela Morrison, except for her blonde hair. Also she was probably ten years younger.

"All six of them were open."

The martini was slipping down my throat like soft white lace sliding over a shiny mahogany table. I must have finished my drink sooner than I expected because in what seemed just a minute or so the second Pamela Morrison was placing another one in front of me. For the first time since I met her, I realized she was dressed in red—a fiery red dress, red stockings and shoes and a red ribbon in her hair. I thought of what the first Pamela Morrison had said about the lovely lady in red who whipped off a dress to show that she was wearing the same color silk underwear. When she raised her hand, I wondered if she had anything planned like that, but she let it rest instead on my head and ran her fingers through my hair, all the time smiling at me. Somehow it was a sad smile.

I really started getting sleepy now. It was time to get some rest. But it was difficult walking. I guess the long ride and the long day were finally catching up with me. I found it hard to keep my knees from buckling, but by catching hold of the railing I was able to stay on my feet.   It was not much farther now. I could see the silhouette of the gate in the distance. Funny, the lights were on again at *The Antepenultimate Act* across the street. Hmmm, at this time of night. Ah, the gate at last. I did not anticipate any problems. Easy now. Just a little push. There. It swung open as easily as a cradle. Just about thirty more feet to the West. The sweet smell of timothy filled the air. I remembered now that they had just recently cut the grass.

I got down on my hands and knees so I would not fall. I felt the cool freshly-turned clay. I rolled on top of it and down to the bottom of the grave. It didn't hurt at all. I felt really at peace. Looking straight up, I could see the skies were alive with stars. It looked like Van Gogh's painting. I took a deep breath and finally closed my eyes. At last I was going to get a good rest. +++++

DRIFTWOOD

I found two odd-shaped pieces of driftwood. They both were ash-gray and smooth as cat's fur but not as soft. One was no bigger than a lady's fan and looked a little like an Indian chief's headdress with a few feathers missing. The other was long and narrow like a fly swatter. It had two holes in the end where the killing part is. Judy would like them because they were different. I stuffed them in my belt and sat down in the sand to watch the sky and the ocean. This time of year the sun comes down fast, sitting on the Pacific like an orange beach ball. It was the middle of September and most of the tourists were gone. I figured I'd have the beach and ocean to myself.

I must have been looking out at the sea for ten, maybe twenty minutes, when I heard him behind me. Well, right then I didn't know it was a him. I just figured it was something or somebody coming my way through the sand. I hadn't been paying much attention at first because I was staring at the afterglow of the sun, little rings of pink and red circling the sky, but as the light faded, I stopped looking and started listening to the silence of the sea. His footsteps were like newspapers skimming along the sand.

I probably would have paid no attention to him and just got up and headed back over the shelf of rocks to my rig, but passing by another human being in an isolated area like this without at least saying *Hello* somehow didn't seem right. Besides, even in the semi-darkness I could see his eyes, white holes in his face staring at me like a scavenger bird on a wooden fence. He was tall and kind of thin, but not exactly skinny, and he was wearing a dark sweater and trousers and white sandals. I couldn't see much of his features except for his eyes because of his scraggly red-brown beard that covered his face like a ski-mask.

He seemed to be pulling something on a string, but I couldn't make it out. I stopped walking for a moment and called out to him.

"Nice night, isn't it?"

He didn't reply, so I decided to move on. There were more and more homeless people around the Oregon coast lately and although most of the poor guys were harmless and just wanted a ride on my truck or some change, once in awhile I ran into one who was off the wall, probably because of drugs, so I figured if this guy wasn't talking, I'd just move on. Pretty as the beach had been when the sun was going down, in the quiet darkness it was getting a bit spooky. But as I passed him, he called out to me.

"Mind yourself on them there rocks up yonder. Efen you slip, you could get hurt real bad."

"Yeh," I agreed. "Should have brought my flashlight. It got darker quicker than I thought."

"Here," he said, guiding my arm, "this is the best way."

He led me across the long flat rocks to the sand on the other side. I could see that he had some sort of animal at the end of the string. He noticed me staring at it.

"Oh, this here is Dipsy-Doo," he said. "Wakes me up in the morning."

He held it up so that I could see. It was a scrawny little bird that looked like she had just flown through a ceiling fan.

"And I call myself Captain Zig-Zag."

"Right," I said.

As if he sensed I had decided that this was enough conversation for one night, he stood in front of me, blocking my way back to the highway.

"Yessir," he said as if continuing a thought, "the trouble with the world today is there is too much violence. You don't believe in no violence, do you, Buddy?"

"Can't say that I do."

"Me too. Y'know Dipsy-Doo and me live alone and people could take advantage on us, y'know what I mean? But even if they did I would turn the other cheek, just like the Bible says."

"You've got a point," I said, edging my way past him.

He reached out and grabbed my arm. His grip was strong. I tried to pull his hand away, but he kept talking as if unaware that he was squeezing my arm like a stalk of celery.

I'm different than most folks. I don't work no regular jobs. But when I need a little grub for me and Dipsy-Doo here, I work a little. Then I go on my way. I can fix all kinds of motors, cut hair, paint houses, pick cotton, take the wicks outta bombs, do plumbing, carpenter work, electricity—you name it. Anything with my hands. Right now I got a good job in this town working on the docks. But after tomorrow I'm going to quit and move on. Me and Dipsy."

"Well, to each his own, as they say."

He looked at me suspiciously for a moment, then seemed to have changed his mind, for he released my arm and put his arm around my shoulder in a friendly way.

"I'll walk with ya a spell, O.K.?"

"Well...sure."

We walked in silence towards my rig, but as I approached it I decided to postpone getting in it for now. I thought of booking a room in the motel next to Mae's Bakery. Could use a shower. But instead I just walked down the highway towards the Laundromat. My companion repeated his dedication to non-violence and began a long description of a beating he had suffered from two strangers with a baseball bat and a lead pipe.

"They hurt me a little," he said, "but not much because the Lawd don't let nobody hurt a peaceful man."

When we were under one of the lamplights I looked into his eyes again. They were like the empty sockets you see on statues in museums. I didn't have any clothes in the Laundromat, but I told him I did and I was on my way to retrieve them.

"I'll come and help you fold them," he offered.

"No, that's O.K. I just have a few shirts and towels."

I ran across the road as a truck came barreling down. The Laundromat was well-lighted, but there was nobody inside. I looked over my shoulder to see if he was still there. He hadn't moved from the spot where I had left him and he kept staring into the Laundromat I could have sworn that his eyes were burning into the back of my neck. For a minute I shuffled the driftwood into a dryer as if it were clothes. Then, lowering my body so the bank of machines hid it, I crawled to the back door and ran behind the row of stores until I reached my rig. I climbed in and locked the door. From time to time during the next ten minutes I peered out of the window looking for him and his bird, but he seemed to have disappeared into the night. I drove a few yards down the highway to the motel by the bakery and booked a room for the night.

***

"I didn't know if you'd still be working here, Mae," I said as I pulled the bakery door open at sunrise, "I haven't had this run in more than a year."

"They can't get rid of me," she laughed. "I'm as much a part of Gold Beach as the sea gulls. Coffee and a buttered bun?"

I grabbed *The Oregonian* from the counter and brought my coffee over to one of the three tables she has for her customers. I had just opened it to the sports section when I heard a car's brakes screech outside. When I looked out the window I saw him standing in the middle of the highway shaking his fist at the driver. He was wearing the same sweater and trousers, his face still covered with his brownish-red beard. Even in the early morning mist I could sense those eyes, or the place where they were supposed to be. He strode in without looking at me and walked right up to Mae.

"Can you sell me a cup of java for six cents? I got a good job here in town, but I ain't getting paid until Friday."

"Your boss won't advance you the price of coffee and buns?" Mae asked. "Where you working at?"

Suddenly he lifted up his sweater and his scrawny bird flew out, screeching its head off. Mae thought it was going for her hair like a bat and ducked her head under the counter. Before I could get up to pull the bird away from Mae, he yanked it back to him by its string and stuck it under his sweater again. Mae looked at him with disgust, filled a plastic cup with coffee, milk and sugar, buttered two rolls and dropped them in a white paper bag.

"Now get out of here, Mister. And don't come back with that bird."

He slowly tucked the lid over his cup and turned to leave. I started to say something, but he looked over my head as if I weren't there. +++++

198

THE WOMAN IN THE FADED CAMISOLE

It seemed that only a few minutes ago it had been a brilliant October afternoon—World Series weather, Mulvaney thought. And then just like that it had turned dark, almost as black as night. A sudden autumn storm was moving in rapidly. The rain seemed poised to fall just above the row of ash trees in the distance. He should have kept going, he told himself. With a little luck he would have made Lancaster by early evening. But he had been thirsty, so he had turned off the Interstate and rode for nearly three miles before he finally encountered a store, on the first floor of a pale green, two-story building.

An old gray driftwood sign announced that ammunition and fresh bait were for sale. Mulvaney got out and was about to try the door, but a handwritten sign scotchtaped to the window advised that the shop was "Closed for two days due to a death in the family." He decided to push on rather than turn back because the law of averages suggested that he was due to pass a store any minute now. He flicked on the high beams. A deer, caught in the light, froze for a moment on the road and then dashed into the woods.

"Graceful creature," Mulvaney mumbled to himself, "but she's not going to make it though the night if she doesn't get off this road."

He was driving slowly because it was hard to see. His eyes were heavy and the road seemed to be forever winding. He looked at his watch and decided to forget about the soda and head for the Interstate before it got really dark in these hills. He pulled into a little path in the woods wide enough for his old Chevvy. Then he threw it into reverse and backed out carefully.

Even though he had just taken this road, nothing looked familiar. When he came to a fork, he guessed left. The trouble was that Mulvaney had taken so many turns since he left the Interstate that now he hadn't the slightest idea how to re-trace his movements. He decided to drive straight ahead in the hope of finding a gas station where he could ask directions. But after a half hour all he encountered were miles of farmland on both sides of the twisting road. No stores, no signs, no people. He had really selected an isolated area. Mulvaney looked at his gas gauge. He had about a quarter of a tank, if the old Chevvy was registering accurately. Well, he couldn't just keep on driving until he ran out of gas. If something didn't turn up soon, he would just have to pull into the nearest farmhouse.

Mulvaney looked at his torn shirt and paint-stained jeans. He wished he had worn a suit or at least a sports jacket. People might be a little frightened seeing a stranger in beat-up clothes knocking on their door on a night like this.

Well, maybe he would find a gas station.

Suddenly the rain came down. Not just a few drops before gradually building up momentum, but all at once. It was as if his old Chevvy was driving in the middle of an enormous washing machine. The wipers couldn't keep up with the downpour and the inside of the windshield began to fog up. He thought of pulling off the road as far as he could and waiting until the rain stopped but was afraid someone might not see him. Not that there was a big crowd on this little road, but the way his luck was going…No, he would go slow. In a mile or two he would find a gas station.

He felt something damp on his leg and reached down to touch it. More trouble. The hood was leaking and the rain was pouring in on his jeans and shoes. Icky. All that has to happen now is for me to run over a big puddle and lose my brakes, he muttered.

At the last second he saw the dip in the road as it turned sharply to the right. But almost as soon as he guided his Chevvy back onto the road, he noticed a light in the distance. Not a bright one, to be sure, but a light. Maybe a couple of them. It didn't seem to be a house either. Must be some kind of a store. Finally.

As he drew closer he could see that it was indeed a store, a rather large one judging from the space between the lights. It was just a few feet off the road. He pulled over right in front of it.

Mulvaney had not felt better about the prospect of encountering another human being in a long time. Earlier in the day when he had been held up in traffic, he had been cursing the human race for producing too many people and cars. But after almost an hour on a lonely road without a sign of life, this store and its owner were going to be a welcome sight. He looked up to see what kind of establishment it was. A weather-beaten old sign read:

Millington General Store
K. Hardwicke, Proprietor
Established in 1872

Must be one of those old-fashioned stores of the 19th century that have been in business for years, Mulvaney mused. He had been to a few of them in Vermont and New Hampshire and enjoyed the homey smells of freshly baked cherry pies and scented candles. He thought he would ask if he could get a hot chocolate and a piece of raisin cake. That would really go well on a night like this. It was still raining pretty hard, so he pulled a newspaper over his head and ran up the old wooden steps to the front door. Probably one of those kind where a bell jingles when you open it, he told himself.

But when he pulled on the door it didn't give. He tried pushing it in. Locked. Mulvaney knocked somewhat timidly on the window. Even if they are closed, they certainly would not mind opening up to give me directions on a night like this, he thought. When there was no response, he knocked again, this time with a little more insistence.

The old wooden porch leaked a little, but he found a dry spot and stared out over his car to the other side of the road. It was too dark to see if it was farmland or if there was a house there. In the old days houses and stores were usually built close to the road. The owner of the store might very well live in a house across the way. Civilization was nearby at last. But he stared out into the darkness in vain until a flash of lightning illuminated the road and the area behind it like a refrigerator door splashing light on a dark kitchen. Surprisingly, there were few trees, but rows and rows of crosses and monuments. Mulvaney had parked across the road from a cemetery.

Staring at his old Chevvy, he thought of something frightening. He had shut the motor off to save gas, but now he remembered that he sometimes had problems starting his car when it was damp or rainy. Water got into the sparks or something. He wasn't sure, because he knew practically nothing about automobiles. That was the big joke among his friends: why did somebody as mechanically retarded as he was own such a dilapidated old car? Right now Mulvaney agreed with their criticism. He had better see if it would start. He was just about to run down the steps to check it when the door swung open.

For a moment he couldn't tell whether it was a man or a woman. What he saw was a tall slim figure draped in the shadows of the doorway. He stared into the darkness for a moment or two before he found his voice.

"I-I saw your sign and thought I'd stop by for some coffee. Or hot chocolate. It's an awful night."

The person at the door, dressed in a robe of dark brown or black simply stared back at him from the darkness.

"I'm tired from driving and I could do with something to pick me up."

"I have no food or drink."

Mulvaney could see now that it was a woman, probably a young woman for her voice was soft and when she moved he could see she walked with grace. He wondered now why he hadn't just come right out and said that he was lost and afraid of running out of gas.

"I realize now you're closed, but I saw the light and—"

"I'm not closed."

"But you just said—"

"I said I have no food."

"Well, you see I turned off the Interstate and the storm broke out suddenly and it was hard to make out the—"

"Come in."

She held the door open and Mulvaney walked past her. As he did he could smell her perfume, one of those scents that made its presence known almost immediately. It reminded Mulvaney of the inexpensive perfume Miss Grayson, one of his grade school teachers, used to wear. The other kids made fun of it, calling it the "cheap stuff they sell at the five and dime," but Mulvaney rather fancied it for the very reason his classmates laughed at it. There was no question that it was perfume, that it was feminine, not just a smell from the garden. Mulvaney liked that. And he was fond of Miss Grayson. She was young and pretty and treated him more like an older sister would than a teacher.

The room was dimly lighted, but he could see two long counters of polished oak. Sitting on the counter nearest him was a huge basket of bright red apples and green, brown, and yellow pears.

"I-I thought you said you didn't have any food," Mulvaney smiled. The woman gestured. Mulvaney interpreted her casual hand movement to mean "Help yourself." He reached for an apple but stopped before he put it in his mouth. It was as hard as a baseball.

"Wooden," the woman said. "Rather nicely painted, don't you think? People use them for centerpieces."

She reached behind the counter and flicked a switch, bringing a little light into the room. Now Mulvaney could see more of the objects in the store, although some of them were lost in shadows. Hanging from the ceiling was a huge old-fashioned sleigh, the kind huskies pull. Between the two long counters were dusty old pieces of furniture—a roll-top desk, a dry sink, two huge armoires, an old oak ice box on which a tattered Sears and Roebuck catalogue lay open to a page advertising ladies corsets and underwear at the turn of the century. Everywhere he looked were relics of the past—bird cages, roller skates, a wind-up victrola, and racks of old clothes, most of them women's. There were long Victorian dresses in black and dark blue, petticoats, huge hats with veils, and high-button shoes. The counter behind Mulvaney was covered with boxes of candles, thread, silk handkerchiefs, and even old postcards. Without thinking Mulvaney picked one of them up. It bore a picture of the boardwalk at Atlantic City, N.J. and on its correspondence side a cancelled one-cent stamp with a postmark dated July 9, 1922. Mulvaney was not going to read the message—despite the age of the card it somehow seemed liked eavesdropping—but his eye nonetheless caught the neat penmanship of what must have been a small girl.

"She was writing to her grandmother to tell her about her trip to South Jersey," the woman at the door explained.

"All this furniture and antiques," Mulvaney said in amazement. "I thought this was a general store."

"It is."

"I mean one that sells coffee and sandwiches."

The woman waved her hand in that same indifferent manner again. Mulvaney noticed that she was wearing long white lace gloves that opened at the knuckles to expose her fingers, white as ivory until they reached the tips, which were painted a vivid red. She walked to a pair of matching Windsor chairs, sat down in one, and gestured for him to do the same.

"It looks so old and delicate, I'm afraid—"

"Don't be afraid," she said. "Sit down."

Between them was an Early American drop-leaf table on which sat a solid brass candelabrum. The woman ran a long safety match along the rough floor and lighted three of the candles. Mulvaney could see that her face had the same pale white ivory coloring as her hands and was highlighted by blue mascara and deep red lipstick. She was wearing a white lace scarf and a long black dress. Her hair was also a deep black and was knotted in a long braid that dangled to her waist. She was a striking woman.

"I got off the Interstate and lost my way. I was looking for a gas station when I saw your lights."

"There are no gas stations near here," she said.

"But you can't be too far from the Interstate. There must be a place for cars and trucks to fuel up."

"Not at this time of night."

"But I'm almost out of gas."

"You can stay here."

"What?"

"I said you can stay here. You can stay with all my treasures."

Mulvaney looked at the woman as she reached up for a Victorian doll that looked oddly familiar to him. Suddenly she stood up and removed her white scarf, exposing her ivory white shoulders. She put her hand into her bosom and pulled out a small black case. Inside was a pair of scissors. She cut off a small piece of her scarf and wrapped it around the doll's shoulders. Now Mulvaney knew where he had seen the doll before: it was a spitting image of the woman with the ivory features.

"Don't you want to stay here? You could have a very bad accident trying to drive in all that rain."

The doll was even wearing the same kind of gown, Mulvaney realized. With the piece of white lace it really looked like a miniature of the woman. Why would she do something like that, he wondered.

"Are you expected somewhere?"

Mulvaney had told his former college roommate that he would arrive tonight for the start of a three-day weekend. Larry's wife had arranged a blind date for him, but that was not until tomorrow night. If the storm was bad they would understand. He could call.

"I was on my way to Lancaster, Pennsylvania. I told my friend I would probably arrive tonight, but with the weather—"

"Then you're not really expected?"

"N-no, I guess not."

"Good. You can stay here."

"Well, that's really nice of you ma'm, but—"

"My name is Miss Hardwicke."

"Miss Hardwicke?"

"Yes. Do you like my dress?"

As she sat down again, she pulled the long gown over her ankles and halfway up the calves of her legs. Either she was wearing white stockings or her legs were ivory-colored too, Mulvaney thought. They were nicely shaped, but didn't seem real. They looked more like a manikin's.

"I have others," she said.

"Others?"

"Yes, others that may be more to your liking."

"Oh, that one is fine."

"It's velvet. Old black velvet, but I have one in black lace. It's right up there."

Mulvaney followed her gaze to a rack of old Victorian gowns. When he turned back to the woman, she was undoing buttons at the back of her dress. She slipped it down over her shoulders and waist and let it drop to the floor. Now she stood before him in a faded white camisole and petticoat, similar to ones he had seen advertised in the old Sears and Roebuck catalogue atop the oak ice box. Her neck and shoulders matched the soft ivory of her legs and fingers. As she moved to the rack of dresses, Mulvaney noticed that the scent of perfume was even stronger than before. It was starting to make him slightly dizzy. She pulled the black lace dress from the rack and held it in front of her.

"It's very old," she said. "All my things are old."

Two grandfather's clocks began to chime the hour almost simultaneously. Startled, Mulvaney jumped up, brushing against the old lace dress which fell to the floor. Whether by accident or unconscious design, he brushed against Miss Hardwicke's camisole. The straps crumbled into tiny white fragments and hung in the air like stardust. Mulvaney stared at her naked breasts, plump as ripe pears but white as ivory. He looked at his feet where the black gown had fallen. Almost all of the tiny designs of lace were disengaged. It looked like the floor was alive with an army of black beetles.

"My bed is in the back of the store," she said. "Come now."

Mulvaney looked into her face. The white dust of the old camisole seemed to be sticking to her skin, covering up her blue mascara and red lipstick. It was as if her features were disappearing into a mask of whiteness. The dust circled around her neck and shoulders. All he could see of her body were white ivory fingers and legs.

"You are not expected," she said. "They will not know you stayed with me."

She pulled at her petticoat and it tore away from her body, the white fragments swirling around the room like snow. Mulvaney tried to get past her, but she stepped in his path. Instinctively he moved forward and seemed to run right through her. He ran across the store, and pulled at the door. She had bolted it. He kicked his foot through the window and raced for his old Chevvy, locking the door as soon as he got in. He turned the key and prayed for it to start. It whined but did not catch. He tried it again. And again. Just as he thought the battery was about to go, the engine kicked off.

Mulvaney had driven about a hundred yards before he realized he hadn't put his lights on. The scent of perfume

was so strong he could hardly breathe. As he opened the window, white flakes of camisole dust eased their way into the October night.+++++

VI.

SEX Happens

It's not true the more sex that you have, the more it interferes with your work. I find the more sex you have, the better work you do

—H.G. Wells

THE HOOKER IN THE HYMN CLOSET

Bannon is the one guy I know who can talk you into doing something absolutely insane and have you convinced that it is perfectly reasonable. You think putting a hooker in a hymn closet of a respectable Baptist Church is off the wall? Bannon would have you believe it's as much part of the everyday norm as Gregor Samsa's awakening to discover he had become a cockroach overnight. And after hearing him tell it, it sounded like something a grown man should be able to carry off without questioning his sanity. As I said, when Bannon strings the words together, they seem to make sense.

***

I waited till Bannon filled up my beer before I resumed the list of objections to his proposal. I learned long ago that if you're going to get on the wrong side of the bartender, it's best to do it with a full glass.

"Look, here I am almost 45 years old and I have not had a steady woman companion for three years until I met Laura," I said, striving to be tactful. "She is a delightful person to talk to, and it doesn't hurt that she is one of the few females in town whose face is as beautiful as her body is zaftig. Who knows what would happen if our relationship were to move out of the platonic stage? That's why I have to decline to participate in what I would ordinarily consider a rather imaginative venture, Bannon."

He put a head on my beer and leaned over the bar in a confidential pose, the way he usually does when he is bulldozing me, an art in which, as I have noted, he is quite proficient.

"You're afraid of old Miss Dipple, aren't you?"

"It's not that I am afraid of her, Bannon, but you know that she circles this town like a horsefly at a picnic. If she ever caught me breaking into the church—"

"Don't worry, Waddensfort, there's no moon tonight. And we don't have to force our way in. I have an associate who can provide me with the key."

"But what if she sees me going into Milady's Boudoir? How many guys pop in there?"

"That's all the more reason you have nothing to worry about. If she is going to spy on you, the last place she is going to look is in a ladies' underwear store in Cartersville. Drink up, Waddensfort. This one is on me."

He was getting to me. After all, it would be a really long shot if old lady Dipple caught me going into a lingerie shop ten miles away. She's a Class A snoop in River City, but she rarely ventures out of town. I wouldn't have hesitated if Miss Dimple didn't live next door to Laura. Bannon seemed to be reading my thoughts.

"What do you care even if by some wild chance she sees you going into Milady's Boudoir? You can always tell Laura you were shopping for a present for her."

I took a sip of the beer, licking the foam that was tickling my nose. Hmm. Bannon had a point. The chances of Miss Dimple seeing me in the lingerie shop were nil. And, as always, Bannon's little caper sounded like fun. I told him I would think about it.

I sipped my beer slowly and began ruminating about the Reverend Winger. I rather liked the old minister, but I have to say that I have never seen a man as stiff as Winger in all my life. He was the type of guy who looked like he always had a mouthful of grapefruit—even when he was smiling. But that didn't appear to bother the ladies who filled the River City First Baptist Church every Sunday to hear his sermons. They seemed to have the attitude that unless a minister had the pained expression of one dragging his way to Calvary with a bad back and sore feet, he wasn't truly a good vicar. Thus no matter how glum and sour the Reverend Winger appeared, and no matter how boring were his sermons, sprinkled here and there with dire prophecies of the proximity of Armageddon, his faithful parishioners followed his every word and glance with dogged admiration.

Bannon pointed out that Reverend Winger's personality of gloom and doom was the secret of his success.

"Henry, you and I don't go in for all that kick-yourself-in-the-teeth-on-a-regular-basis routine with a little feisty flagellation on the side," he observed, "but the old broads eat it up. They've been going to church all their lives, so they have read enough of the Bible to convince themselves that the world is an evil place and anything rotten that happens to them is something they probably deserve. When they reach this stage in their thinking, winning the lottery would probably bring on a heart attack."

"Because of the excitement?"

"Nah. Because of the disappointment. They think good fortune is bad luck because they are pretty heavy on that passage in the Bible that says it's easier for a camel to walk through the eye of a needle than for a rich fatso to squeeze through the Pearly Gates."

"I assume you're giving me a rough translation?"

"You know what I mean, Waddensfort. Anyway, what River City needs is a little excitement to remind the denizens that they are in a new millennium. Look at it this way: it will be our gift to the citizens of River City. I have already done all the necessary research while attending last Sunday's services."

"You went to church, Bannon?"

"Please, Waddensfort. You talk as if I have never been there before. When it comes to research, I go anywhere. Well, what do you say? Are you going to be my partner in this little venture? If it works, lots of guys in River City won't have to waste good drinking time in church on Sundays mornings. Think of it as one giant step for—"

"O.K., just make sure Miss Dimple doesn't get wise."

"No problem. Everything's worked out at the lingerie store. My brother-in-law, Wilheim Glocken-schlater, works there and he'll have his eye out for you. Now here's what I have in mind..."

Bannon, a master at intricate details, had done his homework, so I figured my part in the scheme would be a snap. Wilheim met me at the door of Milady's Boudoir in Centerville with the mannequin.

"My boss will be back sometime in the middle of next week, so you better bring it back Monday," Wilheim had insisted. "And be careful with the underwear. Those panties and bra are made of pure silk."

The mannequin was so realistic looking—it resembled a blonde with long flowing hair—that I wondered if I should leave it in my Ford while I stopped in the YMCA for my daily battle with the machines. The black lacy underwear made the dummy so provocative looking that there was always the chance that some weirdo would break into my car, thinking the answer to a pervert's dream was stretched across the back seat. But I could hardly take the mannequin into the Y. There was always the chance that I might run into Miss Dipple who worked part-time on the desk when she wasn't rehearsing the choir at the River City Baptist Church. There just didn't seem to be a way of escaping that old haybag. Now if Ms. Evers were on the desk, it would be a different story. She has a sense of humor and belongs to the River City Episcopal Church, not necessarily in that order.

Of course, I could have skipped my workout and gone straight to the vicarage. But Bannon wouldn't be there yet, because he had to wait until six o'clock to get his hands on the church key. And I didn't want to sit around in my car in front of the rectory too long. It would look suspicious.

I tried putting the mannequin in the trunk, but it was jammed with athletic gear, and I was afraid of damaging the dummy and her underwear by squeezing her in. Just as I was taking the mannequin out of the trunk and placing it in the back seat, David Bailey, one of the new members of the Y, walked by. Perhaps it was my imagination, but ever since he joined the Y, I have had the feeling that there was something odd about this new guy. I'm convinced that Bailey saw the mannequin. I could understand if he had whistled, laughed, or even made some macho gesture. But he passed the exotic-looking mannequin with the same dour expression that the Reverend Winger brought to services every Sunday. Maybe this guy was a defrocked minister. He certainly had the look of one. Sometimes I get the impression that River City must grow glum faces.

Looking under the back seat, I found an old Army blanket and spread it out over the mannequin so nothing could be seen of her nicely framed body and black silk underwear. Now I could exercise in peace.

Two hours later, showered, shaved, and exercised, I retrieved my wallet and wristwatch from Miss Dipple, who, as I had guessed, was on duty at the desk. She handed them over reluctantly, as if I had stolen my own stuff. I slipped on the wristwatch and placed the wallet in my inside coat pocket. It never would have occurred to me to check its contents. The chance that old Miss Dipple would ever snatch anything from my wallet was about as remote as an accurate weather forecast.

As I was driving to the church, I contemplated Bannon's plan. By now I was completely under his spell and the more I thought about it, the more convinced I was that it would work. Right now the main thing was for Bannon and me to slip the mannequin into the church without being seen. Then all we had to do was to hide it in the tall cabinet by the altar where the Reverend Winger kept his hymn books. The vicar's routine at Sunday service was predictable. As soon as he finished his sermon, he would walk over to his hymn cabinet, open it up, and pull out his favorite hymn book on the top shelf. What Bannon planned to do was remove the shelves from the cabinet so he could fit the mannequin in.

I turned on the motion picture camera of my brain. What a sight this was going to be! I could just picture the scene in the middle of next Sunday's service. The Reverend Winger, as stone-faced as ever, would be just finishing reading a passage from the Bible. He would glare at his congregation, his eyes scolding them for the many indiscretions they had committed since his last Sunday service. Then he would tell the congregation to sing Hymn 112.

"I will lead you," he would say, "as a shepherd leads his flock. Come raise your voices with me and sing 'Let Our Hands be Busy Working for the Lord.'" And he would open the cabinet door.

Then plop. Right into his outstretched arms would fall Wilheim Glockenschlater's mannequin, looking as authentic as a woman from a strip joint with her black lace panties and bra fluttering in the breeze of the two altar fans at the River City First Baptist Church. The dummy was so realistic that even the people in the front row would think he had hidden a hooker in his hymn closet. I hated waking up just to go to church but I was looking forward to making next Sunday's service. It would be worth missing an hour or two of sleep, just to glance up at the choir to see Miss Dipple's face when the mannequin fell into the vicar's arms.

I was so taken up with images of the Reverend Winger with a half-naked mannequin in his arms and the congregation singing off-key "Let Our Hands be Busy Working for the Lord" that I failed to notice the police car that had been following me for the last two miles. My reverie was interrupted by the shrill sound of a siren and the rapidly blinking lights of the police vehicle. I pulled over to the shoulder of the road.

"Your driver's license and registration, please."

"Yes, Officer. But what is the problem?"

"You were doing 60 in a 40-mile an hour zone."

"Oh, I'm sorry. I guess—"

The officer held the driver's license up to the light. Suddenly he placed his hand atop his service revolver. His partner, who was driving the patrol car, stepped out with his pistol drawn. I felt like I was in an old cops-and-robbers movie.

"All right, Mac, step out of your car and put both hands on the hood of your vehicle."

"B-but, officer. I didn't realize I was going that fast. I—"

"Speeding is not your biggest problem, Buster. O.K., stand up straight and put your hands behind your back. Frisk him, Murphy."

Before I could realize what was happening, the second officer had handcuffed me and ran his hands up and down my body in a most embarrassing manner.

"Officers, there must be some mistake. I admit that I was speeding, but surely that is no reason to place me in handcuffs. I am not a criminal."

"Yeah," the first cop said, unimpressed. "Your only problem is that you can't leave the ladies alone."

"I-I don't understand."

"Don't give me that innocent crap, Smart Ass. I know a sex pervert when I see one."

"Officer, you are making an awful mistake."

"This is no mistake. It says sex offender right on your license."

"I can't believe that."

"Well it doesn't actually spell the words out, but it has a red S printed in the right hand corner. The state of Delaware has made it the law that every repeat sex offender must have this designation on his license. O.K., get in the back seat of the police car."

"But I am not a sex offender. I don't even have a regular girlfriend."

The cop named Murphy looked at me dubiously and reached into the back seat of my Ford.

"What's this?" he asked, tugging at the blanket that covered the mannequin.

"Oh, that's—"

But just at that moment he pulled the blanket off the lower half of the mannequin, revealing the bottom of its black lace panties.

"So you're not a sex offender, eh?" he said. "What are you doing with a hooker sleeping in your back seat?"

"Officer, that's not a woman; that's a mannequin."

"Yeh. And I am Madame Curie. In you go into the back of the patrol car, Mr. Bailey."

"Bailey? My name is Waddensfort."

"Your name is what?"

"Waddensfort, W-a-d-de—"

"Don't give me that, Bailey. Your name is right here on your driver's license."

"May I see that license?"

The first officer looked at me suspiciously.

"What's your point?" he asked

"There has to be an awful mix-up somewhere. There's no way my license can say Bailey when I am Waddensfort."

The first cop held the license out for me to read. I guess he was curious what I would say when I saw that the name on the license was indeed Bailey. I stared at the license in disbelief.

"I-I don't understand this. It's imposs—"

The cop named Murphy grabbed me by the arm. "Come along, Bailey."

All of a sudden it hit me. "Wait a second, Officers. Look at the registration."

Reluctantly the first cop glanced at the registration again. It was for a 97 Chevvy. But I was driving an '86 Ford.

"Where did you steal this car, Bailey?" he asked.

"I'm not Bailey. And this is not my car—I mean, this IS my car, but you've got the wrong license and registration."

I didn't sound very convincing and the cops were starting to lose their patience.

"Get in that police car and shut up," the cop named Murphy said. ".I'm taking you down to the station house."

His partner pulled out a pad. "I'll get a statement from the bimbo in the back seat. Call for Louie's tow truck for this piece of junk this guy stole. The young lady and I will ride to the station in the cab with Louie."

I figured it out on the way to the station. Miss Dipple had got my wallet mixed up with the one turned in by that new guy Bailey. I was right about him. He was more than weird; he was a sex offender. What a pickle I had got myself into.

Then, despite my predicament, I broke out in laughter. Officer Murphy in the front seat turned his head slightly in my direction.

"What's the matter, Mac? Are you cracking up?"

"No. officer. I was just thinking of your partner in my car: trying to take a statement from a dummy."

"Dummy?"

"I told you that's not a real person. It's a half-naked mannequin that I was going to put in the Reverend Winger's hymn closet this Sunday."

Officer Murphy took another furtive glance at me.

"So you are traveling around with dummies in their drawers? That sounds like an interesting hobby. And the Reverend Winger collects them too? That comes to me as a bit of a surprise. Who would ever think old Winger was into dummies? But I suppose nowadays just about anything is possible."

I didn't know if he were humoring me.

"Officer, I don't collect dummies. It so happens I borrowed just this one to—"

But Officer Murphy wasn't listening. He was talking to someone on his police radio.

I was being fingerprinted and getting my mug shot taken when the first cop walked in carrying the mannequin over his shoulders caveman style. Her black bra and panties were torn. Officer Murphy and the police photographer did a double take.

"Calm down, you guys, it's not what you think. This is a dummy."

Murphy remembered why I was laughing on the way to the station. He had a hard time holding back a grin.

"Is that's so, Joe?" he asked. "How did the interview go?"

The face of the cop named Joe reddened. He turned to me.

"Listen, Waddensfort. I'll make a deal with you. Keep quiet about this whole thing and I'll let you go. We'll get rid of the fingerprints, the mug shot, and all the records. No questions asked. Is it a deal?"

I didn't see any point in refusing an offer like that, but I was still curious.

"How did you know my name?"

"When I was getting out of Louie's tow truck a bartender named Bannon came up to me and told me your nutty plan of putting this dummy in the hymn closet. He had followed me in his pick-up truck when he recognized your car being towed. Bannon said you must have got the wrong wallet when you checked out at the Y. That guy was some talker, so I figured he might be giving me a line. But when I called the Y they told me they have your wallet and that a guy named Bailey has been complaining that they lost his. I told Bannon I would talk to you and if you agreed to keep your trap shut, we'd see that he got his dummy back and we'd forget the whole thing. Bannon is parked outside. He said he'll drive you to the police garage where we keep the towed vehicles. It'll cost you $50 to get your car back. And here's Bailey's wallet. Drop it off at the Y and you can pick up yours."

After I watched him throw my records into the police shredder, I got out of there as fast as I could, not even stopping to wash the ink off my fingers. On my way out I heard Officer Murphy repeat his question to his partner about interviewing the dummy. I guess things are slow in River City these days.

Bannon didn't want to put the mannequin in the back of his truck because he was afraid it might rain. That's how the half-nude dummy landed in my lap at almost the precise time an old woman got out of her car across the street from the police station. I am almost positive she saw me with the dummy.

"Get going, Bannon. We're being watched."

He tuned to me to see what I was talking about.

"Who's watching us?"

"Didn't you see that old lady getting out of a cab across the street?"

Instead of stepping on the gas, he stopped to take a look. "Well, what do you know about that? It's Miss Dipple."

"C'mon Bannon, move it. If she hasn't seen me already, she will if you don't get the hell out of here."

"Don't worry, Waddensfort, broads that old don't have good eyesight."

"Miss Dipple doesn't need good eyesight. She finds things out by instinct. How do you think she got here just as I was walking out of the police station with the dummy?"

"O.K., O.K.," he conceded, putting the truck into third, "if she badmouths you, this is what you tell Laura: you've got a cousin from Walla Walla, Washington, a lingerie model, who was kidnapped during a fashion show and—"

"Wait as second. Walla Walla?"

"Yeah, it makes it sound more authentic. Anyway, she's rescued by the FBI, but she suffered a memory loss when she was hit on the head by the crooks. All she can recall is her cousin, Henry Waddensfort. Out of nowhere you get a call from the FBI and they—"

I closed my eyes and let the rhythm of Bannon's lingo soothe my jangled nerves. Maybe Miss Dipple had not seen me after all. But even if she had, it would be fun—sort of—to see what would happen if I tried telling Bannon's tall story to Laura. On second thought, I could ask him to tell her. Then I wouldn't have a thing to worry about.+++++

THE CARPENTER, THE WALRUS, THE MARATHON RUNNER, AND SQUINTY, THE IRISH SETTER

"The time has come," the Walrus said.
To talk of many things:
Of shoes—and ships—and sealing wax—
Of cabbages—and Kings—
And why the sea is boiling hot—
And whether pigs have wings."
Lewis Carroll

Sgt. Harry Steinhoffer had never seen anything like it in his 31 years on the force.

A big blob that looked like a walrus, but was probably a man, was wrestling with a little guy in an astrakhan hat with a screwdriver and hammer sticking out of his belt, while a few feet away a honey-haired woman wearing only crystal earrings and unlaced hush puppies lay moaning on the bottom step of the back porch of a fashionable suburban home, her head resting on the tail of a mangy Irish setter who was contentedly chewing on the corner of a pink bath towel.

The sergeant, somewhat overweight, was breathing heavily from running from his patrol car and straddling the split-rail fence. When neither of the wrestlers paid him any heed, he reached for his service revolver and fired two shots in the air. The naked woman, whose svelte figure was surprisingly tanned for this time of year, stirred slightly and then passed out, but neither the Walrus nor the Carpenter paid the police officer any heed, although the Irish setter—but that's getting ahead of the story....

***

The Carpenter

It was not Boris Rutkowski's ability with a hammer and saw that made him a successful carpenter; rather it was his inability with a pad and pencil. Boris couldn't add, or at least he professed to lack this basic skill when he was summoned to give an estimate of a job.

If he were refinishing a basement, for example, he would pull out his measuring tape and record the length of a wall, then climb on his ladder to determine its height. He would jot these dimensions on his pad, wet his pencil with his tongue a few times to make the multiplication easier, re-measure, re-climb the ladder, add, subtract, multiply and re-wet his pencil. While the home owner looked on with wonder and awe, Boris would take off his astrakhan hat, scratch his head vigorously, and throw up his hands as if he had made a decent attempt to discover the origin of the universe but found the task slightly beyond his reach.

"It's no use, Mac. I don't know what to tell you. This job could cost $8,000; then again it could be $20,000, maybe even more. You never know what kind of complications you're going to run into—crooked walls, cracks in the cinder blocks, faulty wiring. With a helper, materials, tax…. you're looking at ten grand, at least. The problem is, Mac, they just don't make houses the way they used to."

And just when the owner would be about to forget the whole thing and tell his wife to find another place for her mother to live, Boris would raise his hand like a maestro telling the violins to break in.

"Look, to be perfectly honest with you, Mac, I don't know how involved this job is going to be. It could be nice and simple; then again I could be getting into a can of worms. Honest to God, I wish I knew. But if you want me to give you an estimate, I'm going to have to protect myself. You know what I mean, don't you?"

"Well then, maybe I should postpone—"

Boris would wait until he saw a glimmer of hope in his victim's eye.

"All right, I'll tell you what I'm going to do. You seem like a nice guy. Now keep this confidential, because I don't do this for everyone. But seeing as your crooked walls make it hard to estimate, I'll work for you by the hour. Now listen to this: I'll only charge $75 an hour and I'll do it without a helper. In today's market that's a real good deal, Mac. This way you only pay for what I do."

"Sounds fair, but just so I can have an idea of how much this job is going to cost me in the end, could you give me an estimate on the number of hours it will take?"

Boris would grunt and talk to himself inaudibly before going back to his clipboard and doodling some more. After a few extravagant strokes, he would smile and turn his palms inward like a bookie being asked for a tip on the daily double.

"I can't promise you anything, Mac. Like I said, this one is hard to figure. But in my heart of hearts I don't think it is going to take me too long. It won't be anything like that twenty grand estimate."

By this time the owner's wife would be standing at the top of the stairs, wondering about the fate of her mother. That's was when Boris knew he had made a sale.

Once he got the O.K. to start working by the hour his whole body would shift into slow motion. He would tap at nails like a xylophonist and saw wood like a harpist. Most owners got nervous as the hours started to mount up, but few of them wanted to call off the job in the middle— what with parts of their houses looking like the aftermath of a terrorist attack. His slow pace was compounded by his penchant for taking on three jobs at the same time, keeping each one in a state of chaos.

Thus Boris made a good living without wearing out much of his equipment, save the lead on his pencil.

The only problem with his success was his wife, Madge. It wasn't that she didn't appreciate the money he brought home from his calculating carpentry; it was her realization that, since they had enough income for a while, it was time Boris worked on their own neglected house. She pointed him in the direction of their porous roof and Boris, finally working for himself, picked up the tempo.

It was while he was on the roof that he discovered the Walrus.

**

Boris soon suspected that it might not be a walrus at all, but his neighbor, Rodney Dalrimple, who lived directly behind him. And on that windy day in March when he looked up from his shingles and down at the Dalrimples' back porch, Rodney forever became the Walrus in Boris's mind. For there was Mrs. Dalrimple, her pale lemon skirts flying high in the air as she raced madly between the flower pots, with her husband in fast pursuit, flailing a huge flounder in the air. Boris soon realized that the gigantic gray blur swinging the fish at Mrs. Dalrimple was his neighbor, Rodney. He mentioned the incident to Madge as soon as he got down from the roof for his coffee break, but his wife said that while he had been "gallivanting all over the neighborhood with his hammer and saw," she had seen several strange goings-on at the Dalrimples, which she could not describe in any detail because she was a good Christian woman. Madge had mentioned this to put Boris in his place for neglecting their home front for so long, but it only added to the new aura with which he regarded Rodney.

Can you imagine that, Madge?" he asked again and again. "That nut must actually think he's a walrus."

Madge looked at the calendar from The Reliable Savings Bank hanging over the kitchen sink. Sunday was four days off.

"I'd say he would do a better job passing for a hippopotamus. Can't you see the similarity in the mouth?"

***

The Walrus

Rodney did eventually catch Melanie Dalrimple that windy morning—just as she reached the top of the stairs. He tackled her in the upstairs hall and they rolled around on the floor for two hours at least, enjoying the bliss that comes to the average red-blooded American man and woman after a highly competitive footrace in lemon-hued skirts and a Walrus suit.

Later that afternoon, when Rodney was changing into his Mary Queen of Scots costume in preparation for a little ballroom dancing, Melanie remarked that she thought Boris might have caught some of their act from his perch on the roof.

"Was he taking videos?"

"No, he was repairing torn shingles."

"Well, you don't have any holes in your underwear, do you?"

"Just one, but I don't think he had a telescope. I imagine he just looked up from his work when you tossed the flounder out the window."

Rodney pulled his long white gown down. It was a little short and his argyle socks were showing.

"You know, Melanie, sometimes I think he's a little nosey. Do you think he's really fixing his roof?"

Melanie shrugged and pulled her husband down on top of her. She was glad he had changed his mind about being Moby Dick. The last thing she wanted to do was re-injure her calf.

***

The Marathon Runner

Melanie was not picky. She enjoyed her husband as Attila the Hun, Minnie Mouse, John Wayne, Henry VIII, Marlene Dietrich, Rin-Tin-Tin and Baby LeRoy, but she had to admit she rather liked him as The Walrus the best. The costume was a lot smoother than she had imagined at first, so it was easy on her skin. When she overheard Boris refer to her husband as the Walrus while the Carpenter was making a deposit at the Old Reliable Savings and Loan Bank, she began calling Rodney by that name as well.

Much as Melanie enjoyed the games she played with her husband, her favorite pastime was running. Although only 38 years old, she had already run 42 marathons and rarely missed a day that she didn't jog at least ten miles, no matter what kind of weather she had to endure.

The only thing that slowed her down was injuries, which were becoming more and more frequent as she neared her forties. She took all the precautions—plenty of stretching before and after her run, a careful vegetarian diet, comfortable clothing, and even occasional visits to her sports medicine physician, whose advice she usually ignored.

"I can't stop running for two weeks," she told him after a calf injury.

"But if you don't, your leg won't have adequate time to heal."

"I'll cut down to eight miles."

"How about walking instead?"

"O.K. I'll walk two miles and jog six."

He would throw up his hands in despair. Melanie kept running, but she slowed down her pace during the length of the injury. For her that was quite a concession.

***

Squinty, the Irish Setter

Melanie named him Squinty when he was a pup because it looked like the poor dog didn't have any eyes. His face was twisted like a piece of used-up sandpaper with two nail holes in the middle. Actually Squinty, a frenetic Irish setter almost constantly on the run around the Dalrimples' two acres of fenced-in yard, was quite healthy and had average eyesight for a 15-year-old dog. The Walrus often made the point that by human standards Squinty would be 105 years old and that no man or woman that age could circle two acres 20 or 30 times a day and only occasionally fall in a hole or bump into a fence post.

What drove the Dalrimples bonkers was Squinty's confusion about doors. He would jump from the couch and bark incessantly to get out to do his business in the back yard, but when one of them would get the door and hold it open for him, Squinty would just sit there and stare up at his benefactor.

"Let's go, Squinty," a tired Melanie would order, shivering a little from the North Wind.

But the dog would just sit there and look up and squint.

"Let's go, damnit."

And still he would sit, stare, and squint. Sometimes he focused his attention on Melanie, sometimes it was on the door of the back porch. When this kept up for a few minutes the Walrus would be called to the scene and together, by a little coaxing, pushing, or cracker-tossing, he and his wife would convince Squinty that it had been his idea to go out in the first place. Once outside, he would break into a gallop, yapping and circling, circling and yapping. It was as if a tiger were chasing him.

Everything would be fine until he decided to return. Then the barking, sitting, looking up, and squinty routine would begin again, only this time from the outside of the back door.

***

It was sunrise on a bright Sunday morning in May, Mother's Day to be precise. All the principals were in place, scarcely more than a hundred feet from the Dalrimples' back porch.

Sgt. Steinhoffer was sipping black coffee from a cardboard container and reading the Sunday paper in his patrol car, which he had parked across the street from the Dalrimples' driveway. He would have been off, but he had offered to work so his buddy, Sgt. Pete Keller, could spend the day with his family.

"My old lady appreciates it, Harry, but you ain't fooling me."

"Whatdya mean, Pete?" Steinhoffer had answered, feigning hurt feelings. "If I had a mother, I woulda taken the day off."

"Your old lady has a mother. You coulda spent it with her."

Steinhoffer had smiled that smile that suggests one is privy to one of the secrets of the ages.

"I just thought this was a day when the mother and daughter like to be by themselves."

And while Sgt. Steinhoffer was reading the colored comic pages, The Carpenter, for somewhat similar reasons, was pounding away on his roof. Madge had wanted him to take her and the kids to Pistillini's Italian Restaurant for Mother's Day, but he had protested that he if he didn't work on the roof while the weather was good he would never get it done. The Carpenter preferred taking money in much more than he did to giving it out, and by working he would not only avoid getting ripped off by Pistillini, but he would be finishing his homework and getting back to the business of pounding nails slowly for $75 an hour. He pulled down his astrakhan hat to protect himself from the early morning breeze and the screams of Madge trying to get the kids up for mass.

Things weren't going as well for Melanie, who was soaking her legs in the bathtub. She had injured her left calf muscle slightly the previous day when a red BMW filled with screaming teenagers had forced her off the road, causing her to twist her leg as she fell in the bushes. If she had not been in pain, she would have tried to race after the car to get its license number. If it turned out that she had to limit her run today, she would go to the high school the next day and look for the BMW in the parking lot.

Rodney was taking off his Julius Caesar toga that he had been sleeping in and putting on his Walrus suit. He knew this was Melanie's favorite and he was hoping that if her leg was bothering her she might opt for some exercise in the bed rather than on the highways. He rubbed the wrinkled skin of the Walrus's hide appreciatively. Yes, Melanie liked it and so did Rodney. It wasn't everyone who could make love to a beautiful woman and boast of having a pair of tusks almost two feet long. He hung Caesar's toga on his side of the closet, being careful not to detach the wide sash on which he had printed the legend *Render unto Caesar the things that are Caesar's...*

And Squinty, snoring on the kitchen floor by the fireplace, was dreaming of a huge cat the size of an elephant chasing him around the backyard. Just as he was about to be smashed by the paws of the gargantuan feline, he awakened and felt the call of nature.

It all began when he sat by the back door and let loose with a plaintive moan...

Rodney heard it, but he was busy zipping up the back of his walrus suit. Melanie waited a minute or two. Then realizing her husband was probably too busy with his costumes to let Squinty out, she slipped into her hush puppies and made her way to the back door. However, as she approached it, she heard the sound of the Carpenter's hammer, so she returned to the bathroom for a large pink towel to drape around herself. When she opened the door for the Irish setter, Squinty just stared up at her and her bright towel.

"O.K., you wanted to go out. Now *go*."

Squinty continued to look at her without moving.

"C'mon, dog, let's go."

Still nothing.

"Damn it, Squinty, I'm chilly. All I've got on is this towel."

Squinty either did not understand her or preferred not to.

"MOVE!"

But Squinty did not like being yelled at. He looked like he might be about to whimper, but he managed to keep a stiff upper jaw and continue to stare at the pink bath towel. Melanie cast a nervous eye towards The Carpenter's house. He had stopped hammering. She wondered whether he could see her from the roof. Opening the door a little wider, she gestured for her stubborn dog to go out. When he still refused, she reached back her leg and took a kick at him.

And then everything happened at once.

Squinty dodged the clumsy kick and ran yapping into the back yard. Melanie twisted her sore leg and fell down the back stairs. Dazzled by the whirling pink towel, the yapping dog and the screaming Melanie, the Carpenter descended his ladder and rushed to the rescue. By this time the Walrus, now fully attired down to his tusks, realized that something was askew and made his way to the back door in time to see the Carpenter closing in on his naked wife. Sgt. Steinhoffer looked up from the funny papers at the sound of Melanie screaming and Squinty barking. Seconds later he was straddling the split-rail fence.

**

It could have been much more serious. The sudden pain in her left calf had caused Melanie to pass out, but she returned to consciousness when Squinty pulled the pink towel from underneath her. Sgt. Steinhoffer, The Carpenter, and The Walrus lunged for it, but Squinty was too fast for them and began tearing around the yard with it, yapping triumphantly. The Carpenter picked up his astrakhan hat and returned to his roof, Sgt. Steinhoffer put his revolver back in his holster and made his way back to his Sunday comics. The Walrus picked Melanie up to carry her into bed. Along the way she hung on to his tusks for support. +++++

VII.
Comic Tales

Comedy is an imitation of the common errors of our life.
—Philip Sidney

CAT-HUNTING

Caspar the Cat reminded me of a cat in a comic strip I used to read when I was a kid. This cat was fond of picking up a brick, winding up like a baseball pitcher, and flinging it at the head of anybody who messed with him. Even cops. I can't remember where he got the bricks or how he seemed to always get away with it. His name was Ignatz and the comic strip was called *Krazy Kat.*

Now that I think of it, he wasn't so crazy. For that matter all the cats in my life have been pretty shrewd and one had to be in top form to compete with them. But none was trickier than Caspar.

Caspar was all black save for a streak of white shaped like the map of New Jersey underneath his whiskers. If you didn't know Caspar well, you probably wouldn't have noticed it because it was so small. From Trenton to Jersey City it was less than a half-inch across. I never would have known Caspar if it weren't for Carrie Benson, who used to stop over our house once or twice a week to exchange gossip with my wife, Bertha. She brought Caspar with her on a little leash, the first time I ever saw a cat on one. It was a good thing too, because at least I knew where he was. He worked himself free once and had a little snooze in my dresser drawer. I could never get his smell out of my shirts, and wound up using four of my favorite tailor-made ones to clean off my windshield on muddy days in March. Carrie thought that was cute. She was always telling us how smart Caspar was and how much he had cost.

When Carrie started coming to our house three and four times a week, and the kids suddenly took to giggling behind my back, I knew something was up. It didn't take me long to realize that it had to do with Carrie. And if it concerned Carrie, obviously it concerned Caspar.

I figured it out in no time. Carrie and her husband, who had a few bucks, were taking a three-month cruise around the world. Naturally that meant they would need a cat-sitter, and since Bertha knew how I felt about cats in general, and creepy little Caspar in particular, neither she nor Carrie would ever ask me. But that, of course, didn't mean they wouldn't try to stick that little cat on me. As soon as I found out the date that Carrie's ship sailed, I was ready for them.

Their modus operandi was simple. When I left for work on the day of their departure, Carrie and Bertha would get together, hide Caspar safely in our house and, once the ship left port, I would be the proud foster father of a cat for three months, whether I sought the honor or not. To make sure I didn't discover the cat when I came home from work, Bertha had Carrie invite me to the bon voyage party in her stateroom on the upper deck. Room 319. Since I had to come there straight from work, they knew I wouldn't find out about Caspar until Carrie and her husband were on their way around the world. It was one thing to know about their sneaky cat attack; it was another to thwart it. I knew what I had to do: get that cat out of my house and return the favor by sneaking it into the Bensons' stateroom just before I left the bon voyage party. Then they would have the choice of trying to keep Caspar in hiding in their cabin for three months or of paying to board him in the ship's hold. They had a lot of money, but I suspected, like some rich people, they were cheap. Otherwise, why would they try to leave their precious Caspar with me, a cat-hater?

My problem was how to get the cat right after Carrie and Bertha hid it in the house and left for the ship. There was no way I could take a day off work, so I had to find someone who would do the cat-napping for me. I called around to a few friends without success. Finally I decided to throw caution to the winds and ask my next-door neighbor.

Marjorie has long been considered the mystery woman of the neighborhood. She doesn't seem to have a husband and is frequently being visited by old women in multi-colored shawls covered with moons and stars. Rumor has it that Marjorie is into fortune-telling and astrology deeper than Nancy Reagan was. Bertha is about the only woman in the neighborhood who talks to her, more out of curiosity than Christian charity. Asking Marjorie was a calculated risk, but I had run out of people.

To my surprise, she was sympathetic with my cause. She had a great fear of cats, which she considered unlucky, and the thought of having one next door to her for three months was worse than having Jupiter in the House of Mars.

"I wish I could take Caspar to the pier for you, but I am scared stiff of cats. I just could not bring myself around to touching him."

I told her I would pay off one of my kids to put Caspar in a basket, close it, and rope it shut, so that all she had to do was make the delivery.

"But he won't be able to get out of the basket?" "I'll have Peter put him in your trunk."

"The cat won't suffocate?"

"Nah. He has breathing spaces all over his body." "O.K., but as soon as I meet you at the pier, I'm taking off. If Bertha ever knew I was involved in anything like this, that would be the end of our relationship. And she's the only one in the neighborhood who talks to me."

***

The timing was perfect. Marjorie arrived in her white Dodge twenty minutes after Carrie and Bertha left. Peter got home from school just in time to see his mother hiding the cat in the washing machine. He put him in a laundry basket, and fastened the top with a piece of clothes line. Marjorie called me at my office to report the basket was in her trunk and to ask me to leave work a little early so I wouldn't be delayed by the rain. The last thing she wanted was to be double-parked at the pier with a strange cat in her trunk. I got there ten minutes before she did. Marjorie's face was flushed as she rolled down her window.

"Please don't ever ask me to do anything like this again."

"Did the cat give you any trouble?"

"Trouble's not the word. From the moment I left your driveway, he's been moaning something awful. *Yeeeeooowwwwwwww!!* Something like that. It sounded like he was being murdered."

"Cats don't like confinement."

"Here are the keys. Open the trunk and get him out of here. Remember I had nothing to do with this."

My plan was to board the ship, pretending the basket was filled with booze or going-away presents. The yowling might present a little bit of a problem, but I had come this far, so I was sure I could muddle through. Contemplating the look on Carrie's face when she returned to her cabin, pie-eyed from the party, to find good old Caspar sleeping on her bed gave me the strength to bring this mission to its conclusion. I turned the key of Marjorie's trunk and pulled it open.

Caspar darted out skittishly like a balloon that had suddenly lost its air. I made a wild lunge at him, but he disappeared under a parked car.

"What'll I do now?" I asked Marjorie. "That cat is supposed to be worth more than three thousand dollars." She took the keys and started the motor.

"That's your problem. Even if I weren't scared silly of cats I wouldn't help you because sure as hell while you're looking, Bertha is going to walk down the gangplank. I can feel it in my bones."

Seconds later her white Dodge was a misty blur slowly dissolving in the shadows of the New York waterfront.

***

Caspar being black was bad enough. But being black at night in the rain was worse. I decided to check the underpinnings of the cars in the parking lot. It was my only hope. I knew cats don't like water, so I figured he would be looking for the driest spot. The only trouble was that there were hundreds of cars. And I didn't have a flashlight.

I've got to keep calm, I told myself. If worse comes to worse I could sell my golf clubs or my season's pass to the Giants. That should be enough to pay for the damned cat. Unless Carrie started pulling stuff about emotional and psychological damages. She has a shrewd lawyer and she knows she could sue me without Bertha getting mad. Bertha would probably encourage her. She's always saying, "My husband is bizarre" and would love to say that under oath. The two of them would probably split the money. What am I saying? I'll find the damned cat. He's got to be here somewhere.

I tried calling him.

"Here, Caspar. Nice Caspar. I've got some milk for you, Caspar, old pal. Meeee-oww, Caspar. MEEEE-ow!" Nothing.

"Please, Caspar. Come to Daddy, Caspar. Come here, Caspar, you rotten son-of-a-bitch!"

A couple of old ladies saw me. At first I thought they were going to help me find the cat, but when I looked over at them, they started walking fast in the other direction. I thought I heard one of them say something about calling the cops.

Ever since I started searching for Caspar, I had the tremendous urge to pee, but I was afraid that the moment I stopped looking would be the very moment that Caspar would reveal his hiding place. Of course,

I could probably look and pee at the same time, but the way those old ladies were talking, I might soon be under surveillance of the police.

All of a sudden I heard the sounds of drunken laughter coming from the gang plank, followed by a couple of toots on the foghorn of the steamer. The bon voyage party was breaking up. Now my problems were doubled: I had to find Caspar and dodge Bertha.

The announcement came over the loudspeaker that all visitors had to be off the ship in 15 minutes. Knowing Bertha, she would be the last to leave, so I had a little time yet. Wrong again. In the first wave of visitors I recognized Bertha's voice. I hit the ground under a Cutlass Supreme. I lay there for a few minutes looking at the bottoms of passing cars in the wild hope of seeing Caspar. One car, slowly making its way towards me, looked strangely familiar. It was a white Dodge. Marjorie!

"Before I got to the Holland Tunnel my conscience started bothering me," she explained. "I couldn't leave you crawling on the ground all by yourself. This is Madame Theresa."

She opened the passenger door and a heavy-set, olive-skinned woman in long golden earrings and a silk shawl with stars and crescents on it emerged.

"It ees pleasure, darling," she said, extending her hand.

"How did you—?"

"She has a place on Spring Street, not far from the tunnel. I have had her out to my house a few times, but I guess you never met her. Madame Theresa is better than St. Anthony when it comes to finding things."

Madame Theresa smiled.

"Unlike Miss Marjorie, I like ze cats. For me, lucky."

"Anything you can do, Madame Theresa, I would certainly appreciate."

She smiled at me with huge ivory teeth.

"The customary donation for cat-finding is one hundred dollars, darling. Cash, please."

She got down on her knees—to look, I think—and Marjorie and I did the same. Just then we heard Bertha's booming voice.

"Look at my husband, crawling on the ground with two gypsies," she announced to her friends. "He's bizarre." She was apparently too bombed from the champagne to wonder what I was doing there and who my companions were. Since she was more familiar with my rear end than

Marjorie's, I don't know till this day if she realized I was cat-hunting with the woman next door. Just as the loudspeaker was proclaiming that visitors had ten minutes to leave the steamer, Madame Theresa walked over to me with Caspar in her arms.

"A nice cat. The white spot ees very lucky."

As I opened my wallet to get the hundred bucks for her, a thought occurred to me.

"Madame Theresa, would you like another hundred dollars?"

"Of course, darling. Times are so hard these days." "Bring the cat to Cabin 319. You can't miss it—they're having a big party there. You should be able to hide him under the bed without anyone noticing you."

Madame Theresa slipped the two hundred dollar bills down her bosom and gave Caspar a friendly little pat. He seemed quite content in her arms.

"It ees pleasure, darling," she said as she made her way up the gangplank.+++++

AT A BAR AT THE CHATEAU FRONTENAC

This is your first night here. I can tell. Before I get half way through my story, you'll ask me to take you to bed. I know. Seven women in this bar, sitting right about where you are now, have already asked me this week. Chances are, the next time you go to the ladies room you'll run into one of them or one of their friends. Anybody who has been here for a few days knows my story and just about all the women want to go to bed with me.

You're laughing. You can see I'm not drunk. This is my second Courvoisier. Do I look bombed? Of course not. And I'm not some sort of an egomaniac, either. Bald spot in the back of my head. Like Prufrock. A little paunchy. Nose too long and chin too short. I'm not kidding myself: I don't turn women on. That's probably one of the reasons—not the most important, to be sure—but definitely one of the reasons I politely refused all seven women. I was flattered, but I didn't want to disappoint them.

The other reasons? Well, it looks like you are in the mood for a bit of my story. Leave any time you want, but I suspect you'll break in at the half-way point to ask me about my boudoir upstairs. The answer has to be the same, but I must admit you are even lovelier than the other seven. I have a weakness for long flowing red hair. Sounds like a proposition, doesn't it? Can't help myself. I like to talk and the only relief I get is by telling my story. I've got what you might call an *Ancient Mariner* complex. Funny, my tale is about a wedding too. Actually, not just a—but I'm getting ahead of myself.

You wouldn't be listening if you didn't think that what I'm going to tell you is a love story. Well, it is. Sort of. Love is rather hard to describe and certainly difficult to categorize, but from what I know and have felt about love, I'd say my story fits that description. At least part of it.

Vivian was the woman with the flaming red hair. I met her at an amateur comedians contest in London, Ontario. Crazy place. Styled after the really big London in England. Had a lot of the same street names—Piccadilly, Victoria, Wellington—and even a Thames River. I was there on vacation with a bunch of guys and she was with her girl-friends from college. She had just graduated from Slippery Rock State Teachers. Yes, there really is such a place.

My friends put me up to entering the contest because they had seen one of my routines that I pull after a few drinks at parties, and Dutchy had the one prop I needed in the back of his car. A huge mallet like the kind you try to ring the bell with at carnivals. To impress your girl. The secret is not in strength; it's in the way you swing the mallet.

The other comedians were good, but I had the good luck of being picked to go last. My act was simple. I went into the kitchen and got a bunch of fruit, eggs, and a container of yogurt. On the outside of the restaurant, they had one of those newspaper vending machines. Dutchy helped me drag it in and we hid it behind the curtain. Then I borrowed a heavy oak chair from the band leader and I was all set.

I put a watermelon on the chair and smashed the hell out of it with my mallet. The people in the first three rows, including Vivian, were squished good with watermelon pulp and juice. Then I set down the tomatoes, eggs, and yogurt. When I plopped the grapes on the chair, I gave them my first spoken line. "You want wine? I'll give you wine."

The audience was a mess, but they were hysterical too. They liked the idea of seeing things smashed. I was War with a sense of humor. When I rolled out the newspaper vending machine, I gave them my second prepared line. "So you put your money in this sucker, but you can't get your newspaper? Or your quarters back? Here's how you…"

My friends chipped in to pay for the machine and in about two months Vivian and I were going steady.

***

I guess the first year with Vivian was the happiest. I don't consider myself a great comedian—I tried out for nightclubs with a few of my routines and bombed—but almost everything I did cracked up Vivian. When my broken-down VW failed inspection for the third time, I stayed on the road by going to a junkyard and buying an old windshield; I played guard on our alumni basketball team in pantyhose; I waged a successful campaign to get Kenchu elected dogcatcher in Hoboken, New Jersey. Kenchu is her golden retriever. When Vivian was laughing, she was happy. And we did have some good times.

We never went to bed, though. I was raised a Catholic and she was a pretty devout one, so the question didn't come up until the night we came in fifth in the marathon dance contest, and on the way home I slipped my hand a little farther than usual up her leg. She pulled my hand away gently, gave me a sisterly kiss and told me that things like that were for after marriage.

It wasn't that she was giving me a hint. I was nuts about her anyway. Besides, we both more or less knew we would be married. The next time we went out—to Ray Connolly's Annual Rain Festival, where, of course, it never rained—we set the date.

Thanks, Andy. You see what I mean? I can't even buy a drink in here. So please don't get the impression that this is my treat. It's been like this since I got here. Quebec is a lovely city and the people are friendly whether you speak English or French, but this hospitality is almost a little too much. Well, cheers.

Vivian may not have been much for premarital sex, but she really subscribed to all the trimmings surrounding weddings. Bridal showers, detailed instructions to the photographers, best man and best woman, a white rug for the center aisle of the church, high mass with three priests, an organist, two soloists, special meetings for the bridal party, presentation of gifts to the ushers, bridesmaids, and priests. The whole bit.

She and her mother went through every old address book they had in their attic and she got me to do the same. We were inviting the plumbers, barbers, and insurance men of our childhood days. Even Sam the candy store man, who was once pinched for selling single cigarettes to teenagers for a penny each, got an invite. He was on her father's bowling team. She wanted me to ask some of my old girl friends, but I drew the line there. Vivian said that weddings come only once in a lifetime and that the people who had been once a part of our lives should be there to help us celebrate the occasion. The bill for the reception was going to be steep, and I offered to pay half, but her parents said that one-third would be more than generous on my part.

You can imagine the crowd at the church on the day of the wedding. Vivian had the addresses of more former dentists, babysitters, and mailmen than I did, so her side of the church was jammed. I wasn't exactly a slouch, but I suspect a few of the people on my side were friends of the bride who couldn't find seats on hers. At any rate I wasn't sure whether I actually knew many of the people sitting behind me. It's hard to recognize your old stickball buddies when they aren't sporting freckles and wearing Keds.

I met Dutchy, my best man, in the sacristy at 9:30. The wedding wasn't until ten, but for some reason I couldn't sleep the night before and decided to get there a little early. Dutchy could see I was nervous and kept telling me jokes about big-bosomed women, but I wasn't in the mood to listen. Father O'Donnell, who was going to serve the mass, popped in at 9:45. Five minutes later Father Spinello and Father Witkowski, who were assisting him, came in to get dressed in their white robes. Everything was set to go at ten.

I took my spot with Dutchy at the door of the sacristy, waiting for the music to start. I wasn't supposed to approach the middle of the altar under Vivian had made it down the aisle and her father had begun to remove her veil. "That's your cue," Father Spinello had told me the night before. "Wait till he touches the veil."

At five after ten I looked up for Maggie Swenson, the organist. She had played the national anthem at the county bowling championship tourney the night before, and, since that's her favorite sport, I thought she might have overslept. But she was there, along with Doug Yonkers and Millicent Cronin who had sung with the Guys and Dolls company in summer stock last night. At the recessional they were going to do a duet of "I'll Be Loving You Always," our favorite song. The church was very still. Father Spinello said everything was on hold until the bride made her first step down the aisle.

10:15.

10:25.

10:30.

Still no bride.

Dutchy called her house, but there was no answer. All her family were here at the church.

Her father asked her mother, but her mother said the last time she had seen her was just before ten. She supposed she had gone downstairs to the bathroom.

10:40.

10:45.

240

Father O'Donnell told me that the church had another wedding at 11. He said he would make the announcement to the wedding guests. I can't remember exactly what he told them, but it sounded something like the announcer says on television when they lose the picture but maintain the audio. "Due to circumstances beyond our control, we have temporarily lost—-"

Something like that.

Dutchy figured we might get a break from Tuxedo Haven if we brought out suits right back and explained we had only worn them a couple of hours. Either that, he said, or we could ask the 11 o'clock wedding party if they were short on ushers. In those days Dutchy would do almost anything for a few free drinks. He hated to see the wedding shot down in front of his eyes after all the hours he had spent memorizing the toast to Vivian and me. I just wanted to leave there fast. I was getting a lot of dirty looks from Vivian's relatives and Sam, the candy store man, seemed really infuriated. He had bought us a pop-up toaster with slots for six slices of bread. Must have set him back a bundle.

Nothing doing at Tuxedo Haven. Tony, the manager, explained that the suits still had to be dry cleaned and pressed. He said he was sorry that the wedding didn't come off and told me if I decided to try it again with someone else, he would give me a ten percent discount.

It was a hard day to get through. All afternoon I kept thinking how pretty Vivian would have looked throwing her garter, cutting the cake, and then having the last dance with me before we left for New York to spend our first night together in the Plaza Hotel. When we booked our honeymoon suite, the room clerk let us take a look at the room. All night long over more martinis than I can remember I pictured Vivian in the nightgown I had bought her—black with red lace around the bosoms— getting into the big brass bed next to me at the Plaza. I kept saying to myself that this was the night we were finally going to do it.

My hangover was so bad the next morning that when the phone rang I thought it was the doorbell. I had to go down to the superintendent in my underwear because when I went out in the hall to see who it was, the wind blew the door shut and I was locked out. Max was annoyed because he usually slept late on Sundays. Also I don't think he was happy at being a guest at my no-show wedding.

The phone was ringing when I got back in my apartment. It was Vivian. She had counted 32 rings. Was I all right? Why hadn't I answered the phone? Was I angry with her?

My head was pounding so hard that I didn't remember until the doorbell rang two hours later that I had agreed to let Vivian come over "to explain things."

Vivian hadn't the slightest idea why she hadn't gone through with it. There was no question of her loving me, she said. Hadn't we been going together for so long? And all the people we invited? Almost everybody she had ever known since she was in the crib. At five minutes to ten she decided to step outside to have a little talk with herself. To thank God and the Universe for this great moment in her life. And then? Every time I asked her she broke out into tears. I kept wiping her eyes with the tablecloth my Aunt Winnie had sent us. For some reason she seemed extremely sexy when she was crying, and for a moment I thought of reminding her what we had planned to do last night in the Plaza, but something told me to just stay with the tears and the tablecloth. When she came up for air, she asked me to help her compose a letter to send to all her friends and to give her a hand wrapping up the presents and sending them back. How could I refuse? I told her I would stop by her house the following night.

In a few weeks we were going out again. Nothing serious. A movie now and then. Sometimes we'd go dancing. Besides the long flowing red hair, she had green eyes and dimples as round and soft as her breasts, which she let me touch now and then. For old time's sake we went to Ray Connolly's Rain Festival again. This time it rained and I proposed to Vivian one more time.

The next few months were pretty happy ones. We decided not to invite as many people this time, but we did include most of Vivian's relatives, her father's dentist and Sam the candy store man. I estimated the church would be about three-quarters full. We stayed with the high mass and the three priests, with Fathers O'Donnell, Spinello and Witkowski all agreeing to the same assignments as before. We noticed that when the wedding presents started coming in a little less than half the people re-cycled the old presents. I got my hand a little farther up Vivian's leg a couple of nights. She was still for basic chastity before the event, but I think she had loosened up a bit.

We decided to do it on the anniversary of the wedding that didn't come off. This time it was on a Sunday. Just about everything was the same, except we pushed it back from ten to twelve. Dutchy drove me to the church at 11:30 and I took my position in the sacristy waiting for Vivian's father to pull up her veil. I don't know why, but I wasn't nervous this time. I kept thinking how Vivian was going to look later on at the Plaza in that black nightgown with the red lace around the bosoms. About a minute before twelve I looked up at the choir. Maggie Swenson was there. So were Doug Yonkers and Millicent Cronin. Father Spinello winked at me from the back of the sacristy. Dutchy peeked out and told me that it looked like there were more people than the first time. Standing room only in the back of the church and along the sides. Probably some people had wondered in off the street. Just curious, I guess.

12:05.

12:15.

12:20. I heard Vivian's mother sobbing in the front row.

12:25.

12:30.

12:45. Father O'Donnell told me there were no more weddings scheduled for that day, so he was willing to wait a little longer, if I wanted him to. He said it was lucky we hadn't decided on another Saturday wedding because two funerals had been booked for yesterday.

12:50. Sam the candy store man was the first to leave. Pretty soon the center aisle was jammed, wreaking havoc on the rented white rug.

I appreciate that look. And you do have lovely legs. But I was telling you the truth about the seven other women. You can ask Andy here. See, that's the third drink he has bought us. There are some things I just can't explain, because I have more than a boudoir upstairs. It's a seven-room suite. The best in the *Chateau Frontenac*. President Roosevelt stayed there when he met with Winston Churchill during World War II. I don't think you believe me. Have it your way. I told you I was a guy who just loved to talk.

It was three months before I heard from Vivian. Even then it wasn't actually her. Early in the morning Max asked me if I would be home around six as usual. At the time I didn't recognize how relieved he was when I told him yes.

The doorbell rang and there were two red-haired women in mini-skirts. One played the violin while the other sang, "What can I say, Dear, after I've said I'm sorry?" A week later Vivian called and asked me to help send the wedding presents back again.

When we met, she didn't try to explain and I didn't ask her to. After we got them all wrapped I told her I would take them to the post office and when she didn't call again, I thought I had finally seen the last of Vivian.

***

One of the benefits of falling out of love is that you get a lot of work done. When I stopped thinking about Vivian all the time, I had nothing to do so I figured I might as well pay attention to my job. I'm a pharmaceutical salesman. When people ask me what I do, I sometimes tell them that I deal in drugs. Boy does that get their attention! Actually all I do is visit doctors' offices and tell them about our company's latest products. They're usually busy, so I just slip them a few brochures and samples of the newest drug and leave. You'd be surprised how many of them start passing out the samples without knowing much more about it than it says in the little flyers. I'd never go to a doctor myself unless I was in really bad shape. But I have to admit a few of them were nice. They'd let me in to see them without making me wait my turn with the patients, and they acted as if they were really interested in what I had to say.

Our company had a contest for its salesmen. The one who made the most visits in a two-month period would win a three-week vacation to Quebec right in the heart of Winterlude. I wasn't even trying for the prize, but as I said with Vivian gone I hadn't much to do but visit those gloomy doctors' offices. Early in the morning, late at night, you'd always find me next to a potted plant with last month's *Reader's Digest* or *Better Homes and Gardens* on my lap. Other guys played cards or watched football on TV; I translated the Latin on the wall for old ladies with hemorrhoids. It passed the time.

Just before Christmas I ran into Vivian again. Almost literally. It was one of those wild rainstorms that really belong in late September or October—wind howling, rain rolling out of the heavens so fast you'd think you were under a waterfall. I was on my way to a gynecologist with a new lotion when I saw her crossing the street. The wind lifted her skirts up to her neck and knocked her down right in front of me. I carried her into my car. She kept saying that she was all right, but this time I didn't take no for an answer. I drove her to my apartment. You should have seen Max's eyes as I got in the elevator. I told her to take off her wet clothes and I would put them in the dryer in the basement. All she had on was an old sweater of mine that reached almost to her knees and a pair of white jogging socks. Her hair was still drenched, but I don't think I've ever seen her looking as attractive.

You know, you're just like the guys when everybody first started going on dates. "Didja make out?" we would ask each other and almost always we would lie, turning a goodnight kiss into a night of passion. Well, I'll tell you the truth. When I brought her clothes up from the dryer, she made no effort to get dressed. We sat there on the bed and talked for a long time. She said that perhaps her problem was the formality of weddings themselves and maybe we should just live together. All the time she was talking she was casually putting her clothes back on, as if she had been getting dressed in front of me for years. I was positive that if I had asked her to stay she would have, but for some reason I put on a pair of dry socks and drove her home. The next day, for the first time in weeks, I visited but a handful of doctors, skipping my evening calls completely.

This time we decided to make it really simple. One priest, no white rug, no mass, no invitations to casual friends. Vivian's mother was dead now so there was little pressure to contact all the relatives and insurance men. Sam the candy store man had moved to Florida and Father O'Donnell had been assigned to the Bishop's office. Father Spinello, the acting pastor, suggested a casual ceremony on Tuesday afternoon. No one has weddings on Tuesdays, so ours would be truly unique, he said.

Vivian made up the invitations herself. She sketched two long-stemmed roses on each side of a small piece of white cardboard and wrote in her own hand: "We are please to invite you to our wedding on Tuesday, Jan. 12th at—" She made an asterisk after our signatures and requested that no presents be given. It wasn't that we were afraid of all the wrapping and mailing again. We were really sure this time. Both of us. It was just that this would make it more of a spiritual affair. Besides, there was not going to be any reception.

A week before the wedding, my company announced that I had won the trip to Quebec. Father Spinello was impressed. It seemed like the heavens wanted to make up for all the bad luck in the past, he told us. The good lord takes away, but the good lord also gives, he said.

Something like that.

The guys at work knew about the other weddings, of course, so they chipped it to add some extra trimmings to our trip. A gourmet dinner and orchids on the plane, a chauffeured ride from the airport to here, a case of 100-year-old champagne waiting in our room—just about every nice touch you can think of. The boss heard of it, and changed our room to the Roosevelt suite. This was going to be a honeymoon the likes of which no one had ever had before, he told the board of directors at the meeting where they displayed a chart of my 1,043 visits to doctors' offices.

As I said, I knew there wasn't going to be any slip-up this time, but Dutchy, who was my best man as usual, got his younger sister to drive Vivian to the church just in case. From my spot in the sacristy I could have sworn there were tears rolling down Maggie Swenson's cheeks as she got ready to play the first chords of *Here Comes the Bride.* I closed my yes and pictured Vivian, as lovely as ever strolling down the aisle holding her father's arm. but instead of wearing her white wedding gown, she was dressed in the flimsy black nightgown with the red lace around the bosoms. . . .

***

When I looked out the window at the Quebec airport, I was amazed. The gang at the office had outdone themselves. There was a 25-piece orchestra playing *I'll Be Loving You Always*. . .as the attendant opened the door. And at the end of the platform stewardesses had stretched out a long white rug, bigger than the one we had in church at the second wedding.

Then over the loudspeaker comes a voice:

"Bonjour, mesdames et messieurs. Une couple des Etas-Unis est juste arrivé sur le vol le numéro neuf cents treize. Ils ont juste été maries. . ."

I could only make out a few of the words, but I got the gist of it. Anyway, in a minute or so—even while some folks at the airport were crying out *"Vive la couple!"*—he was saying in English,

"Ladies and gentlemen, just about to disembark from Air Canada Flight 913 is a young couple who were married but a few hours ago. Let us welcome to Quebec the newlyweds, Mr. and Mrs. Bunky Bottomley!"

One of the stewardesses opened the door. A young woman in a pink miniskirt and black pantyhose stood shivering on the top step with a dozen red roses. I stepped out and accepted the flowers, holding them over my head as a fighter holds his gloves after a fifth-round knockout. The folks on the ground kept straining their eyes for the bride, but all they saw was me. I was probably the first guy in the history of Canada who ever went on a honeymoon by himself.

The bandleader was confused. I kinda felt sorry for him, so when his boys got to the end of the song, I sang out,

Not for just an hour,
Not for just a day,
Not for just a year
But always.

I kissed the woman in the pink miniskirt on the left cheek and held the roses close to my breast all the way to the Chateau Frontenac. I change the water every day. They're still fresh.

Come on, now. I told you twenty minutes ago what you would want to ask me. You don't? Well, that's refreshing. I guess, to be honest, I'm slightly disappointed. But you'd like to see the Roosevelt suite, you say? Because of its historical significance. Surely you're pulling my leg. No sex, you insist. Neither of us are in the mood. You'd just like to sit around for awhile. Half hour or so. Have a nightcap. Room service would do anything for me. I know. Well, it's a refreshing idea. You know me: I love to talk. But I can listen too. And I wasn't kidding you about your long red hair. Just like Vivian's. Well, I am flattered. Honestly. What a nice thing to say to me.

I mean it. I really think you're kind. And different than all the rest. I'd love to have you upstairs with me. Even for just a half hour or so. But, you know. Some things are really hard to explain. I honestly enjoyed talking to you. Probably see you walking along the Rue St. Louis one of these days. I'll be here for almost two more weeks.

G'night now. +++++

WHAT I DID FOR SOUP

I *had* to be nice to Archie. And Archie was the last guy in the world I wanted to be nice to. His voice was a fingernail running across a blackboard; his unexpected presence was steaming doggy doo underneath brand new shoes.

Worse yet, the times Archie made it into my life were the times I needed so much to be alone.

I'd come home from New York on the 6:22 on a summer's night, my shirt sticking to my back from the humidity, weary from writing ad copy on the advantages of Massey Ferguson tractors on large farms or Doctor Schull's foot pads on small feet. All I wanted when I finally made it to my liquor cabinet was a double gin on the rocks with a slice of lemon and a quiet place to sip it while I read about the Mets.

I knew about the planned invasion of Archie long before I arrived home, of course, but there just didn't seem to be a way to dodge him. Twice I had taken a later train and walked home from the station, but in each case Archie was waiting for me on my front steps. Another time I tried entering my house from the rear, but Archie caught me on the back fence just as I was ripping the trousers of my Brooks Brothers suit. That guy had a sixth sense. And he also seemed to know that although I might elude him from time to time, once he found me I was committed to stay and talk to him.

Now I'm not against conversation. It goes well with double gins. But Archie didn't drink and he didn't converse. All he did was talk.

Not the usual blabber either. Archie's world was soup, and he could rattle on about the number of vegetables in Progresso's Minestrone the way a bookie could spiel off the odds at the seventh at Saratoga. In the beginning I had a vague interest in the variety of soups his company made, but after a while his monotonous, grating voice started to suck the flavor right out of my gin.

Other guys might have been able to tell Archie to get lost, but my situation was different. Bertha and I had eight kids, ranging from ten months to ten years. They weren't what you would call *bad* kids, but they were extraordinarily active in the neighborhood. The long and short of it was their various antics had alienated all of our neighbors.

Except two: Archie and his wife, Catherine, who for reasons which still escape me had never had their lawn mauled or windows broken by our little gang of eight.

"You simply have to be nice to Archie," Bertha insisted. "He and Catherine are the only ones on the block who still talk to us."

That was a slight exaggeration, but basically it was true. And Archie knew it.

I was stirring the gin around with my pinky and taking greedy little finger licks when Archie popped up from behind the tree where I was sitting in my backyard.

"Today was some day, Ben," he said. "Must have hit 93. Still, they say it isn't the heat but—"

I took a stiff belt of gin to block out the rest of his cliché.

"So guess how much soup I sold today, Ben."

"I don't like guessing, Archie; it gives me warts."

"Well, I did 150 in Scotch Plains, 75 in Garwood. I tell you, Ben, it was a great..."

He had stopped talking, and in the middle of a sentence, no less. My ears had become so conditioned to his special whine that the sudden silence was unsettling. I looked up and noticed that he was observing me like a butterfly-chaser examining a specimen.

"Say, Ben, do your kids like soup?"

"Archie, they like anything they can swallow, including Vaseline and shaving cream."

"Really?"

"Well, you know, there are eight of them and they're always in competition for whatever food is around. When we go to the supermarket, they sit in the shopping carts eating the stuff out of the packages before we get to the check-out counter."

When Archie got excited the pupils disappeared behind his eyelids, leaving only the dirty whites of his eyeballs. He was excited now.

"Ben, you can be the Garwood Grocery Store."

"I can be *what?*"

"The Garwood Grocery Store. I'll order extra soup for Garwood, but sell it to you. Wholesale. Your kids will love it. We have 53 varieties."

I took another sip of my gin. The booze was helping to make Archie disappear a little, but I knew I had to say something.

"Sounds good, Arch."

"The only thing is, Ben, since you are going to be the Garwood Grocery Store, you'll have to pay me as soon as your order comes in. I can't charge it to my account."

"O.K., Arch."

"I'll drive it right to your house in the company van. But you'll have to help me unload and carry it in. I have a heart condition, y'know."

"I know, Arch. I'll do the lugging. Well, thanks a lot. See ya around, O.K.?"

To my surprise he took off. I was on my second gin, quietly congratulating myself on getting rid of him so quickly when he showed up again, this time carrying a pencil and clipboard.

"I told you I'd get the soup, Arch."

He looked pained.

"But you've got to tell me what *kind*. We have a large variety, you know."

"Ah, any kind. The kids eat anything that's not moving."

"And how many?"

"Hmmm. Eight kids, eight of each. In that way there won't be as much fighting."

"Let's see. Do you think they'd like artichoke chowder?"

"Oh, yes."

"How about asparagus soup?"

"Sure."

"Bean?"

I hesitated. The plumbing had been acting up lately.

"Better pass on that one, Arch."

He jotted something on his clapboard and moved on.

"Carrot?"

"Yup."

"Celery?"

"No problem."

"Chicken gumbo?"

"You bet."

"Cream of Mushroom?"

"Why not?"

And so it went on for awhile. When he finally got to zucchini broth, I sighed in relief. I had never realized there were that many types of soup. But my time was not wasted. This would save a lot of lugging from the supermarket, and some money too.

"I can't tell you exactly when this shipment will arrive, Ben. There may be a strike down South and that could hold up deliveries, but when it comes you'll have to pay me right on the barrel head because you're—"

"I know, Archie, the same as the Garwood Grocery Store."

I took another sip of gin. It was the first conversation I had ever had with Archie in which we had communicated anything, even though it was just a little soup deal. Archie wrote on his clipboard again and, to my surprise and joy, got up to go.

"Well, Ben," he gushed. "It's been a pleasure. A real pleasure."

The purchase of the soup had another unexpected dividend: Archie stopped coming over for awhile. I had expected to see him the very next evening with a few cartons of soup in his company van. But I was well into my second martini without a hint of Archie. And he was home, too; there were lights on in his house. And so it went the rest of the week. The gin never tasted as good. I was in such an upbeat mood that I agreed to take Bertha and the kids to see her mother the following Sunday. She was almost as hard to take as Archie, and Bertha insisted on staying late because she hadn't seen her in awhile. But I got by; I took my trusty gin along.

I guess that's why I didn't hear the alarm the next morning.

"O.K.," I told Bertha, who was shaking me furiously, "I'll take the late train today."

"Late train or not, you still have to get up," she said. *"Right now!"*

"Why?"

"Archie is here."

"What does he want?"

"He has some soup for you."

"Can't he come back later?"

"He says you promised you would help him unload as soon as he delivered it. You know he has a heart condition."

I fought my way out of the bed so I wouldn't have to hear again how Archie and Catherine were the only ones on the block who tolerated the kids. I threw my red and white checked bathrobe over my shorts and went out to see the soup man.

"Just like I promised, Ben."

"O.K., Arch, lemme start taking it in."

He looked at me suspiciously.

"Remember what I said, Ben."

"I don't remember well this early in the morning. What did you say?"

"I said you are the same as the Garwood Grocery Store."

"O.K., I'm the same as the Garwood Grocery Store."

"That means you have to pay me now. In cash."

"Well, all right. I'll have to go inside and get my wallet. How much do I owe you, Arch?"

He looked at his clipboard.

"That will be exactly $996.46. There's no tax on soup."

"What!"

"Cash, please."

"Archie, how the hell do I owe you $996.46 for *soup?*"

"Remember, Ben, you promised—"

The window opened and Bertha called out to me.

"Ben, may I see you inside for a moment, *please?*"

Bertha enjoys a good scream now and then. It relieves some of her frustration. I could see she wanted to scream, but couldn't do it with Archie just outside the door.

"Are you fighting with him?"

"No."

"Don't lie. I heard you."

"He wants me to give him $996.46 for soup."

"You've got to give it to him then. He and Catherine are—"

"Where am I going to get that kind of money?"

"Write him a check."

"I can't just write a check. I've got to have $996 in the bank first."

Bertha was silent for a moment. I knew she was thinking of how to pay Archie, not why soup suddenly cost more than washing machines.

"Well," she said finally, "you'll just have to take out a loan. The bank should be open by the time you drive there. Now don't keep Archie waiting."

Why I did it, I don't know. Maybe it was the hour, maybe it was Sunday night's gin, maybe it was the force of Bertha's will. And, of course, Archie's. At any rate twenty minutes later, my checkered bathrobe more or less camouflaged by my olive green raincoat, I found myself sitting in front of Mr. Quigley's desk. He's the one in charge of the loans; I had dealt with him before on other loans. With eight kids, borrowing money is old hat. But I always had the impression that Mr. Quigley never liked approving my loans because he always threw in a few extra questions at me. You'd think it was *his* money.

I had rattled off my numbers—address, phone, area and zip codes, social security, army serial number, checking account, credit card numbers, blood type, the number of other debts, safety deposit box number, salary, mortgage number, car registration, the number of kids, the works...This was Mr. Quigley's niche in life: to see people squirm as he jotted down all their numbers and then to sit back and ruminate a little over the fiscal feasibility of lending someone like me anything more than fifty bucks. After the numbers came the questions about my health, the type of work I did, the condition of my house...I thought of one question that was about to be asked. I was actually looking forward to it.

"And what, Mr. Browning, is the purpose of the loan?"

"To buy soup."

"To buy soup," he repeated after me and began to jot it down on the bank questionnaire.

Suddenly he looked at me.

"Wait a minute," he said. "You can't have a loan to buy soup."

"Who says?"

"Mr. Browning, please."

I shrugged my shoulders.

"Now what is the purpose of your loan?"

"To buy soup."

He flicked his little pince-nez over his nose and raised his pen at me as Sister Theresa in the fourth grade used to do.

"Mr. Browning, I have to list the purpose of the loan. Now you can have it to buy a car, to make repairs on your house, for medical expenses..."

He looked at me with a touch of hauteur in his eye.

"You can even have it to consolidate your other loans."

"I know, Mr. Quigley, but I happen to want it to buy soup."

"Please, Mr. Browning, your voice is carrying."

"Look, if you want me to lie about it, go tell your bank that I'm using it to research a way to remove unwanted snot without a handkerchief. It just so happens that the purpose of my loan is to purchase $996.46 worth of soup."

"But why—?"

"I like soup."

"This is highly irregular. I think I may have to bring this matter up with Mr. Prescott."

"Are you saying you don't want to loan me the money?"

"Yes—I mean, no. I mean, I just can't believe anyone would buy $996 worth of soup."

I stood up and opened my raincoat, revealing my checkered bathrobe and a few curly tufts of brown hair from my chest. By the first teller's window Mrs. Vanderbetter from the PTA saw me, but turned around quickly when I glared back at her.

"Look, Mr. Quigley, would I be here this early in the morning in my bathrobe if I didn't need $996 in a hurry? Right now as I'm talking, there's a little runt of a salesman in front of my house with his company's van loaded to the brim with soup. If I don't buy it, my wife and I say good-bye to the only neighbor on the block who still speaks to us because of our loud-mouth kids. Go ahead, get your Mr. Prescott, I'll take him down to my driveway to meet the soup man if he thinks I'm lying."

Mrs. Vanderbetter looked my way again. So did the two ladies behind her on line. Mr. Quigley pulled out his handkerchief to wipe his brow.

"Oh, all right, Mr. Browning. Loan approved. I could lose my Christmas bonus for this."

When I was loading the soup I realized what had happened. I had thought I was ordering eight *cans* of each kind of soup; Archie had brought me eight *cases*.

They weren't ordinary little cans that you see on the shelves of the supermarkets. These were No. 10 cans, as big as the ones they put Dole's Pineapple Juice in. I think Archie tricked me in order to make the Garwood Grocery Store set some sort of company record.

There was no room for the soup in the pantry, so I had to put most of it in the cellar. I told Bertha that at least we would know that we always had food in the house. But after a few days had passed and the kids had knocked off about twenty cans of it, Bertha said that they started to complain they were getting tired of soup.

"How come they go through 50 jars of peanut butter every month and never get tired of that?" I asked.

"Peanut butter is different. You just do not comprehend the juvenile mind."

"Yeh, but of the all the different kinds of soup Archie sold us, they must have a few favorites."

"They do—leek and won ton soup."

"Well use up all those cans up first."

"I can't."

"Why not?"

"I guess you haven't heard of the contest. *Why I Like Progresso Soups in 100 Words of Less.* The winner gets a bicycle."

"What's that got to do with won ton soup?"

"To enter the contest you had to tear the label off three Progresso cans and—"

I closed my eyes and pictured the mayhem in the basement: Eight kids ripping the labels from hundreds of No. 10 soup cans. Now we would not only be having Archie's soup at every meal, but we wouldn't know what kind of soup it was until we opened the can. We would in fact be engaged in Russian Roulette of the soup can.

"You mean they won't touch the soup unless they know what's inside the can ahead of time?"

"Well, that's about the size of it. And that's not the only thing. It's damp down in the basement and those cans are going to get a little rusty. The kids would never eat soup out of rusty cans."

I pictured myself down the cellar every month with a Brillo pad scrubbing the rust off to protect my $996.46 investment. The longer the soup hung around, the more I was going to have to Brillo it.

"Look, Bertha, maybe you can slip a little soup into everything they eat—sandwiches, salads, mashed potatoes, and pumpkin pies. They shovel the food in their mouths so fast they never know what they're eating anyway."

It worked for awhile, but after a month the kids refused to eat anything with soup in it. And we couldn't fool them either because they took turns watching Bertha cook. She even tried sneaking off to the bathroom with the can opener in her brassiere, but one of the kids spotted her through the keyhole. So we stopped serving soup in our house.

We tried The Salvation Army and the Red Cross, but they both turned it down because of the missing labels. Same with the Foreign Missions. When the nun came down our cellar and saw all the soup stacked up to the ceiling she looked at me suspiciously.

"I may only be a Sister of the Sacred Heart, but I want you to know that the Catholic Church has no intentions of being a front for a drug ring."

I think she might have been kidding, but I'm not sure. She lifted up her veils and got out of our cellar lickety-split.

That was ten years ago. I've told my story to so many people over a few gins that it got to the point that I was able to get the pile down a little by giving them a few cans of soup for Christmas, Thanksgiving, birthdays, anniversaries, Secretaries Week...Our friends would never dare serve the soup, of course, but they use the cans for book-ends, paperweights, trivets—things like that. Archie's soup has become conversation pieces like pet rocks used to be.

By the way, Archie's heart is still going strong. He sold his house a month ago, and new people moved in last week. I heard that the guy who bought it is a salesman too, but I swore to myself that I would never in a million years ask him what he sells. And if he tries to collar me when I come home on the 6:22, I will duck him if it means putting a fence ten feet high all around the house. Even Bertha agrees with me on that.

+++++

A HARD PERSON TO FIT

I believe in signs and there were three of them staring me in the eye. I had a red light, there was a parking spot right along side of me—really rare for Hoboken—and the shoe store didn't seem busy as far as I could tell. I checked my sneaks. Aw, why not, I told myself.

She saw my surprised look. I had my choice of about two dozen chairs. The only ones occupied were the one she was sitting on and two others by salesmen reading magazines.

"I don't know where the hell the people are, Miss," she said, half by way of apology, half by way of defending herself. "But just wait. Christmas Eve, when all of us want to get home, they'll be all over the place like flies in an outhouse. Want a pair of flats or heels?"

She must have said that automatically because I certainly didn't look like anyone who ever wore shoes, let alone a dress. I had just been jogging and was wearing my red running suit, ski cap, and blue Nikes.

"Just running shoes. Like the ones I have on, if you have them."

She whistled as she looked at my Nikes.

"You must run a whole lot, huh?"

"Just about every day."

"Why?"

I didn't have an answer for that one, mainly because she surprised me with the question, I guess. I tried to adjust my tone so that my answer would say between the lines that it was nobody's business why I ran.

"It's—it's just something I always do. That's all."

"Well, it can't hurt. Probably does you some good—as long as you can duck the cars and the muggers."

"I'm careful."

"What size do you take?"

"Men's or women's?"

"You wear both?"

"Yes. Size 7 in men's usually fits."

"Usually?"

"Well, yes. It depends upon the shoe and the shoe company."

She got up and walked to the back of the store. One of the salesmen, a guy in his mid-twenties with kinky black hair and tortoise-shell glasses, waved at me and smiled for no logical reason, but I waved back. I felt like an idiot.

On the floor near where she had been sitting was a book with a woman wearing black stockings, garter belt, and half-opened red raincoat on the cover. I picked it up. It was called The *Listerine Lunatic*. She was on Page 147. As she came back with four boxes of shoes, I was at the point where a woman in a red raincoat, possibly the one on the cover, was being ushered into a middle-aged bachelor's town house after she had told him her car had broken down outside his door in the middle of a raging rainstorm.

"It's trash," she said, putting down the shoes in the chair next to me, "but what the hell isn't nowadays?"

"The Diane in the story seems naive. Is she?"

"She knows her way around."

"Is she a prosti—?"

"Naw, she's no hooker. She's the Listerine Lunatic."

"What's that?"

"She goes around seducing guys and when she gets them hot and naked in bed, she pulls a little Saturday night special and a tiny scissors from her garter belt and orders them to cut off a few of their pubic hairs for her. Then she makes them lie face down in their beds while she pours a bottle of Listerine mouthwash all over their rear ends. She hasn't been caught yet and I'm on the seventh chapter. I've got two men's sevens and two women's eights. My name's Theresa, by the way."

The sevens were just a little too small, although the left foot on one of them fit perfectly. The eights were big enough but too narrow. Apologetically I told Theresa that running seemed to have made my feet wider for their size than the average woman's.

"That makes sense because my feet are wider than average, too," she said, "but mine got that way from lugging too many cadavers."

"Cadavers—you mean dead people?"

"Yeh. I don't have any half-sizes in women's. Do you want to try a nine?"

"You were carrying around *dead* people?"

The guy with the tortoise-shell glasses looked up at that. When he saw me turn in his direction, he waved again.

"I was doing it for my boyfriend. I was between marriages at the time and this guy was an anatomy professor at St. George Medical College in Grenada. He needed the corpses for his school work. People would donate their bodies to science and he and I would fly all over the United States to pick them up. He had some kind of a grant."

She took one of the women's shoes and started bending it back and forth—to try and stretch it, I supposed.

"Just you and the professor?"

"Oh, we'd get a little help at the funeral homes and airports, but basically it was Jimmy and me."

"I guess you really have to like someone to go all over the country with him with a plane load of cadavers."

She picked up the other shoe. Instead of bending it back and forth, she eased her hand inside it.

"Oh, Jimmy was all right. We had some good times together. He was different from anyone I ever went out with. I mean, you would think that a guy who was a scientist and all—a guy who spent so much time with dead bodies would be a—"

"I know what you mean."

"Yeh. But he wasn't morbid at all. He had a pretty good sense of humor. Sometimes he could be a little off-the-wall and other times he'd be quiet and would sit for hours reading poetry to me. Can you beat that—an anatomy teacher talking about seabirds and rainbows?"

I was starting to get a little chill from my run. That usually happens to me when I go too long without taking a shower. I knew I should have waited until later to shop for running shoes, but the store looked empty so I thought I could get it over with in a hurry. I never could understand those women who spend whole afternoons shopping for scarves and belts. Theresa didn't have any shoes in the back that would fit me; I sensed she was trying to stretch the woman's eight just so she could talk awhile. I wanted to get home so that when Raymond called to ask me to watch his session with Mrs. Farrington's German shepherd, I could tell him I wasn't feeling well. I was just about positive that he was going to call and the last thing I wanted to do was observe a grown man talking to a dog. And yet, instead of getting up, for some reason I just sat there listening to her.

"His favorite poet was a guy named Donne. A Limey, I think. I can still remember one of his poems because Jimmy would say it over and over again.

> *Go and catch a falling star,*
> *Get with child a mandrake root*
> *Tell me where all past years are*
> *Or who cleft the Devil's foot*

"I used to hear a song about catching a falling star and putting it in your pocket. I never knew the songwriter swiped it from this old Englishman till Jimmy told me. He said they have stuff about the root of the mandrake in the Bible. It was supposed to help knock a woman up. Can you believe that?"

"It doesn't sound like your standard *begats* and *begets*," I agreed.

"But it's in there. Jimmy showed it to me. In the Old Testament. He said the poem was about all things that were impossible unless—"

"Unless what?"

"Unless you really believed in them. Boy, those poets sure can write some shit, can't they? Want to give these babies a try now?"

I slipped on the women's eights again. The left one felt O.K. and the right one seemed a little better than before, but maybe it was because I was itching to get out of there so I could take a shower. I thought of buying them and keeping them for walking shoes. That way I could leave. But I hesitated too long.

"He knew all the pilots and flight attendants that made the Grenada run. I mean, if a guy is constantly loading up your plane with dead bodies you've got to remember him, right? On one trip me, Jimmy and two flight attendants who had been drinking with us earlier in the evening took a couple of cadavers out of their crates in the baggage room and snuck them into the passenger section. We propped them up in seats and stuck magazines in their hands. It was a night flight and hardly any passengers were booked. The pilot, Capt. Grayson, one of Jimmy's buddies, may have suspected what we were up to, but then maybe not. They say he was heavy into pills, but that's another story. Do they feel any better?"

That was my chance, but I blew it. I should have said "Fine," and let her finish her story about the air-borne cadavers at the cash register while I paid, but instead I just stared at her uncertainly.

"Looks like you're a hard person to fit. So was Jimmy. I mean, I never sold him shoes; I wasn't in this business then. It was just that he was the kind of guy who was always dreaming of this and that, but he was leery of the regular down-to-earth stuff. I used to tell him, 'Jimmy, you keep looking up at the stars and your feet's gonna be covered with doggie-doo.' Where was I? Oh, the stiffs on the plane. Would you believe that about a half hour out of Newark a little guy with a black moustache and a pack on his back stands up and pulls a rod? 'This is a hijack,' he says. 'Don't nobody move or I'll blow your ass off. And don't try to touch me; my back is wired with dynamite.'"

"Oh my God!" I said. "You must have been scared stiff."

"Everybody freezes, like he says. But there's only a few people in the front of the plane so he walks down to the back where me, Jimmy and the corpses are. He must have been nearsighted because he looks right at them without blinking an eye. But when he turns around the dynamite on his back smashes the head of a corpse that had been involved in a pretty bad auto accident and was only hanging on by a few threads. The impact more or less decapitates the cadaver, sending the head rolling down the aisle like a bowling ball."

"That was weird!"

Theresa smiled at the little bit of winter sun that had just then peeped in through the store window, as she re-lived the image of the spinning head.

"Yeh, but it got the job done. The little guy with the moustache passed out and his hijacking days were over. When we landed they brought him to the mental hospital at Grenada."

"Is that the——?"

"Yep, the same one," she said, anticipating my question. "The one Reagan's commandoes bombed by mistake when they invaded the island. Can you imagine that for luck? Here's this guy who probably plans his hijacking out carefully for months. Figures out when it's quiet at the airport, when there's a flight without many passengers, when he's dealing with a pilot who has been known in some circles for taking a couple of pills now and then. The set-up seems perfect. A half-hour into the sky and he gets up to make his pitch. He's caught everybody by surprise, only to run into a plane loaded with dead bodies. Then they cart him off to a mental ward and a couple of months later the United States bombs the hell out of his hospital. Hey, that doesn't even happen in the movies."

"Why did he try to hijack the plane? Was he a terrorist?"

"We never figured out what his motive was. Maybe he was just bored. It turns out his gun was a water pistol and the dynamite was a stove pipe. Jimmy visited him in the hospital a month after he was admitted and they told him the guy was doing so well they put him in charge of the inmates' education program. He had been a high school principal before he cracked up. I never heard if the poor bastard survived the bombing or not. Want me to take another look in the back for your size?"

"Maybe I'll just leave my name and number and you can call me when you get some shoes that you think will fit me."

"Sure. No problem. But it won't be until after Christmas."

"That's O.K."

I started putting my shoes back on. Usually when I take a lot of someone's time in a store and wind up not buying something, I feel a little guilty. It's silly, I suppose, but I haven't been able to kick that habit. But Theresa didn't seem to mind. And yet I imagined she was a good saleswoman despite herself. Reaching into my pocketbook, I pulled out the little pad Raymond had given me, jotted my name and phone number down, and handed it to her.

"That's a Union Township number, right?" she asked, gazing at the slip of paper.

I nodded. Despite my slight chill, I wanted to know what happened to Jimmy. I knew I could ask her outright and she would tell me. Still I thought if I waited a minute or two she would blurt it out on her own. But she just kept staring at the piece of paper I had handed to her.

"Raymond Ragsdale, Canine Conversationalist," she read aloud. "This guy talks to dogs?"

"Well, he teaches them manners. He uses that title on all his advertising. I keep telling him he ought to specialize in training dogs for the big shows where the money is, but Raymond isn't interested in that."

"But he talks to them, right?"

I asked myself why out of all the little scraps of paper at the bottom of my pocketbook I had to pick one with Raymond's letterhead. I could have put my name and phone number on the back of a gum wrapper.

"Oh, I guess he talks to them, but they certainly don't talk back to him."

Theresa smiled. "You never can tell. There's all types of talk, y'know. Sounds like an interesting guy. Jimmy had a golden retriever named Casey that was a walking encyclopedia. He'd—"

She looked out the window and seemed to be staring at the sun again. Or maybe she was picturing Jimmy playing with Casey.

"You said before that you met Jimmy when you were between husbands. I guess you married someone else."

"Yeh. It was one of those spur of the moment things after Jimmy and me had a fight. Jimmy had wanted me to go to Prince Edward Island with him to grow potatoes. Said that it was as much fun to watch the rows and rows of white flowers on the potato plants as it was to eat them. But my kids didn't want to leave their schools. The marriage didn't last and I tried to contact Jimmy. I traveled to Grenada, Prince Edward Island, and lots of places we had talked about. But he didn't leave any traces. Then one day I read a little piece about him in the New York *Times*. Imagine Jimmy in the *Times*! He and another guy named Rambottom were killed during a storm on the Gaspe Peninsula in Canada in one of those small planes. They were involved in some sort of a program to save the seals. Guess looking at the advertisement of this canine conversationalist made me think of it. I'm sure Jimmy would have talked to the seals. This guy Ragsdale a friend of yours?"

"Yes. Well, actually we're engaged."

I thought I caught a quick look of surprise which seemed to say "Do people still get *engaged?*" But maybe I was wrong. At any rate she hid her feelings pretty well.

"So when are you getting married?"

She stopped to laugh, this time at herself.

"Sorry," Theresa said. "I don't know why the hell I've got to know everything. You know, I even wiretapped one of my own kids. But what the hell, I had to. Hardly anybody tells the truth nowadays."

Before I could stop myself I was asking her what her kid had done.

"All of a sudden I began to realize I was missing a hell of a lot of my drawers," she said. "I tapped my oldest son's phone and discovered that he was operating a *Panty-of-the-Month* club for the kids of Hoboken High School. You see, when I was working part-time for the Byrne Detective Agency I learned to wire-tap and—"

Four people walked in the store at once. The guy with the tortoise-shell glasses signaled to Theresa for help. It was a perfect opportunity for me.

"So you'll call me when you get my size," I said.

Despite myself I hesitated again. The new customer, a middle-aged woman in a black mink sat down two chairs from me. Out of the corner of my eye I could see her glancing at the jacket of *The Listerine Lunatic*, but when she saw me watching her she quickly looked down at her shoes, as if she had just discovered they were on her feet. Theresa nodded to her to indicate that she would be right there and turned to me once again.

"I'll be in touch after Christmas," she said. "It was nice talking to you."

I smiled and left. When I got out in the street I glanced at my watch. It wasn't as late as I thought. If I took a quick shower I could make it over to Raymond's kennels in time to see him training—or talking to—Mrs. Farrington's German shepherd. I smiled as I anticipated how surprised Raymond would be to see me.

Just before I got in my car I took one last look at Theresa through the store window. She was kneeling down with her right hand shaped to form a gun as kids do when they are playing cops and robbers. The lady in the black mink was watching her intently. I supposed that Theresa was now back with the Byrne Detective Agency for a little while. +++++

THE CATHOUSE ON FIFTH AVENUE

It took Sarah more than a half century to find out, but once she learned the secret, she was determined never to forget it.

When she was twelve, for instance, she put a lot of faith in Mr. Schillington, the manager of the Rialto Movie Palace. He always took time out to talk to her when she came in with her girl friends to see the Saturday double features. Sometimes when she bought a large, twenty-five-cent Hershey Bar in its rich brown packaging, Mr. Schillington waved away her quarter and said softly.

"G'wan, it's alright. Take it; it's alright."

Once or twice when Mrs. Taylor, the cashier, was sick and he sold the tickets, he let her in free. So Sarah didn't think anything of it when he asked her to stop in to see him in his office after school so he could give her a signed photograph of Clark Gable.

When he stuck his hand underneath her dress and tried to pull her panties off, she screamed and ran out of his office. But she didn't tell anyone. Not even her mother.

Three years later Todd Barrows, the captain of the Winslow High football team, tried the same thing on their second date. She wasn't as frightened of Todd as she was of Mr. Schillington, for by this time she had heard a lot about it. But when it was all over, she was disappointed, and after their third date she began to realize how conceited Todd was, so she stopped going out with him.

By the time she was modeling slips and brassieres for the Neuberger Department Store, she had come to the conclusion that a girl didn't have to have all those tingly sensations up and down her spine to know that she wanted to get married. When David Neuberger happened to walk through the store while she was modeling a black lace bra and panty set and asked the floor manager "Who's the blonde with the cute figure?" Sarah knew how she was expected to act. She smiled sweetly when he talked about the store's expansion plans over dinner, was more reserved with him in his apartment than she had been with Todd Barrows in the back seat of his Packard, and subsequently let him succeed where Mr. Schillington had failed, once David assured her he had "serious intentions." He was the oldest son of the three Neubergers and his father was ailing of late. The Neuberger Department Store was one of the largest in Westchester County and the family was indeed planning to expand.

And so they were married.

David wanted children, so she gave him children. One of each. When David III finished Harvard Law School, he joined a prestigious law firm specializing in divorces in Los Angeles. He visited Sarah and his father every other year on the holidays. Sometimes he even brought the children. Debby married the scion of a shoe manufacturing company in Italy and after her divorce made her home in the French Riviera. Sarah never heard from her after she left the country.

Without a son to run the department store, David sold it and he and Sarah bought a 16-room apartment in a co-op on Fifth Avenue in New York City for four million dollars. They needed the extra rooms for the four servants they took with them from their estate in Westchester County.

Even though the Neubergers certainly were rich enough and seemed to come from the correct society, they never were accepted by their seven neighbors who also owned large luxurious apartments in the co-op. David hardly noticed it because he was frequently out of town "looking for new places to invest his money." Or so he told his wife. Sarah suspected that her neighbors' aloofness might have had something to do with her background and her choice of clothes. She made a few attempts to invite her neighbors to dinner or to share the Neubergers' boxes at the opera, but did not get any takers.

"Oh, that's very kind of you, Mrs. Neuberger, but my husband and I always go yachting on the weekends," Mrs. Boyce-Bentley had told her.

"Oh. Well, how about next Thursday?"

"That's the meeting night for the board of trustees of the museum. Anthony is chairman, you know."

The Kensingtons weren't interested in spending a Sunday afternoon with them in their heated boxes at Giant Stadium, the Fitzgeralds were seldom home, according to their butler and maid, and the Parker-Groats said they would love to go to the opening at the Palace with them, but they were flying to Stockholm that night. The other three families were so reclusive that they didn't even list their names in the directory in the lobby. David was of the opinion that they were foreigners whose activities were of such a delicate nature that they did not want their business known. Occasionally Sarah would see a middle-aged Japanese couple or a group of gray-haired Chinese men and women whom she did not recognize coming into the building late at night and taking the elevator to the upper floors, so she assumed these were what David called "the three mysterious families upstairs." She even went to the trouble of leaving little notes by the doormats of each of the "three mysterious families," inviting them to lunch, but when she checked a few days later, she saw the notes had not even been picked up. One day Sarah gathered up all the theatre, opera, and sports tickets she had purchased for her neighbors and gave them to the day doorman, asking him to divide it up with his associates on other shifts.

And so Sarah watched the soaps during the day and the sitcoms in the evening. Since she was aware that David had two or three women on the side, she was not surprised when the wine and women in his life caught up with him at the age of 63 and he suffered his second—and last—heart attack. David III stopped by on the day of the funeral to pick up his share of his father's fortune. Debby's lawyer in the French Riviera arranged for his client to receive her share through the mail. Sarah had her husband's body cremated. One night after two grasshoppers and a Harvey Wallbanger she tossed his ashes from her balcony when the wind was blowing south in the direction of the Boyce-Bentleys' living room two stories below.

**

It was Brunhilde the cook who heard about the kittens. They had been left on her sister's doorstep in her flat in Brooklyn. Both were coal black with a little streak of white on the neck. They were so cute she couldn't resist bringing them home to show Mrs. Neuberger, who hadn't been feeling well lately. Once she saw the two little bundles of black fur, Sarah went crazy for them. It was the first time in her life that she had ever fallen in love.

One was a male and the other female, so she called them Tristan and Isolde after the two famous lovers of Wagner's opera and the medieval Celtic myth. David had taken her to the opera years ago and Sarah had been impressed with the constancy of the love of Tristan and

Isolde. Indeed, the two little black kittens seemed a good deal like their namesakes—always playing together, jumping up on each other, and following each other around.

"You know, Brunhilde," she told her cook, "I have a feeling that these two are going to be with one another until the day they die."

As if in response to her observation, the kittens put their little paws around each other. Brunhilde started to hum a waltz and tap her feet and Tristan and Isolde moved across the floor like dancers. Sarah looked on, delighted. That night she took them into her large brass bed with her. After that they slept with her every night.

Sarah gave the two kittens the run of the apartment. She seldom went out to shop or go to a play, but when she did she entrusted Brunhilde to the care of Tristan and Isolde. The cook had the authority to hire anyone she needed to help with the animals, so she persuaded Dr. Alice Heidgert, her sister's veterinarian, to become Mrs. Neuberger's live-in cat-doctor. When the vet demurred for a minute or two, Brunhilde told her she was authorized to give her a contract for a $250,000 a year, plus a month's paid vacation at one of Mrs. Neuberger's European estates, if she could locate a reliable vet to fill in while she was gone. It didn't take Dr. Heidgert long to pack her toothbrush, a few sets of underwear, and move in.

These were probably the happiest days in Sarah's life. She was not pressured to entertain important guests, she did not waste hours of her time worrying about the snobbery of her neighbors or David's infidelities, and she no longer had to fret about what was going to happen to her children. Instead, she spent most of her day with Tristan and Isolde, watching them lap up milk, play with balls of string, and jump up on her lap for a few hugs and kisses. She didn't care how much money her various investments were bringing in, or even what the weather was like outside. Her world began and ended with her two cats. They were performers on a stage without a curtain, playfully leaping about the furniture, chasing each other around the apartment of seemingly endless hiding places, always assured of the warm applause of their audience, Sarah and her entourage of servants.

And so she laughed until she cried, marveling at their gambols as an aficionado of the arts applauds a rip-roaring comedy. Tristan and Isolde sensed they were forever on stage and didn't seem to mind it a bit, especially since their every action was cheered and rewarded with little snacks of shrimp and lobster. Sarah felt she was in her prime—surrounded by loyal servants and warm, cuddly cats in a luxurious New York apartment with everything from a view of the East River to bullet-proof windows.

And just as suddenly as she rose to the riches of the elite of Manhattan, she slipped quietly into the obscurity of its dead. While playing with her beloved cats, she felt a sharp pain in her chest. Tristan jumped into her lap and rubbed his whiskers gently against her breast. Isolde lay at her feet, touching her mistress's ankles lightly with her black furry ear. Sarah sobbed once, twice, and it was all over.

***

She had been anticipating it for some time and wanted to make sure that she took care of her trusted servants and, of course, Tristan and Isolde. No one else had been a part of her life. Six months before she died she had even taken the time out to wire her two children that there was no point in their going to all the trouble of flying in for her funeral, because they were not in the will. And so she was waked in her apartment with Brunhilde and the other servants welcoming the few old friends who stopped by. After a decent interval, Mr. Dunleavy, her lawyer, assembled the servants in Sarah's library for the reading of the will.

"Mrs. Neuberger was quite generous," he said. "She has left a legacy to everyone here, which in each case is a fortune in its own right. You will be pleased to know that she has noted in the will that you were each good and faithful servants.

"However, there is one condition that Mrs. Neuberger insisted on, and until this condition is fulfilled, the money bequeathed to each of you will be held in escrow in a trust fund."

The group waited patiently for Dunleavy to explain the condition. None of them wanted to be the one to ask that it be spelled out, for fear of seeming eager and crass. Dunleavy, anticipating their feelings, hesitated for a moment and then continued.

"As everyone here knows, Mrs. Neuberger was deeply attached to her two cats, Tristan and Isolde. She asked that they remain here just as they were when she was alive, because this is the only home they have ever known. And she wants all of you to share the responsibility of caring for them. You will be paid your regular wages plus a 20% increase."

Dunleavy removed his reading glasses and looked at each member of the group.

"Mrs. Neuberger asked me to make regular visits to inquire on the condition of Tristan and Isolde for the rest of the animals' lives. After both of them have died and have been given proper funerals, the trust funds will be released to each of you. The only condition for an earlier release would be an emergency in which the funds were needed to guarantee the happiness of Tristan and Isolde. However, I cannot conceive of any such possibility, since the cats have all the care they seem to need, as well as the run of this huge apartment. Besides, all of you are paid so well that you could easily take care of any exigency that might come up. Mrs. Neuberger asked me also to apologize for the many precautions she has taken, but all of you who share her love for Tristan and Isolde can surely understand why this was necessary."

He closed his briefcase, indicating the meeting was over. As he was putting on his topcoat, he suddenly remembered something.

"Oh, the apartment itself is part of the will and it was Mrs. Neuberger's wish that you each be co-owners of it after the demise of Tristan and Isolde, at which point you could either continue to live here together or sell it and divide the receipts of the sale equally."

As he was buttoning his top coat, Tristan and Isolde, almost as if they knew they had been at the center of an extremely important discussion, each took an affectionate bite at his shoelaces. Mr. Dunleavy bent over to pat them on the heads. He reserved a more business-like wave for Mrs. Neuberger's now-wealthy staff.

"I'll see you soon," he said as he made his way to the door.

****

The quartet of servants, the vet, and the two cats were living comfortably in the large fashionable Fifth Avenue co-op until Tristan jammed a tennis ball down the toilet off the master bedroom and Brunhilde couldn't get Benny the regular plumber and had to call one she found in the *Yellow Pages*. Going down the lift, Mrs. Boyce-Bentley overheard him telling Higgins, the elevator operator, the experience he had locating a rubber ball that "some dumb cat had dropped down a terlet." It wasn't long before Mrs. Boyce-Bentley told Mr. Kensington who told the Parker-Groats. A half hour later the phone was ringing off the hook in the office of Mr. Teedle, the building manager. Cats were not allowed in the co-op.

Mr. Teedle contacted Mr. Dunleavy and reminded him of the clause in the contract the Neubergers had signed.

"Well, of course, you must know, Mr. Teedle, that the Neubergers no longer live in the co-op."

"I never quite understood the arrangement Mrs. Neuberger made with her servants."

"I wrote to you and explained that it was Mrs. Neuberger's wish that her servants remain."

"Yes, but you didn't say anything about cats."

"I sent you a photocopy of the section of the will that applied to Mrs. Neuberger's pets, Tristan and Isolde. Didn't you read it?"

Mr. Teedle suspected that he hadn't. In his business he was forever getting letters and Photostat copies of something or other that he didn't get around to reading.

"I don't have your letter available right now, Mr. Dunleavy, but the point of the matter is that your clients signed an agreement never to bring cats into the co-op."

"My clients are dead, Mr. Teedle."

"Oh my God," Teedle sighed to himself, as he hung up the phone and reached for his stress pills.

***

Tristan and Isolde made the front page of the *New York Post,* and *The Daily News,* both papers using headlines appropriate to their taste and their readership. The *News* headline read *Luxury Cathouse in Trouble* and the *Post* went with *Illegal Pussies on Fifth Avenue.* Brunhilde checked with Mr. Dunleavy before allowing the photographers in. He told her it might be better to cooperate than to deny the tabloids a made-to-order story. Hopefully, he said, the public would be on the side of the two cats.

Mrs. Boyce-Bentley was furious, especially with the photo of Tristan posing with Isolde on the mahogany toilet seat. She demanded that Mr. Teedle enforce the contract immediately, insisting that if the cats were not removed, court proceedings would be instituted at once. Teedle called Dunleavy who in turn visited Brunhilde and the staff of servants.

"It's a sticky question," Dunleavy said. "The Boyce-Bentleys, Kensingtons, and others have us legally because of the No-Cat clause is in the contract that the Neubergers signed. Even though they are dead, you have to abide by what they agreed to."

"But we are also bound to live under the conditions of her will," Dr. Heidgert, the vet, argued.

"True," Dunleavy agreed. "And if you are forced out of here, you may have other beneficiaries of the will arguing that you are not entitled to the trust funds Mrs. Neuberger left for you because you did not stay here with the cats."

"But that's a Catch-22," Brunhilde objected. "It's not fair."

"Perhaps, but that's not unusual for the law. That's one of the reasons there are so many lawyers."

"Couldn't you argue for us that if Tristan and Isolde are evicted, those of us who cared for them may eventually lose our trust funds?"

Dunleavy shook his head. He told Brunhilde he was sympathetic with her position, but could not make this argument against other beneficiaries of the will that he was bound to execute.

"Where did they ever get such a crazy rule banning cats from their own house?" Brunhilde asked.

"The *they* you are talking about, Brunhilde, is all the tenants of the co-op. They are the ones who voted on the No-Cat rule."

"You mean if they had another vote, they could change the rules?"

"I don't think it would do you any good, Brunhilde. The Kensingtons and Boyce-Bentleys carry a lot of weight around here."

Brunhilde nodded her head grimly. If Mrs. Neuberger herself couldn't dent the snobbish society of this co-op, what success could her servants expect?

After Dunleavy left she sat on her stool in the kitchen where she had planned so many meals since Mrs. Neuberger had hired her years ago. The thought of eventually leaving here after the cats had died bothered her, but now she was faced with the reality of having to leave this beautiful apartment almost immediately—by the end of the month. Well, one thing was certain: no matter what happened, she would take Tristan and Isolde. She knew the others would agree, because Brunhilde was the closest to the cats. She loved them every bit as much as Mrs. Neuberger did. These were not just cats, she told herself. They were more human than most of the so-called people that she knew.

Tristan looked at her sympathetically, almost as if to say he was sorry for causing all the trouble by dropping the ball down the toilet. Brunhilde picked him up to hug him and, seeing Isolde by his side as usual, picked her up as well. In so doing she knocked her pocketbook off the counter, spilling half of its contents on the kitchen floor.

"See what I get for loving you characters so much?" Brunhilde said to the cats, picking up her lipstick, change purse, and keys.

As she closed her pocketbook, Tristan and Isolde kept staring at her pensively as cats are wont to do.

"What are you guys up to now?" she asked, following their stare. "Oh, you're telling me I forgot something."

Brunhilde noticed a small manila envelope that had fallen underneath the sink. It was her copy of the section of the will that applied to her and the others who were caring for the cats. Absent-mindedly, she opened the envelope and took a look at it, thinking to herself that it was hard to believe that Mrs. Neuberger would have let something like this happen to her cats. But when she came to the part where the conditions of the trust could only be broken if the happiness of Tristan and Isolde was threatened, she jumped out of her chair so suddenly that even the casual cats stepped back in surprise.

"That's it!" Brunhilde shouted. "That's it—oh thank you so much, Mrs. Boyce-Bentley for the threat! And thank you, you loving creatures."

She picked up Tristan and Isolde and hugged them again. The cats seemed to like it, but after Brunhilde did it for the second and third time, they looked just a trifle bored. Tristan and Isolde enjoyed a bit of affection as well as the next one, but basically they were sophisticated cats.

***

All the publicity in the *News* and *Post,* and even a little one-column story entitled *Feline Follies* in the business section of the staid *New York Times,* brought the press to the lobby of the co-op, where the meeting was held. The Parker-Groats tried to bar the reporters and photographers, but they were shouted down by Brunhilde, Dr. Heidgert, and the servants. Mr. Teedle was too cowed by all the pressure to object forcefully to their presence, only asking them to be quiet and not take movies or still shots until the meeting was over.

"According to our by-laws, any one member of the co-op can ask for a meeting to consider a change in the rules," Mr. Teedle began nervously. "Since we have had such a request, I now call our meeting to order to vote on the question, namely: Should owners be permitted to have a minimum of two cats in their apartments? The by-laws, as you know, call for an open vote. I will now call the roll of owners. Mr. and Mrs. Cecil Boyce- Bentley."

A tall, thin man in rimless glasses stood up.

"The Boyce-Bentleys vote *No,* Mr. Teedle.

Teedle made a mark in pencil on his chart.

"Mr. and Mrs. Bernard Fitzgerald."

A young attractive woman in her mid-thirties stood up.

"My mother and father, Mr. and Mrs. Fitzgerald, have asked me to cast their vote as an abstention," she said.

Mrs. Boyce-Bentley looked at her husband in surprise.

"I think they had a little spat," he explained.

"Mr. and Mrs. Kensington," Mr. Teedle called out.

Both Kensingtons stood up. Brunhilde noted to herself that she never had seen the two of them together before.

"The Kensingtons vote *No,* Mr. Teedle."

Teedle marked the vote.

"Two votes *No,* one *Abstention.* Mr. and Mrs. Ernest Parker-Groat."

A heavy-set man, scarcely five foot tall and almost that wide around, leaned on his cane and prepared to arise slowly and painfully.

"No need to stand up, Mr. Parker-Groat," Teedle said. "We can hear you."

Parker-Groat settled back in his chair, less grateful for the opportunity to remain seated than irked by having his condition made the center of attention.

"The Parker-Groats will always vote *No* to having pesky, unsanitary animals in our building."

A little burst of cheering and clapping broke out.

"That's three votes *No.* Mr. Peter Dunleavy, representing the estate the late Sarah Neuberger."

Dunleavy stood up and waved his open palm towards Brunhilde.

"I defer to Ms. Brunhilde Jensen, who, with her staff now occupies the Neuberger co-op, and has full voting rights, according to the by-laws."

Brunhilde stood up and looked at Alice Heidgert and the others who shared the apartment with her. Finally she glanced lovingly at Tristan and Isolde, who were playing at her feet. This was her big moment. She was surprised that she wasn't nervous.

"I cast four votes *Yes!*" she said proudly, her voice becoming less shaky as she said the *Yes!*

"Four votes *Yes*, three votes, *No*, one *Abstention*," Teedle mumbled, almost automatically.

"What did she say?" Mrs. Boyce-Bentley screamed incredulously.

"I think she said *four* votes for eliminating the cat restriction in our by-laws," Mr. Kensington said.

"That's impossible," Mrs. Boyce-Bentley objected. "Each co-op owner has one vote. That's the rules. Tell her that, Mr. Teedle."

"Oh, there's no need to explain that to Ms. Jensen. She is well aware of—"

"Then why in God's name are you allowing her to vote three times?"

"I am not *allowing* her anything she isn't entitled to, Mrs. Boyce-Bentley."

"This is ridiculous," Mr. Parker-Groat objected. "She just gets one vote the same as the rest of us. Now let's get the goddam vote right, Teedle."

But Teedle had heard so many cat complaints in the last two weeks that he seemed inured to them and had got to the point of almost enjoying the pettiness of his clients. Normally he would have been frightened by Mr. Parker-Groat's threats; now he looked forward to watching his face when the discrepancy was explained.

Mr. Dunleavy stood up, hesitantly.

"Should I explain, Mr. Teedle?"

"Please do."

"Quite simply, ladies and gentlemen, the reason Ms. Brunhilde has four votes is that she and the group she represents own four co-ops here. You see, she purchased the apartments of the Hayakawas, Yang Sangs, and Yondo-Hondos, all of whom vacated their co-ops during the night. I have the deeds here, should any of you want to examine them."

Mrs. Boyce-Bentley was stunned. She had never even met the Asians who lived on the top floors, and here was this cook or maid or something not only meeting them, but buying their apartments.

"I just don't know what the world is coming to," she sighed, wondering whether to sob or sneer.

Mr. Teedle gave himself the luxury of staring for just a moment at the crestfallen faces of the Parker-Groats, Kensingtons, and Boyce-Bentleys. All the pomp in their countenances had shriveled away like sun-drenched tomatoes. For a split second he was tempted to feel sorry for them, but he quickly recovered from the temptation as he remembered the acts of abuse he suffered from them.

"There being no other business, the chair is looking for a motion to adjourn."

"I so move," Ms. Fitzgerald said.

"A second?"

"I second the motion," Brunhilde called out.

"The meeting is adjourned. Thank you everyone."

Slowly the residents made their way towards the elevator. Brunhilde glanced down at her feet. Tristan and Isolde looked up, waiting to be scooped up into their mistress's arms for the ride upstairs. At long last they had become the resident cats of the co-op. Legally. +++++

THE MADWOMAN OF MURRAY HILL

Wilbur's two biggest problems were, not necessarily in this order, his teeth and his wife. His teeth were disintegrating because over the past ten years he had been grinding them down in his sleep. Wilbur himself was the antithesis of his teeth. He was more than six-foot-four and weighed about 250 pounds. When he opened his mouth his row of tiny teeth peeked out at the world like a midget picket fence in front of a four-story mansion.

His problem with his wife was minor compared to some of the things that come between spouses. In fact, Myrna did not consider it a problem at all. Wilbur tried to ignore it and sometimes it seemed to disappear for awhile. But sooner or later it would crop up again and Wilbur would make a half-hearted effort to deal with it. He held out the vain hope that it would somehow just go away, but over the last year it seemed to get worse.

Myrna, in short, was looking for God. When she first mentioned it to Wilbur, he more or less took it in stride.

"So?" he replied.

"So?" she repeated. "Is that all you have to say?"

"Well, what am I supposed to say? You want to find God. Who doesn't?"

Myrna looked at her husband suspiciously.

"Don't you, Wilbur?"

Wilbur was watching the opening game of the season between the Mets and the Pirates at the time, and his wife's questions were breaking his concentration. But he did not want to appear uninterested, so he shook his head in agreement.

"Sure I believe in God. Who doesn't?"

"Lots of people don't, Wilbur. Otherwise we would not have all this hate and violence in the world."

Wilbur was trying to see if the Met runner sliding into home plate could knock down the Pirate catcher and jar the ball out of his hand. Myrna picked up the remote control button.

"May I shut this off for a minute, Wilbur, so that we can talk?"

The picture faded before he could reply. It looked like the Pirate catcher had dropped the ball, but he couldn't be sure.

"Well, I don't go to church or any of that stuff, Myrna, but that doesn't mean I don't believe in—the Almighty. You don't go to church yourself."

"It's not a matter of going to church, Wilbur. God doesn't stand in the pulpit or sit on an altar rail and check attendance like a high school principal. He, She, or It is not confined to a church."

Wilbur nodded.

"I see."

"God is everywhere, inside you and inside me."

"If you know where He is, why are you looking for Him?"

"That's just it, Wilbur. I want to believe God is everywhere, but I have never seen God. That's the frustrating thing about it."

Wilbur reached for the remote control switch.

"Well," he said, watching a Pirate outfielder misjudge a fly ball, I guess you just got to keep trying, Myrna. He's bound to show up one of these days."

Myrna was as relentless as a greyhound in her pursuit of God. She read books on theology, philosophy, and parapsychology; she joined yoga and meditation groups; she visited psychics and faith-healers. There were times when she thought she was getting hot on the trail, but in the end she came to the same conclusion: God was probably out there somewhere, but she didn't seem to be getting any closer in her quest. Watching Wilbur going about his routine of selling policies for Providence Insurance Company by day and watching baseball games and grinding his teeth by night was a little disconcerting to Myrna until the day she came up with an idea to alleviate her loneliness and stop her husband's teeth from fading away at the same time.

"Wilbur, do you know why you are grinding down your teeth?"

He hesitated. There was something in her tone that suggested she was going to tie his shrinking teeth with God.

"How should I know? I'm asleep when it happens."

"Exactly. You are all tensed up. You are trying to relieve your tensions by grinding your teeth. And do you know why you are so tense?"

Wilbur agreed that he was a little up tight, but he attributed that to the Mets' losing seasons.

"No, Wilbur, you are tense because, like me, you are looking for God and cannot find Him."

Wilbur knew that God was the last person he was looking for, but he saw no point in admitting that to Myrna. Besides, if he told her the truth, it somehow wouldn't sound right. He had nothing against God and, as a matter of fact, would not mind seeing Him pop in any time He was in the neighborhood. But Wilbur, while not willing to consider himself a skeptic, did not think God had the time to get involved with people like Myrna and him. He was convinced that she was wasting her time with this God-business, but he didn't know how to tell her. So he went back to his teeth.

"You've actually seen me grinding my teeth?"

"How can I avoid it? Your whole mouth turns into a snarl and you keep mumbling something like 'Getting closer, gettin' closer.' You know, Wilbur, you may be nearer to God than I am, and I've been looking for so long. Somehow that doesn't seem fair."

Wilbur wondered how much longer this was going to go on. By the time he got the remote control switch back from Myrna, the game would be in the sixth inning.

"Well, Myrna, you have a good point. Can I watch the game now?"

"Wilbur Judge, I don't think you're listening to a word I'm saying."

"I am, too. You're saying that God is grinding my teeth down."

"I am not saying that it is God, Wilbur. God doesn't do such things. You are the one who is grinding your teeth down."

"Yeah, that's what Dr. Rumson says."

Myrna appraised her husband carefully. She had long ago learned that timing was nearly everything in life. This seemed to be the right time.

"Next week a famous psychic is coming from Chicago to address our Women's Club at our regular monthly meeting. The name of her talk is—let's see; I have it right here somewhere."

Wilbur looked on dispassionately as she rummaged through the top drawer of her desk.

"Oh, here it is. Her topic is *You Never Know what's Going to Happen When You Begin the Search for God.* What do you think?"

"I don't know, Myrna. Why do you need to hear a spiel like that? You're looking for God all the time."

"I wasn't thinking of myself, Wilbur."

"Oh. You mean——?"

"Yes."

"Well, gee, Myrna...I don't have to search for God. I know He's *around* somewhere and I'm happy with things just the way they are."

"Then why are you grinding your teeth?"

Wilbur reached for the remote control, but Myrna picked it up from the table just as he stretched his hand out for it.

"C'mon, Myrna, the first inning has started already."

"Will you come, Wilbur?"

"Come where?"

"To my Woman's Club meeting."

"But I'm not a woman."

"Men can come too."

"When is it?"

"A week from Wednesday. At eight o'clock."

"At night?"

"Of course. You wouldn't be able to go in the daytime."

"I'll miss the Met game."

"One night won't hurt you, Wilbur. Madame Ranevsky has never been in our area before."

"Who?"

"Madame Ranevsky, the famous psychic. She's coming all the way from Chicago."

"Just to speak to your women's club?"

"Well, not exactly. One of our members found out that she was going to be in the area on other business, so she was able to get her to agree to speak to us. Her works have appeared in all the New Age books. We were very fortunate to get her."

"Fortunate to the tune of a couple of hundred bucks, I'll bet."

Myrna hesitated, thought about it, and blurted out:

"Actually her fee is $1,000."

"Are you kidding?"

"Madame Ranevsky usually charges twice that much, Wilbur. She is giving us a break because we're a charitable organization."

"Do I have to pay anything?"

"No, Wilbur. You get in free as my guest. It's a great opportunity. And you may be able to stop grinding your teeth."

Wilbur grunted and shrugged his shoulders.

"Just this once, Myrna. Now can I have that channel-changer?"

***

It turned out that Wilbur didn't go to work the Wednesday that Myrna's Women's Club was to meet. He ground one of his bridges loose during the night and called the dentist as soon as he got out of bed. Betty told him Dr. Rumson would see him at noon.

"But it just needs a little cement. I can't go to work this way."

"I know, Mr. Judge. But he is at the all-day health meeting called by the governor. Dr. Rumson said if there were any emergencies, he would see them on his lunch hour."

Wilbur grunted. He just realized that today was Wednesday. Rumson 's all-day health meeting was on the golf course with the other dentists. He was surprised that he would even come back for emergencies, for the links were twenty miles from Murray Hill.

"How come he has enough time to break away for lunch and still get back to his—to his all-day meeting?"

"The meeting is right here in Murray Hill. At the regional high school, just three blocks away. That's why Dr. Rumson is able to come back for you. See you at noon, Mr. Judge."

Wilbur was convinced that he had just been given the old runaround. He couldn't remember the governor or any big-wig politician ever coming to Murray Hill ever since he had been living in the town. Besides, if they had the big meeting in the high school, what would they do with the students? That woman had some spiel. Funny thing about it was that Betty was not only Rumson's secretary, but she was also his mother. She covered up for him better than a bullet-proof vest.

He hadn't realized the dentist had his mother working for him when he first started going to the young dentist, for Betty was one of those mothers who did not look much older than their sons. Besides, she seemed too calm and peaceful to ever have been a mother. She was forever bidding him *Gooooood* Morning and *Gooooood* Afternoon and asking him about Myrna, the insurance business, how he was feeling, how Pinkerton his cat was making out, and if Myrna's purple azalea bushes were still blooming. What's more, she had such a saccharine voice and ready smile that she seemed a nun rather than a parent. If she were a mother at all, she would be more of a good-looking Mother Theresa or Mother Cabrini than a mother of a grown-up man.

As he suspected, she was waiting for him with a smile, her pen fixed solidly in her right hand, and his chart spread out in front of her when he climbed up the steps to Dr. Rumson's office at noon.

"*Gooooood Morning,* Mr. Judge. The doctor is just washing up. He will be with you in a minute. Would you like a copy of the latest *People* magazine? There's a wonderful story about General Schwarzkopf's teddy bear collection. Would you believe he has stuffed animals imported from every country in the coalition?"

"Naw, I think I'll just look at *Sports Illustrated.*"

"*Woooooonderful,* Mr. Judge. You'll just love the swim suits—blue, yellow, violet. Such delightful colors."

At that moment her son buzzed her and she rushed into his office with her charts calling out cheerfully:

"Coming, Dr. Rumson."

Suddenly the front door swung open about a foot and a huge head, a woman's, slithered its way through the opening. Atop the head of wiry black hair was a cavernous purple hat with a lone white feather protruding from it, creating the impressing of Medusa in a chapeau

"Dr. Zatcher wants you to move your car."

The voice that came from the enormous head was surprisingly soft. Wilbur looked over to where Betty was sitting, but saw she was gone.

"There is no one here right now. They're all inside," he volunteered to Medusa.

The woman pointed to Wilbur.

"*Your* car," she whispered and closed the door.

Wilbur got up uncertainly. All the time he had been coming to Dr. Rumson he had never heard of a Dr. Zatcher. He assumed he was a new doctor who had rented an office upstairs. The parking spaces bore the names of the tenants in the building, but since the parking area was large and there were always empty spaces, no one seemed to pay any attention to the individual designations. As he closed the door behind him, he saw the lot was relatively empty again. The woman with the purple hat, now connected with the rest of her body, was standing next to his Nissan. Her body matched her head; she was almost as tall as Wilbur, perhaps even taller if he counted the white feather.

"I don't mind moving my car for Dr. Zatcher, lady, but there are parking spots all over the place."

"You don't *mind*!" the woman exclaimed. This time her voice was several decibels higher.

"No, I don't—"

"*MOVE IT!*"

"What?"

"I said move your goddamned car before I chop your spine off," she screamed, her once-muted voice sounding like a trolley car screeching to a halt.

Wilbur looked at her with disbelief. The woman with the Medusa head had a torso like a refrigerator and legs like tree stumps. She was raising a long black lead pipe over her head as if she planned to smash the hood of his Nissan with it. Or maybe him.

"Wait a second, lady. What—?"

"Move it, maggot. *MOVE IT!*"

Wilbur hesitated. The woman swung the pipe at the left headlight. Seconds later broken glass flew about the parking lot like shrapnel.

"Hey, Lady. You've got a problem..."

"You're fucken-A right I have a problem. I'm a psycho."

That was enough persuasion for Wilbur. He ran up the steps into the dentist's office and a smiling Betty, discreetly chewing *Dentine* and talking to a patient in a red lumber jacket.

"Why, Mr. Judge, I thought you had run away with our swimsuit edition."

"You wouldn't believe what just happened to me in the parking lot."

"Oh, Mr. Judge," she smiled cheerily. "Something seems to be always happening to you. First you grind your teeth, then your run away with the swim suit—"

Wilbur looked out the window at his car. The woman was gone. This might be the best time to make a break for it.

"Look, Betty, I think I'll cancel my appointment. I'll come back another time."

"But Dr. Rumson is all ready for you. You don't want to go around with a bridge missing from your mouth. Here, give it to me and I'll clean it."

"No, I've gotta go."

"Oh, Mr. Judge, you know that Dr. Rumson doesn't hurt. You've been here so many times before and—"

"It's not that. It's the woman in the parking lot. She—"

"What woman?" Betty asked.

At that point Medusa swung the door open so viciously it nearly flew off its hinges. Betty started to say something, but swallowed her gum instead.

"You Wet Wick!" she screamed, swinging her lead pipe over her head. "You Bedpan—"

It happened quickly. Dr. Rumson, the man in the red lumber jacket, and Wilbur converged on the woman with the purple hat and eased her out the door while Betty slipped the safety lock on.

She told me she was a psycho," Wilbur said to Rumson.

"I saw her once before," the dentist said. "She is a patient of Dr. Zatcher upstairs. He's a psychiatrist. I think that's where she went."

From outside the window came the sound of brakes screeching. Medusa emerged from a Mercedes shaking her fist.

"I gotcha now, Slopbucket."

She had parked her car perpendicular to Wilbur's, blocking him in.

"You might as well get your bridge cemented, Mr. Judge," Betty observed. "I think you're going to be here for awhile. Do you want to read about General Schwartzkopf's teddy bears while the cement is drying?"

Dr. Rumson had Wilbur's bridge cemented in place in fifteen minutes, but he couldn't leave because Medusa was upstairs with the psychiatrist.

"Dr. Zatcher asked us to give him a little while to calm her down," Betty smiled. "Then I'm sure she will move her car."

Wilbur looked at his watch.

"I took the day off just to get the bridge in. I've got a few things I want to do at home."

"Oh, I understand, Mr. Judge. But if you'll just be patient a little longer everything will be *allllll* right. Would you like to see some *New Yorker* magazines?"

"Nah."

"*National Geographic* or *Better Homes and Gardens*?"

Wilbur shook his head and passed also on *Newsweek LIFE, Popular Mechanics,* and *Prevention.* Looking about furtively, Betty reached into the bottom drawer of her desk and pulled out a *Playboy.*

"Even better than the swimsuit edition," she smiled mischievously.

***

When Wilbur became bored with the magazines, she brought him tea and cookies.

"Could you check with the shrin—with Dr Zatcher again?"

"I think I'd better give him a few more minutes, Mr. Judge."

"But I've been here an hour and a half."

"I know. Would you like me to see if there is anything in the fridge that I can make a sandwich with?"

"That's O.K. The cookies filled me up. Why don't we just call the police and have them tow the car away?"

"Oh, you know how the police are, Mr. Judge. Swirling lights and sirens and all that kind of thing. It might make the poor woman worse."

"Poor woman? With a Mercedes?"

"Dr. Zatcher says it's a rented car."

"You still need money to rent a Mercedes."

"I know. He said she is really a rather prominent woman. She came here all the way from Illinois just to see him."

"No shrinks out her way?"

"Well, Dr. Zatcher is a specialist. Besides, I think she wanted to keep her condition confidential."

"She'd better stay away from parking lots then."

"Oh, Mr. Judge, you're simply a scream. Are you sure I can't get you some more tea?"

Wilbur shook his head and wandered out into the hallway. As soon as he opened the door, he could hear Medusa screaming in the upstairs office.

"I don't think he's making any progress with her. Why don't I take a look at her car to see what company she rented it from and you can call and have them pick it up?"

"Oh, I wouldn't go near her car, Mr. Judge, if I were you."

"Why?"

"She can see from the upstairs window. While the cement of your bridge was drying Dr. Rumson stepped out on the porch and walked towards her car. When she saw him, she charged down the stairs and almost knocked him off the porch."

"She needs more than a psychiatrist; she needs someone to put her in straitjacket. And she came all the way here to get help. Where did you say she was from?"

"I think Dr. Zatcher said Chicago."

It had been a frustrating afternoon. Wilbur had not got out of the dentist's office until three o'clock. He had to hide in one of the back rooms until Dr. Zatcher felt that the woman with the purple hat had "reasonably calmed down" enough to drive her Mercedes.

"If she had looked in the window and seen you there, it might have started her up again," Dr. Zatcher had explained to Wilbur, after offering his apologies and agreeing to pay for the smashed headlight.

"What set her off?" Wilbur had asked.

"I'm afraid it would be unethical for me to discuss the case of a patient," he had said. "I feel I can tell you, however, that other than these occasional lapses into aggression, she is a professional woman and comes from a very talented family. Today was just a temporary aberration."

Myrna had been out getting her hair done for her women's club meeting while Wilbur was in the dentist's office. She got caught in a rainstorm on the way home and was so distracted by her damp hair that she was only half-listening to Wilbur's saga at the dentist's office. He decided to wait until tomorrow to tell her with all the vivid details so that she could get the full flavor of his adventure.

"Well, that was quite an experience, Wilbur," Myrna said as she took the pot off the stove. "So. Are you looking forward to hearing Madame Ranevsky?"

Madame Ranevsky! The thought hit him like a lead pipe to the solar plexus.

Of course it could be strictly coincidental, he told himself as he swirled spaghetti around his tongue. Madame Ranevsky was from Chicago and so was the weirdo in the parking lot. Myrna had said she had agreed to speak to her club because she was going to be in the area anyhow "on other business," someone in the women's club had said. Could that "business" be a trip to Dr. Zatcher? The shrink had said that his patient was an important member of society, but that would also apply to Nicky the garbage man because when he went on strike everyone in town realized how important he was, Wilbur reflected.

"Say what does this Madame Ranevsky look like, Myrna?"

His wife regarded him curiously before passing him the brochure from the women's club with the guest speaker's picture on the cover. Wilbur thought she had small eyes like the woman with the lead pipe, but the picture was really too dark to tell. She was also wearing a humongous hat, but this one didn't have a feather.

Because of the rain and the damaged headlight, they were a few minutes late, so they followed the time-honored tradition of taking seats in the back. There was no one on the stage except Mrs. Flannery, the women's club president, who was introducing the evening's speaker as Wilbur and Myrna slipped into their seats.

Wilbur glanced at the program and read Madame Ranevsky's background. He had to admit that on paper it looked as if she knew what she was doing—a Ph.D. from Johns Hopkins University in abnormal behavior patterns, credit for helping solve four puzzling crimes by giving advice to the Chicago Police Department after psychic meditations, three books published by Simon and Schuster. It was hard to believe that someone with that background would smash cars with a lead pipe. Mrs. Flannery was finishing up.

"...and her subject is *You Never Know What's Going to Happen When You Search for God.* Ladies and guests of the Murray Hill Women's Club, it is my great pleasure to give you Madame Ramona Ranevsky, doctor of abnormal behavior, renowned psychic, and friend of women everywhere."

There was a burst of applause, as crackling as a fire of dry twigs, as a tall, heavy-set woman in a wide-brimmed black hat made her way across the stage. Most of the women stood up. Wilbur stayed in his seat, grateful for the huge human shield. He slipped his large gray cap back on, pulling it down as far as he could. As the women began sitting down again he heard a melodic voice as clear as a silver bell. He looked over the head of the person in front of him. The speaker resembled the woman in the parking lot but there was something different about her that he could not put his finger on. At any rate she didn't spout out the weirdo's screeching rhetoric. Madame Ranevsky's voice was smooth and velvety.

When she spoke Wilbur was surprised to find himself at ease. He lifted his cap from his eyes an inch or so and allowed himself to relax. Why he had ever thought that the woman with the lead pipe would turn out to be Madame Ranevsky was beyond him. He began to think that the experience had been so traumatic that it had caused his imagination to think of things that were hardly possible.

"Yes, ladies and friends of the Murray Hill Women's Club, God *does* work in mysterious ways. And we'll going to talk about that now. And when I am finished speaking, I have a little surprise for you. Now picture yourself riding on horseback to Damascus with St. Paul and..."

Wilbur found himself nodding his head. It had been a trying day and Madame Ranevsky's voice was so soothing. Myrna was tempted to nudge him to wake him up, because she was afraid he would snore. But Wilbur sat quietly in his chair, breathing very softly. Myrna wondered if he was getting Madame Ranevsky's message in a subliminal way. She had not seen him so peaceful in a long time. It was only when Madame Ranevsky was finishing up that she dropped the smooth hypnotizing tone of her address.

"So. Next time you look into the beautiful pink petals of a gardenia, remember you are looking into the face of God. And now for that surprise I promised you."

Madame Ranevsky looked to the wings and waved her hand.

"I know many of you are familiar with the work of Dr. Maria Waldron on occult phenomena, but it is not generally known that we are sisters. She had business in your community today, so she flew from Chicago with me. Maria, will you come out a say a few words to these lovely people?"

Wilbur sat upright in his seat as a tall, heavyset woman in a humongous purple hat, carrying a long black umbrella, walked onto the stage. Wilbur pulled his cap back over his eyes and slunk down in his seat.

The woman in the purple hat looked over the audience without speaking. Wilbur was convinced that she was staring at him. She shielded her eyes from the klieg light illuminating the podium and stared at the back of the auditorium. Clearing her throat, she tilted her umbrella forward slightly towards the audience.

But Wilbur wasn't fooled. He knew a lead pipe when he saw one.+++++

HOW TO STOP SMOKING

The next train for Watkins Falls? Mister, you got a good hour and a half, if it's on time, and it ain't on time but two, maybe three, times a month. Least not when Billy Saunders is running the engine. Not much at keeping schedules, Billy ain't. But he's got a good head on his shoulders. As the saying goes, you may not get there as fast, but you *do get* there. Yes siree, that's what counts, ain't it? Everybody is in such a danged hurry nowadays to get from here to there, and as soon as they get there they want to get to some place else without taking time out to enjoy where they got to in the first place.

But you ain't in any particular hurry, are you? I didn't think so. You don't look like them people that come down here from New York City and think they can push a few buttons and the whole town'll snap to like a bunch of recruits on a drill field. Make yourself comfortable. Harry's on the can right now, but he'll be back in a few minutes. If you ain't et yet, you might try some of his huckleberry pie. Actually, his old lady makes it. It's the best danged pie in Dalton's Corners. I'd take it easy on the coffee, though. The first cup goes down all right, but the second usually sticks in your throat like ticks on a dawg's ass.

Thanks, I don't smoke. Neither does Harry or Thelma. That's his wife. As a matter of fact, Buddy, there's not many people in this here town that smokes. Funny, ain't it? You'd think in a little burg like this most of the folks would be smokers. Well, they was—until what happened to Fuzzy Koenig.

Fuzzy? He's what we call a ghost rider; he drives the hearse for McGinty's Funeral Parlor. Fuzzy used to carry one pack of butts in his left shirt pocket, another in his right, and a third in his coat jacket. And he kept another in the back of the hearse, just in case he got caught short. That guy really liked his smokes. And when he was smoking, almost everybody else was too.

Look, lemme get you the coffee and huckleberry pie. Sometimes when Harry goes to the can he forgets about the rest of the world. He's got the Farmer's Almanac, The Sporting News, and a few of them there girlie magazines in there. Keeps 'em hidden in the tank in a plastic bag so Thelma won't find them. She's out picking berries today, so Harry knows that if anything comes up, I'll handle it for him. You can just put your money in that cigar box there. Thirty-five cents for the coffee and a dollar for the pie. As you can see, this ain't no high class place, but the prices are fair.

Go ahead, light up. I didn't mean to say you couldn't smoke in here. It's just that almost everybody in town threw their weeds away after they heard of Fuzzy's experience.

You sure you want to hear what happened? Well, you got time. Your train ain't even at Prairie Junction yet. Anyway, Fuzzy has this job to drive a corpse to the Veterans Cemetery in Prout's Point. That's about 65 miles from here, but the burial is free for veterans, so Fuzzy gets a couple jobs there now and then. You don't have to be kilt in one of them wars to get in the graveyard; all you have to do is serve overseas when one is going on. Then when you croak, the government takes care of you. Pretty good deal, right?

When Fuzzy gets those long jobs, he usually asks me to ride with him. He tells me it's to break the monotony of the Interstate, but I'm wise to him: he's afraid of taking a long trip with no one in the car with him but the stiff in the back. Now that may sound funny 'cause Fuzzy has been working for McGinty's for twenty years now, and you would think that after all that time around corpses his job would be a breeze for him. After all, I betcha he has seen more of the dead of Dalton's Corners than the living, but Fuzzy don't like to be with them alone for a long time in that big limo he drives. He would never admit this to anyone, but I know him better'n most folks do.

To tell you the truth, I ain't so happy being around stiffs either, but when I take those trips with Fuzzy, he always has a six-pack for me. After the second beer, I forget that there may be a ghost riding in the back.

Another coffee? Like I said, it might stick in your throat like a ball of molasses. But, what the hell? Everybody's different. Don't worry about it—the second one is on the house.

So we've been riding about forty miles when Fuzzy has to go to the can. He pulls in for gas and heads for the bathroom. I decide to create my own *Used Beer Department* in the woods behind the station. Naturally I'm finished way ahead of Fuzzy, so I grab a newspaper and take my seat on the passenger side of the hearse and start to catch up on my reading when this guy—he looked like one of them there Okefenokees that live in the swamps—comes up to me and asks if we are going as far as Parson's Meadows. That's just before we get to the cemetery, so I say, "Sure, hop in. But you'll have to sit in the back with the corpse because there's only room for two people up front—me and my buddy Fuzzy."

That seems to be OK with the Okefenokee. You know, strange as he looked, he spoke O.K. He sounded a little like one of them there English professors. Most of them are weird too, wouldn't you say? Anyway, he piles in the back and he's sound asleep before Fuzzy is back from the terlet. By that time I'm into my fourth beer and feeling no pain. Sometime after Fuzzy got behind the wheel I musta dozed off myself, because the next thing I know we're in Bakersville by the state line, and I know we ain't got far to go.

Fuzzy is puffing away so much that the front of the hearse is covered with blue smoke. It was so bad I was beginning to wonder how he could see the highway. He seemed to be in some kind of a trance, probably from staring out at the road for so long. I figgered I oughta start talking to him about something he was interested in, so I could keep him alert. I was just about to ask him if he thought Whitey Witkowski's wife Mamie was getting any on the side when the dangest thing happened. The Okefenokee with the English accent tapped on the window and asked:

"Do you mind if I smoke?"

Mister, in all my borned days I never saw a normal-looking face turn white as a jack rabbit in heat like Fuzzy's did when he heard that voice coming from where the casket set. It just then came to me that I never did tell him about the fella in the back, who musta found Fuzzy's extra pack of butts. As I said, Fuzzy was always a little askeered of driving the hearse with a dead body in the back. I didn't have no time to explain, because afore I knowed it Fuzzy steered the hearse off the road, across the shoulder and into a field of grazing cattle. Would you believe it, the critters didn't even run, so it was up to Fuzzy to keep missing them until he finally stopped the hearse by ramming it into a chicken house. Boy, you shoulda seen those feathers a-flying! It looked like it was snowing in July. It musta have been a powerful building because none of the chicks got hurt. Neither Fuzzy nor the Okefenokee in the back got more than a few scratches. I got a whack in the leg when the casket broke loose and came through the window at me. I couldn't walk right for a week, but McGinty's insurance covered all our injuries and he got a brand new hearse out of the deal.

But Fuzzy ain't never been the same after that. I never did have the nerve to tell him that I invited the Okefenokee into the hearse in the first place. Fuzzy figgered the guy must have been a drifter who had been attracted to the hearse by the cigarettes he had hidden in the back.

But he said he could never light another cigarette without thinking of that voice coming at him from the casket. He hasn't had a cigarette since that day. After seeing a big chain-smoker like Fuzzy give up the weed, some of the other men folks started swearing off smoking too. And then before long the women folks were giving it up too.

Me? I never smoked in the first place. But I'd never give up my six-packs. Can you imagine how it would be to ride in a hearse through a field of cattle—right smack into a henhouse—without a drink?

Hmmm. According to Harry's old Regular clock, which most of the time is right, you've got thirty-five minutes afore the Watkins Falls train arrives here. Liked that huckleberry pie, huh? Why don'tcha have another piece?

Thelma's been baking those huckleberry pies for twenty, maybe twenty- five years now, but she wouldn't have baked a one if it weren't for that big black bear what wondered down from the mountains one afternoon and walked right in the front door while Thelma was talking on the telephone to her Uncle Egbert—actually he's not really her uncle, but ever since she was six and a half, he...." +++++

VIII.

Love Comes in Different Packages

All you need is love.

　　　　　　　　　　　--John Lennon

THE CEMETERY LADY

The bitter winter wind was rustling the vagrant leaves around the tombstones as Mrs. Watson parked her old 1985 Ford by the side gate of the Ironwood City Cemetery. She gave her accelerator pedal two long taps before she shut the motor off. Her late husband had told her long ago that this made it easier to start up the car again on cold nights. And this surely was a freezing night. She was fond of her old Ford. It had never let her down when she traveled to and from cemeteries on icy winter nights like this.

Mrs. Watson stepped out of her car and reached for her collapsible shopping cart. Once on level ground she stuck her head back in the old Ford and with an effort managed to pull out a huge plastic bag, dropping it to the ground. Now came the toughest part: lifting it into the cart. She bent her knees and reached for the bottom of the bag, edging it up along the side of the car until she could bring part of it to the top of the cart. Then with a final push, she dropped it into her shopping wagon. Exhausted from her battle with the bag, Mrs. Watson stepped back a pace to get her breath. She surveyed the front of the cemetery. Except for the riot of the dead leaves, everything seemed peaceful and orderly inside. But Mrs. Watson knew that despite the stillness, somewhere among the myriad of monuments and simple crosses in this ancient cemetery living creatures lurked, and she was determined to find them tonight.

There was a full moon, this frigid January night. Mrs. Watson looked at her watch. It was ten minutes before midnight. This was her third and last cemetery visit of the evening. Now if only old Pete the custodian had remembered to leave the gate unlocked, as he had promised. Pete was the octogenarian caretaker, a man who always wore a dark suit and tie every day on the job. Yet he was not as lugubrious as he looked, nor as forgetful as he led people to believe. Indeed he was in a way the antithesis of a cemetery. Robust and active, he gave the impression that Death was on a holiday. Mrs. Watson wasn't really worried about the gate; she had known Pete for a long time and he was well aware of her nocturnal walks around the cemetery.

Old Pete was true to his word. The gate was shut tightly and secured by a heavy padlock, but as she reached for it Mrs. Watson could see that he had not snapped it closed. She entered with her cart and, once inside, closed the gate, being careful not to squeeze the padlock shut. She carried a small flashlight with her, but she did not think she would need it tonight. The moon hovered above her like a gigantic street light. Besides, she knew her way around this cemetery; she had been here many nights before this.

For five minutes or so she pushed her cart along a ragged dirt road that wound its way among the gravestones. The clanging of her wagon over the bumps was the only sound she heard. She stopped and strained her ears, listening for a familiar cry. But there was none.

Just as she was about to wheel her wagon down the road again, she heard it, a long, plaintive moan, shattering the stillness of the cemetery. It was coming somewhere from her right, perhaps two hundred yards away. That would be the eastern end of the cemetery. She turned her wagon off the road and followed a path through the tombstones.

Mrs. Watson made her way carefully over the ground, uneven in places due to the ravages of winter. Once again she stopped to gain the direction of the moaning sound. She stood there solemnly in the moonlight in her ragged brown cloth overcoat, army boots, and baseball cap, not unlike the statues and monuments that surrounded her on all sides, wary sentinels in the lonely cemetery. Her patience was rewarded because moments later the moan, this time more melancholy and somewhat unearthly, interrupted the somber quietude of the night.

Now was the time to move very carefully, Mrs. Watson told herself as she reached into the huge bag in her wagon. She pulled out a handful of nuggets and dropped them into her cavernous overcoat pocket. Resting her cart next to the tombstone of *Ezekiel Burnside (1756-1784)*, she moved cautiously in the direction of the moan. Suddenly she heard a flutter of small feet and she reached for her flashlight. Crouched against a crumbling headstone was a frightened little white puppy who appeared to be a mix of a German Shepherd and a yellow lab. As Mrs. Watson approached, he lifted his leg and let out another mournful cry.

"All right, little fella, come here for some goodies," she coaxed, fingering the nuggets.

The dog stared at Mrs. Watson for a moment and ran behind a gravestone.

"Come on, nice doggie," she called after him. "I'll bet you haven't had anything to eat all day today."

As if he had heard her attempt to persuade him, the dog peered out from the side of the graveyard marker and stared hard at the first human being he had encountered on this fiercely cold night. But as Mrs. Watson took another step in his direction, he found shelter behind a towering statue of St. Francis of Assisi. Mrs. Watson smiled, thinking to herself that this dog knew who his friends were.

Now that he had seen her, she knew he would come for the nuggets once she moved away. As with all the dogs she had seen this evening, she wanted to try to coax him to come with her so that she could give him a warm place to sleep for the night, but she sensed that he was afraid, and she wouldn't be able to catch him when he ran away. Better to leave some nuggets here in front of the statue of St. Francis and continue walking through the cemetery in search of other dogs. She left a little pile of nuggets on the ground and moved on. As she reached a bend in the dirt road, she turned around to peek. The shepherd mix had found the food and was having his first meal of the day.

**

Following the path leading to the northern section of the Ironwood City Cemetery, Mrs. Watson recalled that it was just forty years ago that she had found and befriended her first stray dog, a collie mix, while taking a short cut through the cemetery late at night. She gave him half of the loaf of bread that she was bringing home for her next morning's toast. Younger then, she was able to catch the frightened dog when he tried to run away, and she took care of Tombstone, as she named him, until he died in her arms 15 years later.

The rescue of Tombstone had been the beginning of a long career of befriending stray dogs. On subsequent trips through that cemetery she discovered that people used graveyards as depositories for unwanted pets. Mrs. Watson soon realized that this was one of the worst places for dogs, there being no shelter or source of food.

So she began feeding and taking care of as many animals as she could—dogs, cats, birds and an occasional rabbit, chipmunk, and squirrel. But it was the stray dogs that she carried the most food for, because she knew that most of these animals had once had a home and were not as skillful in finding food in the wild as other animals. When she was too old to work, she had to husband her small Social Security payments carefully so she would always have enough money to buy food for the animals. When the strays in the cemeteries were numerous, she had to work part-time as a waitress in an all-night diner to buy food for them, but she always arranged with her boss to be off-duty for an hour or so every night to give her time to feed the animals in the cemetery.

Sometimes on freezing nights she was able to persuade dogs to come to her, and she brought them home to the warmth of her small cottage. At one point she had as many as ten dogs living with her at the same time. Somehow she managed to find food for all of them and still pay her taxes and utility bills. Mrs. Watson was gifted with patience and all her dogs were well-trained, clean, and obedient. But most of all they were loving, every single one of them. Frightened as they were when she first encountered them in the cemeteries, those who lived with her soon transferred their fear to love and became lifelong friends of their benefactor.

***

Now as she walked along the ragged path with the brilliant moon lighting her way, she thought about the collie mix she had seen here last night. He reminded her so much of Tombstone. One night he had taken her food, but she was unable to keep up with him when he ran away. She had a feeling that she would run into him again this evening. It would nice to have a doggie again with so many of the features of her beloved Tombstone. Mrs. Watkins was certain that the collie mix she had seen last night needed a home badly because he looked so thin and malnourished and his fragile body had been shaking in the bitter cold. Her big fear was that he might not have made it through the night. She hastened her step and anxiously pushed her shopping wagon between the graves. If he is still alive, I will find him and bring him home, she told herself. She already had a name picked out for him. She would call him Digger, an apt name for a dog, she thought, and certainly an appropriate one for a dog found in a cemetery.

Mrs. Watson was nearing the grave where she had seen Digger last night. *Ebenezer Crabtree (1772-1821)*, the tombstone read. He might be somewhere near here, because it didn't seem likely that he would wander too far from the place where he found nourishment. She tried calling.

When that brought no response, she reached into her pocket for her whistle. Taking a deep breath, she blew into it with all her might. She heard the echo in the distance. Then silence. She waited a minute or so more and blew again.

Now she was in a quandary. If she did not move on, she would not have the opportunity to find more dogs on this bitterly cold night. But if she left this spot, she might not see the dog she was going to call Digger, for she felt certain he was in this vicinity, since this was where she dropped off food for him in the past. She would wait a few more minutes, just in case. Despite her army boots, her feet were beginning to feel cold. She walked briskly in a little circle, pushing the cart in front of her.

"Digger, Digger," she called out, feeling a little foolish because the dog obviously did not know his name. "Come on, doggie, I have some nice nuggets for you."

She stopped to listen. The only sound she heard was the rush of the wind and the crinkling of leaves gliding over the graves. She was just about to resume her odyssey through the cemetery when she thought she heard something behind her, something like footsteps. As she turned to see what it was, she felt a sharp pain in the back of her head, and she fell forward landing face down on the cold earth.

***

It did not look like Mrs. Watson was going to make it at first. She spent two weeks in the Intensive Care Unit of Ironwood City Hospital before she was able to see visitors. The first one she spoke to was old Pete the caretaker who discovered her body on the frozen ground the morning after the attack.

"Digger and the rest of my dogs," she sighed. "I've got to get out of here so I can feed them."

Old Pete put his hand on her shoulder. "You must stay calm, Mrs. Watson. The doctors here said you almost didn't make it."

"But, Pete, the poor animals will starve if I don't—"

"They are all taken care of, including the collie mix you call Digger. I've been keeping them in the cemetery's mausoleum at night. It's heated in there. I let them out early in the morning before anyone comes."

"You could be fired, Pete, if anyone finds out."

"When you're in your eighties, getting fired is not one of your main concerns. And don't worry about the dog food. Some of the cops are feeding the animals since you've been in the hospital."

"The police! I don't understand."

"Well, they felt bad when I mentioned you had an old Ford, and the hospital staff told them there was no car keys with your belongings. The police figured that the mean person who attacked you also stole your car. But they called him something else other than a mean person."

Mrs. Watson smiled. Old Pete was just as careful with his language as he was with his appearance. And she appreciated his willingness to get into trouble by letting the cemetery's dogs in the mausoleum.

"You tell the policemen that it was very nice of them to feed the dogs while I'm up here. Some people say police officers are cold and indifferent. This certainly shows that they are not."

"I suppose that's true, Mrs. Watson. But I think your dogs had a hand in bringing out the goodness in them."

"I don't understand."

"Didn't anyone tell you how they found you in the cemetery?"

"Just that I was unconscious, lying on the ground near the grave of Ebenezer Crabtree."

"And they didn't tell you why you didn't freeze to death on that bitterly cold night?"

Mrs. Watson sighed. She sensed what old Pete was going to tell her before he even opened his mouth. But she wanted to hear him say it.

"When I walked through the cemetery that morning I didn't see you at first, just the cart," he said. "It was overturned and all the dog food was gone. Then I looked over by Ebenezer Crabtree's grave and saw a huge pile of fur. There must have been five or six dogs lying on top of you to keep you warm. The doctors said that probably saved your life."

+++++

NOVEMBER RAIN

*And it seemed as though in a little while the
solution would be found, and then a new and
glorious life would begin; and it was clear to
both of them that the end was still far off,
and that what was to be most complicated and
difficult for them was only just beginning.*
Chekhov: The Lady with the Pet Dog

K ing Farouk was at her usual position, peeking out the side of
her living room window. Laura was tempted to look up and
wave good-bye, but she knew as soon as she turned around her
mother would slip her head behind the curtains. Mick sensed what his
daughter was thinking. He gave her a little kiss on the forehead as she
slid into Boyle O'Reilly's yellow Kharman Ghia.

"Don't worry about King Farouk, Laura," Mick said. "Just remember
I'm always in your corner."

Laura smiled at her father. In his youth he had been a state amateur
boxing champion and his vocabulary was filled with jargon of the ring
and personages from history. Although he considered *King Farouk* a fitting
nickname for his headstrong spouse, he did not refer to her with malice.
In Mick's mind she was a tyrant with a good heart, even though she had
not spoken to him since Boyle and Laura started going out together.

Boyle O'Reilly had never dated one of his students or, for that matter,
any student in the university until Laura took his *Elizabethan Literature*
class in the summer. After a little farewell party for his students at his
apartment when the course was over, he summoned up the nerve to ask
her if she would have dinner with him. To his surprise and joy she told
him she would be delighted to. Since then they had been seeing each
other every weekend. Today, a brisk Saturday in mid-November, they
were leaving the city for a ride in the country. They had nothing in
particular in mind, except to take a last look at fall's finery before a heavy
rain undressed the few trees still bearing cloaks of autumn gold.

Mrs. Quivaux, as King Farouk was known to the people in her neighborhood and the parishioners of her church, did not approve of Boyle because he was much older than her daughter and worse still was divorced, and therefore must certainly be excommunicated, she thought. Mrs. Quivaux followed the rules of the Catholic Church diligently. She was one of the few people in Our Lady of Perpetual Chastity parish who still did not eat meat on Friday.

"He is much too old for you," Mrs. Quivaux objected. "Besides, he was married before. He's tainted now. Would you buy second-hand clothes?"

Laura hadn't understood that. She had never been interested enough to make a distinction between new and used clothes. Perhaps that was why she had never thought very much about what Boyle had done before she met him. She knew she enjoyed being with him and let it go at that. It was only when her mother complained about him that Laura's thoughts drifted a little into what it would be like being with Boyle a month from now. But she always came back to the time she was most interested in, the here and now.

Laura was wearing a pale blue dress, partly hidden underneath her navy raincoat. Boyle was glad that neither the dress nor the coat was long enough to hide Laura's lovely legs, delightfully wrapped in off-black stockings. The dress brought out the blue of her eyes. Laura looked radiant today.

Boyle steered his old Kharman Ghia off the highway and took a country road which followed the path of a river. The sun slipped behind a bank of clouds. Boyle said it was like a day in Ireland where the sun came out for a short time, followed by dark clouds, rain, and then the sun again. They passed a sign which read:

Tice's Farms
Fresh Apples and Cider
Turn Left at the General Store

Boyle looked at Laura. "Do you want to stop? You know what they say about keeping the doctor away."

Laura smiled. Somehow the juicy flavor of an apple seemed a good match for a day like this.

"I'm in the mood for a few apples," she said.

Tice's Farms was a reflection of Keats's *season of mists and mellow fruitfulness* where the apples were bending *the mossed cottage-trees.* Everywhere Boyle and Laura turned there were apples—in bushel baskets, boxes, and on the ground. The pungent aroma of the fall fruit filled the air. In between the overflowing bushels were barrels of cider surrounded by children bearing paper cups.

"Would you like some, Laura?"

"It smells delicious," she replied.

They each drank two cups of cider and then bought a bushel basket of apples. It started to rain, so they returned to the Kharman Ghia and sat there quietly, luxuriating in the vivid aroma of the apples in the back seat.

Boyle didn't know if it were the softly falling rain or the incense of the apples which had taken on an almost aphrodisiac quality. At any rate neither spoke for several minutes, although each felt the strong communication between them. The rain began to fall a little steadier now, beating a light tattoo on the canvass roof of the convertible. Boyle reached across the seat and took Laura's hand.

"Laura—"

"Yes?"

"Do you want to come—?"

"Live with you and be your love?"

At that moment Boyle wanted nothing more, but he could not believe what the two of them had said, with an assist from Christopher Marlowe. He squeezed her hand.

Laura smiled. Somewhere in the faded rotogravure of her brain was the image of King Farouk spouting out something about the everlasting pain of Hell women suffer when they marry divorced men. But her mother only lingered there a split second. Laura was charmed by the pungent aroma of apples in the back seat, and the pleasant pressure of Boyle's hand.

There were dozens of things to talk about, countless pieces to fit together, and dreams to consider, but each remained silent, fingers entwined, lost in the mystical beauty of the lightly falling November rain. +++++

MATCHING EARRINGS

McElaney remembered that on Saturdays under the west side of the Burnside Bridge there was an open market that stretched out for several blocks down to the Williamette River. It was a crisp morning for June, so it would be fun taking a walk down through Waterfront Park and then moseying over to the market. The best way to forget that you're a long way from home was to mingle with the people where you are, McElaney told himself. He had been to the Saturday Market two summers ago and he recalled it as a pleasant experience. Nothing really happened, but maybe that's why he remembered it so fondly. He had spent the good part of a Saturday in mid-July walking by the river, watching a volleyball tournament, wolfing down a hot dog and then a double dutch chocolate cone, and sitting under an umbrella at a sidewalk cafe, drinking beer and listening to a few street singers who passed the hat around when they finished. He recalled a young blonde woman in a short tight-fitting red dress doing an imitation of Marilyn Monroe singing "The River of No Return." He wondered if she would be there again. The chances were remote, but perhaps he might see one of the waitresses who had served him the last time he was in Portland. He checked the part in his hair over the mirror by the door, told Mrs. Cantwell he was going for a walk and would not be home until early evening, and began walking along Clay Street, past the terraces and cascading water of Ira's Fountain on his way to the park.

As he approached the first stands under the girders of Burnside Bridge, it occurred to him that he might find a present for Phoebe. Her birthday was three weeks away, but if he saw something she might like, he could pick it up now, hold it for a week or so, then mail it. If he got something small, he could probably fit it in an ordinary envelope and send it by insured mail.

A woman was selling freshly baked Dutch apple pies. The sweet scent of the warm fruit and thick crust titillated McElaney's taste buds. He hadn't had breakfast and was tempted to ask the woman if he could purchase a single piece. If he bought the entire pie, he would be tempted to finish it off before the day was over. He hastened past the stand and made his way to a jewelry display.

This fellow seems to have a wide variety, McElaney thought. Since Phoebe collected pierced earrings and necklaces, he had a good chance of finding something for her here. Of course, there was always a matter of taste. He noticed a few women looking at the jewelry. If he found something he liked, he might describe Phoebe to them briefly and get their view on what might appeal to a woman of her style.

McElaney chuckled to himself. He was smiling at the irony that these women, whom he hadn't even met yet, might have a better idea of what would appeal to Phoebe than he did. Of course, it was only jewelry, but symbolically it was still interesting. Especially if they picked out something that would never have occurred to him, and Phoebe liked it.

The salesman was a short man with a friendly, but weary, countenance. McElaney judged by his graying temple and dark complexion that he was about fifty years old and a native of India or Pakistan. He looked up at McElaney as soon as he approached the stand.

"May I help you, sir?"

"I'm looking for a necklace. Not for me."

The man smiled and so did McElaney. He wondered why he had found it necessary to explain that costume jewelry was not his style.

"Your wife, perhaps? I have some nice 14 caret necklaces over here."

"Actually, it's for my daughter. She's 28 years old and the mother of a three-year-old girl and—"

McElaney smiled again. He was a little off-the-wall to ask this fellow to select a necklace based on the age of his granddaughter.

"I see," the merchant said thoughtfully. "Perhaps—"

"My daughter likes unusual things. She not only wears them, but she collects them."

"Would you like something so different that there is little chance that she has ever seen anything like it before?"

"Well, yes. That sounds interesting."

"This way, please."

The vendor led McElaney to the far side of his stand. On the way they passed the three women who had been examining earrings and cuff links. They stared curiously at McElaney as he passed them.

"This might interest you, sir. Imported from India. Brass beads corroded by acid and strung by dental floss. Does the color of the corroded beads look familiar to you?"

"Why, yes. It reminds me of something, but I can't place it."

"Maybe it is because we are about 3,000 miles from it now. You are from New York, perhaps?"

"New Jersey."

"Ah, good. I was thinking of something that lies right between New York and New Jersey."

"The Statue of Liberty!" one of the other shoppers exclaimed. She was a young woman with light brown hair, wearing a blue flowered summer dress.

"That's right," McElaney agreed. "I knew that color looked familiar. But you corrode them deliberately. I like the effect."

"I was struck by it myself," the woman in the flowered dress said. "I'm a little older than your daughter, but if she likes things that are different, I am sure she will find this delightful. It would go well with outfits of almost any color."

"Did you import them from India?" McElaney asked.

"The brass beads," the merchant said. "But I made the rest of the necklace myself."

McElaney took it and held the beads up to the light. It was curious that one could corrode something and make it beautiful, he thought.

"Is your daughter athletic?" the vendor asked.

"Why, yes, she is. She played field hockey in college. Why do you ask?"

He shrugged his shoulders.

"I don't know. The thought just popped into my head."

"If she's athletic, she might like something like that," the woman in the flowered dress said.

The vendor saw McElaney's confusion.

I don't think this lady means that your daughter would be apt to play tennis in it. Possibly she means that this seems the type of necklace an athletic woman would likely wear when she was relaxing."

McElaney nodded. He could see the point of the vendor and the woman. There was something basically simple and yet refreshing about the necklace. He could picture Phoebe wearing it with a strapless cocktail dress on a cool summer evening after she had spent a day swimming in the ocean.

"How much?" he asked.

"Thirty-five dollars. Plus the tax."

"Fair enough," McElaney replied. "You don't by any chance have matching earrings, do you?"

"I'm sorry," the dealer said. "I had one pair, but someone bought it from me as soon as I opened this morning. You said you're from New Jersey?"

"Yes."

"Are you going to be in the area for awhile?"

"Just until tomorrow night. I'm coming back to Portland in a month or so, but I wanted to send these to my daughter for her birthday."

"I can make you another pair, but I won't have the chance to do it until some time next week."

"That's O.K. The necklace is fine. I just thought as long as I—"

The vendor reached down under his counter for a pad.

"If you would like to give me your daughter's address, I can mail the earrings to her when I finish them. You want the same color?"

"Yes. Well, that's awfully nice of you. Here, let me pay you for them. And the postage, of course. How much do I owe you?"

"Please. Just pay me for the necklace. $37.45. The earrings will probably be about the same price, but let's wait until your daughter receives them. Then you can send me a check. Here is my card. My name is Patel. Richard Patel."

"Really. I have no objection to paying for the earrings now. I'll be doing that eventually anyhow."

Patel took the slip of paper from McElaney and slipped it into the cash register.

"In this world nothing is absolute," he said. "I have plenty of material and I will have the time next week to do it. But just in case something comes up, it is better that I do not take the money until the job is completed."

"Well, that certainly is nice of you. And this way she will be getting two packages in the mail."

"You won't be giving the necklace to her in person?"

McElaney shook his head.

Patel looked a little sad. He seemed on the point of saying something to McElaney, but apparently changed his mind at the last minute. To distract attention from himself, he opened the cash register and took out the address McElaney had given him and copied it down on his little pad. Then he ripped the sheet out, folded it up, and placed it in his wallet.

"My memory is starting to slip," he explained. "I find I always need an extra copy of every piece of paper that is important to me. In that way I have two chances, if I forget where I put it. It seems like lately I have been drinking daily from the River Lethe. The curse of old age."

"You don't look very old," McElaney observed.

"What you look and what you feel, my friend, are two different things. I am 52, but I confess that I feel twenty years older."

McElaney had put the necklace in his pocket and was about to leave, but for some reason he hesitated. He had the impression that this man wanted to talk. The three women seemed to sense it too, for they moved on, the woman in the flowered dress smiling at McElaney and telling him she hoped his daughter enjoyed the necklace.

"Maybe you need a little holiday. A friend of mine used to say that besides their regular vacations, all people should take a few extra days off a year for their health—for their mental health, she meant. It is hard to gauge what all this stress does to a person—up early every morning, running the rat race all day long, and then trying to cram a few hours of relaxation at the end of the day."

The vendor smiled, but without joy. It reminded McElaney of a baby's laugh when it was suffering from gas.

"I can't take a few days off."

"That what most busy people say, but I bet if they stopped doing whatever they thought was so necessary, the sun would still rise in the East the next morning."

"But with me, it is impossible," Patel said. "This is my busiest season. When people are on vacation, they tend to buy more. I'm going to be picking up my imports and dipping my jewelry from Monday till I set up my stand again next week. "

McElaney sighed.

"Maybe you'll get a chance to take it easy in the winter."

"That's when I go to the Florida flea markets."

"Well, I must say you do nice work. Perhaps you should charge more for your jewelry. It seems that necklace would sell for much more than $35 in a store."

Instead of answering, the merchant stared over McElaney's shoulder for a moment or two.

"I need a liver transplant, but I can't risk the operation because of my sugar."

The man's remark seemed to hang on the air like a spider on a thin web. McElaney realized the man wasn't working for money, but for life.

"Everyone gets satisfaction in different ways," Patel said. "I have no family—just a few distant relatives back in India—so I don't really need the money. If I keep the prices reasonable, people buy my jewelry and that's what I like. Each of us has something to do, I suppose, and my job is making jewelry. It gives me pleasure, even as it frustrates me."

McElaney nodded. Having made his point, he didn't know what else to say. He told the vendor he would be dropping him a check in the mail when the earrings arrived and that he would be back in a month or so to Portland and would probably be taking another stroll to the market.

"Will you be here?" McElaney asked.

Patel smiled.

"That's the heart of my busy season," he said.

"Perhaps I shall see you again then," McElaney said.

"Perhaps."

McElaney tipped his cap and made his way to the street to the north of the trolley station where he had visited the outdoor cafes and listened to the street singers. He wondered if he would see the woman who did Marilyn Monroe imitations.

***

McElaney had almost been tempted to bring the necklace to Phoebe himself. He had toyed with the idea for a moment, and then rejected it. For one thing, even if he had visited Phoebe before her birthday, there was always a good chance that her mother might have been there. And even if he had been lucky enough to catch Phoebe alone, he doubted if she would have cared for a visit. The mail was much less complicated. He had dropped her a little note with the necklace and asked how she, Jim, and little Cynthia were getting on. This way she would know that he had remembered and maybe she might actually be glad to hear from him. As the days passed without a word from Phoebe, he realized he was being an optimist; she had rarely responded to any of the notes or little gifts he had sent her over the years.

He used to be annoyed when she didn't answer his letters. His view at the time had been that if anyone should have been miffed, it should have been he. He had divorced her *mother*, not Phoebe. And after the divorce he had tried his darndest to continue the warm relationship they had enjoyed before. But it wasn't easy, because every time he had taken her out when she was a teenager, she had begun the evening by acting as if she had been programmed by her mother to be indifferent to him. In all honesty, he told himself, it might have been his imagination. But in those days he couldn't get over the observation that she was hostile when he first picked her up, but pleasant and even friendly when it was time to bring her back home, especially when she had been with him for a week or so.

These days he really didn't care for a response. He had gotten used to her attitude and discovered it had its advantages. There was no emotion or hysteria this way. At least when he wrote the letters, he couldn't be interrupted. Every now and then he found himself wishing that she would reply once in awhile, but he thought it would be silly to stop writing to her because she didn't answer his letters. He wrote to her because he wanted to. That was clear enough.

Suddenly it dawned upon him that for once he might have to call her to see if she had received his present. Not the necklace, but the earrings, which Patel, the vendor in Portland, should have sent to her two weeks ago, around the time of her birthday. He had forgotten about the earrings. Maybe he should assume Patel had mailed them on and just pay him. He fished in his wallet for the vendor's address and began to write a check for $37.45, when for some unaccountable reason he stopped and tore it up. Why, after all these years, he had decided to visit Phoebe was beyond him. To see if she got the earrings seemed like such a feeble excuse. He would call to check if she was home first. But when he picked up the phone, he found himself asking the attendant at the airport the time of the next plane to Boston.

***

It had not been so bad. Phoebe had been surprised to see him after all these years. He couldn't say that she was pleasant or unpleasant. Jim was away at a sales convention, so McElaney suspected she was glad for a little company. He had had fun playing piggyback with little Cynthia, who surprised him with the extent of her vocabulary. He asked Phoebe if she remembered when he played piggyback with her, but instead of replying she left to check something in the kitchen. She did seem to like the necklace. It was the first thing he had given her in years that she had acknowledged. He was explaining to her about the way Patel the vendor from Portland used acid to discolor the brass beads when he remembered why he had come.

"No, Dad, I didn't receive any earrings. Just the necklace."

A week later when he was on assignment in San Francisco, he called Phoebe to see if the earrings had arrived. She told him they hadn't, but that she had worn the necklace to a neighbor's dinner party and several people complimented her on it. Father and daughter chatted aimlessly for a few minutes. When Phoebe began replying to his questions in monosyllables, McElaney told her he would check with Patel on the earrings. He was about to hang up when his daughter asked him to wait so she could bring Cynthia to the phone. He talked to his granddaughter for nearly a half-hour until she accidentally disconnected him.

After he hung up, he tried the phone number Patel had given him, but there was no answer. Off and on over the next two days, he called the number, but the phone just kept on ringing. He was going back to Portland over the weekend. He thought he would stop in at the market and see what had happened. The night he flew to Oregon, he called Phoebe to tell her he was still on the trail of the earrings. She laughed. It was the first time he had heard her do that in years.

"I'm not the only one who is interested to see if you locate those earrings, you know," Phoebe said.

"I don't understand."

"Little Cynthia is always playing with my necklace. I told her I might have matching earrings some day, and she kept screaming 'I wanna wear the ear-drops.' Somehow she has confused Jim's Vicks nose drops with my earrings."

This time McElaney laughed. When he hung up, Phoebe told Jim that she had almost forgotten how her father sounded when he wasn't serious.

***

McElaney could hear the rain pounding on Mrs. Cantwell's roof when he woke up. The weatherman had predicted clearing later in the morning, so McElaney decided to get a little more rest before he set out for the market by the bus depot. When he went back to sleep he dreamed that Phoebe and Cynthia were flying through the air with him on the back of Superman, who dropped them off in front of the outdoor cafe where the woman was doing a Marilyn Monroe imitation. When he let go of Superman's cloak and took a good look at him, he saw that it was really Mr. Patel, the jewelry merchant. McElaney was surprised to see that his temples were no longer graying and that his eyes did not seem tired or troubled.

Mrs. Cantwell insisted that he have bacon and eggs before he left.

"You never eat a thing, Mr. McElaney. I know what's going to happen. You'll get hungry and stuff yourself with hot dogs and ice cream cones. That's not the way to be living, y'know. You need some good solid food, especially with this strange weather we have been having. Rain, sunshine, hot, cold. Now sit down there next to Mr. Peterson."

By the time he finished a second helping of scrambled eggs, and a third coffee, the skies had cleared. McElaney thanked his hostess and made his way down Burnside Street, past Powell's Bookstore, to the market. Patel wasn't in his usual place. He toured all the stands, looking carefully at the jewelry counters in the event that Patel might be bending down to get merchandise. But none of the other stands had wares as exotic as Patel's. He turned quickly at a light tap on his shoulder.

"Pardon me, but are you Mr. McElaney?"

It was a short heavyset woman with blonde-gray hair. McElaney recognized her as the person who ran the bakery counter.

"Why, yes."

"Mr. Patel asked me to keep an eye out for you."

"As a matter of fact, I was looking for him. Is he—?"

The woman shook her head sadly.

"He's in Good Samaritan Hospital. I'm afraid he's in a bad way. He has a problem with his sugar."

"That's too bad. I was trying to get him to slow down when I saw him last. So it doesn't look good for him?"

"I saw him this morning. He's in the intensive care unit. Anyway, he asked me to give you these."

It was the brass earrings. Patel had treated them to match the green of the necklace McElaney had given Phoebe.

"Oh, they are very beautiful. My daughter had been looking forward to these. I'll write you a check for Mr. Patel."

The woman waved his checkbook away.

"Mr. Patel said he wanted them to be his birthday present to your daughter."

"B-but."

"Really, Mr. McElaney, he has no use for money now."

McElaney nodded.

"I suspect he never had," he said. "When did he make the earrings?"

"The day before yesterday. He had started them before, but something kept coming up. He finished them in the hospital."

McElaney reached for his pen and the little pad he always carried with him.

"Could I have his floor and room number in the hospital? I should go there and thank him. And see how he is."

"That would be nice, Mr. McElaney. He has no relatives, you know. But if he is still in intensive care, they may not let you see him. It's Room 418. Fourth floor."

McElaney thanked her and walked towards the river, looking for a cab. He passed a pay telephone in the street and dialed Phoebe. She answered on the second ring.

"You've located the earrings?"

"Yes, Phoebe, as a matter of fact I—"

"Dad?"

"Yes?"

"Is the man who made the earrings all right? Mr. Patel?'

"I'm not sure, Phoebe. I'm going to see him now. What made you ask about him?"

"I-I don't know, Dad. Just a feeling I had. He's in a hospital?"

"Yes. Do you—?"

"Do I *what*?"

"Oh, nothing, Phoebe. I just thought you might have another feeling. How's Cynthia?"

"I dare not tell her about the earrings. She's been asking me for her nose-drops all day. Oh, Dad..."

"Yes, Phoebe."

"I-I think everything is going to be all right."

McElaney hung up the phone and hailed a taxi.

"Good Samaritan Hospital, please," he said. +++++

FROM FLAUBERT....WITH LOVE
(For Patricia)

L ike most living creatures, Flaubert did not particularly welcome death. When he had difficulty breathing and found it a burden to get to his feet, Flaubert realized that his time was up. He knew Tricia and Tom Bardell, the two humans he lived with, would have a hard time carrying him to their car because he had been gaining weight lately, so Flaubert fought the good fight and struggled to his feet. Before the Bardells' amazed eyes he managed to get up, walk across the kitchen to the back porch, descend the six steps to the driveway, and climb into the old Ford Taurus.

It was three in the morning and no vets were available, so the Bardells drove Flaubert to the all-night animal emergency hospital in Watertown. The vet, a tall woman in her early thirties, did not seem optimistic. She asked an aide to help her wheel Flaubert into the X-ray center, leaving the Bardells to wait anxiously. It did not take the vet long to come back with her diagnosis.

"I'm afraid cancer has spread throughout his body."

"B-but he seemed fine earlier today. We were playing Frisbee with him this evening."

"Golden retrievers are very stoical. They endure pain without complaining. He probably went after the Frisbee to please you."

"H-how long does he have?" asked Tricia, her voice trembling.

"A day possibly. Then again he may not last through the morning."

Flaubert looked up at them. His eyes seemed to say that he understood the helplessness of the situation. In human terms at least. The vet left so the Bardells could ponder the awful decision they had to make.

***

It had been a peaceful death for Flaubert cradled in Tricia's arms. Even in that split second as life was drifting into eternity, Flaubert knew what he had to do. And he looked forward to the challenge.

Now dreamers and optimists may think that Flaubert wound up in some kind of a Doggy Heaven. That did not happen, of course, although Flaubert made a speedy trip to another dimension. It was not, as the dreamers would imagine and hope for, a land of unlimited bones and people crackers. Nor were there great fields to run through and endless Frisbees to chase, each one flying just inches over the dogs' noses so that catching them were as easy as eating—if you will excuse the expression—a hot dog. Actually there was no food in the land Flaubert was flying to because in this Canine Utopia there was also no doggy-do, so the animals never had anything to be embarrassed about. Here the term *pooper-scooper* was an anachronism.

What Flaubert encountered was something he had always suspected when he was living life as a dog on earth: this new life did away with all the patronizing towards dogs that even decent human custodians condescended to. No more humiliations such as the orders to sit, beg, stay and come. No more baby-talk such as "Nice little doggie; give me your itsy-bitsy paw, Sweetheart." Not that Flaubert and all the other dogs in this Canine Hideaway were unappreciative of the intentions of their former custodians; they realized the limitations of the human brain. After all, these so-called "owners" were living in a world of politicians, tax-collectors, and dog-catchers. The dogs in Canine Utopia were ever grateful for the love and affection they had received in an imperfect world. No, the experience on earth was interesting and it was a wonderful feeling to be in loving hands, Flaubert reflected, but now it was time to enjoy a new experience.

***

One of the things Flaubert liked about his new adventure was being able to learn without being taught. He appreciated the training that Tricia and Tom had deemed necessary to give him as a pup, but he found it much more fun to find out things for himself up here. No more was there the danger of causing grief to Tom or Tricia by an overzealous act, such as chewing the leg of a mahogany table or biting into the complete works of Shakespeare. Up here he could devour a good book the way humans did, and he soon discovered that reading was one of the few pleasures of mankind that was worth emulating.

He discovered the canine library on his own and was soon racing through works as diversified as Chekhov and Chickamatsu. He found that he not only could read in the language that gave him his name, but also in Russian, Japanese, and all the languages of the seven continents of the world below.

Flaubert, of course, was partial to his namesake and to the many great writers of France from Molière and Rabelais to Giraudoux and Camus. He would hear Tricia and Tom talking about them and couldn't understand why they did not read some of their works to him. They knew that he couldn't read at the time, having never gone to school since formal elementary education was restricted to children. How ironic, he mused! Dogs with endless curiosity were deprived of formal education while children—most of whom, at least—with tons of free books at their disposal paid for by the city and state, seldom showed an inclination to read even the most intriguing works.

Now that Flaubert had loads of time, no longer being obliged to chase Frisbees and tennis balls, he snuggled up on an ethereal couch, not unlike the ones courtesans were wont to recline on down in the world below, and opened up *Madame Bovary,* feeling an obligation to begin with his namesake's most famous work. He moved on to Gide, Sartre, Beckett, and Camus and then to the playwrights, reading aloud all the parts of Giraudoux's *Madwoman of Chaillot* and Molière's *Tartuffe* to the amusement of two cocker spaniels and an Irish wolfhound.

Much as he enjoyed his new estate, Flaubert did not forget his friends from Planet Earth. He knew how sad Tricia and Tom were when he had to leave so suddenly. Both of them loved to stand on their back porch and toss his beat-up old yellow Frisbee to him. How happy it made them feel when he leaped high in the air bringing it down like an outfielder gloving a baseball just before it cleared the center field fence! Flaubert remembered well the joyful expressions on their faces when he raced back to them with the Frisbee between his teeth. It doesn't take much to amuse humans, he mused.

Still, he had to admit that he enjoyed pleasing them. And the doggie biscuits that followed his sensational catches weren't bad either. Every now and then he would peep down from under a canine-shaped cloud to see how they were doing. They looked so downhearted. He was flattered, of course, that they cared so much for him and his memory, but he did not want to see them so depressed. Who would ever think that his racing ten miles an hour to pull down a Frisbee would make them so happy? He was almost tempted to go back down there for an hour or so and catch a few for them. But that would be only temporary and when he had to leave, they would be saddened again. No, he would have to come up with something better. Something more lasting. He was determined to employ all the new knowledge he was gathering in this Canine Utopia. Although he had not the slightest idea how he could help them, he was confident that with a little research he would come up with a plan. For a start he would read Brecht, the Bardells' favorite writer. He selected *Galileo* from the Canine Library.

When he finished reading the play, he sighed the sigh of a reflective golden retriever. Shakespeare's Puck was right when he noted "What fools these mortals be!" Galileo had made his point as clear as a star-lit night: the earth revolved around the sun, not the sun around the earth. Of course, it was easy to see this from up here, but Galileo had let them see for themselves through his marvelous telescope. But the obvious is sometimes the most difficult to understand.

Hmm, Flaubert sighed again, but this time a more cognitive sigh. What is the obvious way to make Tricia and Tom happy again? To bring me back, of course. But that is not feasible, Flaubert realized. Still...

He went back to the library and began reading biographies of his namesake, coming to the conclusion that the more he knew about the other Flaubert, the better the chance he would have of helping the Bardells. There must be a clue somewhere in the writer's background. And so he read on, determined to be the universe's best-read student of Gustave Flaubert. Hmm, he sighed again. It was a lucky thing for him that the Bardells' did not give him that first name too.

The more he read of the several biographies of the writer Flaubert, the more the canine Flaubert kept seeing references to that famous short story writer and novelist, Guy de Maupassant. How curious, he thought. Apparently the writer was a close friend of de Maupassant's mother. A *very* close friend, it seemed. Hmmm. Apparently for that reason the writer Flaubert took de Maupassant under his wing, helped him to become one of France's best-known writers. How nice of his namesake, Flaubert the golden retriever mused.

He treated de Maupassant as if the younger writer were his own son.

But wait! Perhaps he *was* his own son.

The dog Flaubert became a bit shocked by his own discovery because he recognized that made him...But no, it was his *namesake* who could well have been the father of a bastard. A splendid bastard at that, judging by the many famous short stories he created.

Flaubert needed time to think so he took a walk along Canine Boulevard. He could feel he was on the very edge of things...just a synapse or two away from a plan to help his old friends, Tricia and Tom. Now if I followed the boudoir steps of my namesake and fathered a son, he thought, I would have a golden retriever puppy to send down to the Bardells. They wouldn't have me, of course, but they would have something close to me.

Flaubert sighed. Ah, if it were only that simple. Mating would not be a problem because he had seen a beautiful golden retriever bitch strolling along Dogwood Drive. But just like the U.S. Postal Service back on earth, shipping would be a hassle. After she had the puppy, how could he make sure that little Guy de Maupassant—for that is what he would have the Bardells call him—would land safely in New Jersey. Especially with all the heavy air and motor traffic the state was experiencing lately. He decided to take a little nap and sleep on it.

He awoke, breathless, having chased three hundred battered yellow Frisbees at the same time. What a dream! There is no getting away from the past, Flaubert mumbled as he rubbed the sleep out of his eyes. Three hundred Frisbees! He was tempted to sigh *Wow!* But he had a few days ago taken that interjection out of his vocabulary because *Wow!* was the second half of his old doggie expression and he was a sophisticate now.

Three hundred Frisb—That's it," Flaubert cried out, wakening a snoring St. Bernard in the process. "But I only need one."

It didn't take long for Flaubert to find a shiny new yellow Frisbee. He sunk his teeth into it and twisted it about a bit until it was a little frazzled around the edges. Then he collected some old leaves and mud to rub into the Frisbee to mellow it a bit. The next step was that beautiful bitch from Dogwood Drive. That was the easy part.

***

A few months later everything was in place. Flaubert fetched the nicely aged yellow Frisbee in his left front paw, for he was a southpaw, and sent it flying into the universe. Next came the gorgeous puppy, almost as handsome as he, Flaubert reflected. Off went Guy de Maupassant into the universe after the Frisbee, heading straight for the back porch of the home of the Bardells. Flaubert could hardly wait to see the expressions on Tom and Tricia's faces as the young puppy came dashing into view. Gifted with the splendid genes he inherited from his father, Guy de Maupassant would probably catch the Frisbee just before it reached the first step. +++++

TRANSFER

Morgan checked his watch. 10:20. The bus was already seven minutes late. It was supposed to arrive at Kinzer Junction at 11:55 in time to transfer to the midnight train heading for the city, according to the timetable. That was playing it close. He wondered if the train would wait if the bus were late. How frustrating it would be, if after all their planning, one little glitch should wreck everything.

It began to rain, so he huddled under the tiny wooden shelter the bus company provided. Fortunately it was not coming down hard. Still the rain added to the sense of loneliness he felt standing there in the darkness at the point where five winding country roads met.

When he was not looking down the road for the Quakertown bus, Morgan was glancing at the road behind him where his house lay nearly two miles back. It had taken him nearly a half hour to make his way here on foot. All the time he had been looking over his shoulder whenever a car passed by. It was doubtful, of course, that Susan would be on this road. She had called him at work to say she was leaving for her gun club meeting in Cedarville, and that was ten miles in the other direction. Still, she had been suspicious of him lately and might have just driven north up the road a quarter of a mile and waited until he left the house so she could follow him. But only six cars had passed down his lonely road in the last half hour and none of them had been Susan's Audi. Morgan told himself if she were following him, he would have seen her Audi by now.

In the distance to the east he saw a light flicker on the horizon. It had to be a truck or his bus, Morgan thought, because it seemed too bright a light for an automobile. He moved out of the tiny bus shelter to get a better look. It was not a truck. As it came closer he could see the familiar roof lights of the Quakertown bus. At last. He was finally on his way.

"Do you think we will make the train at Kinzer Junction?" he asked as he boarded the bus.

The driver, his eyes weary from straining to see through the wind and rain, now coming down heavier, responded with a grunt.

"If this damn rain eases up."

***

Morgan pulled his raincoat collar around his ears and made his way down the aisle. He felt relieved when he did not recognize any of the passengers, most of whom seemed to be drowsing. The only one who looked up at Morgan was a rather thin passenger in dark glasses and a long olive green raincoat with a black cap pulled down to the eyes. Why would anyone wear sunglasses at night, Morgan wondered. He was glad that there were but a handful of passengers on the bus. Not many folks in Kincaid County traveled at this time of night. Morgan went to the very back of the bus and took a seat by the window. The only other passengers in the vicinity were an elderly man with a cane and a heavy-set woman in her early fifties who was sitting directly in front of him. She was sound asleep. Morgan felt a little less nervous. He was safe back here, he mused. No one could see him and from his position in the rear he could keep his eyes on everyone in the bus.

He rubbed his forehead with his handkerchief. It had been close to freezing outside but he had been perspiring profusely. He told himself to be calm. He had passed the first phase without any problems. If he could just control his nerves, everything would be all right.

So far so good. He had worried about the possibility, albeit a remote one, that someone who knew Susan and him might be on the bus. Of course, one of the sleeping passengers might be a friend of Susan's that he had never met. Once in a while a few of the women from the Kincaid Ladies Gun Club would pop in the house with Susan after target practice, but he had never paid much attention to them. They seemed to him the antithesis of the concept of *ladies.* They reminded him more of burly truck drivers who rode 18-wheelers from coast-to-coast. By contrast Susan looked like a beauty queen. She still had the same trim figure, limpid blue eyes, and the appearance of a winsome personality. Yes, Susan easily gave the impression of an easy-going beautiful young woman, Morgan mused. That was the Susan he thought he had fallen in love with, but it did not take long before he realized that behind that naïve façade was a shrewd, cold woman. It had taken only a few months for Morgan to discover this, but for reasons he still could not fathom, he had stayed in the marriage for these past seven years. He wondered if the women from the Kincaid Ladies Gun Club saw Susan as he saw her.

Well, it was doubtful if any of Susan's gun friends were here now. He had not seen any big burly women as he walked down the aisle of the bus. He would watch carefully at the next stop as new passengers came aboard. But so far so good. It was at least twenty minutes before they would stop at Digby Falls. He might as well try to relax.

The only one he wasn't absolutely sure of was that thin guy in the black cap and long olive green raincoat. He didn't look familiar, Morgan told himself, but in the dim lighting of the bus it was difficult to get a good look at him, especially with those dark glasses on. Could he be one of Susan's friends from the gun club?—but no, he didn't look like a guy who got his rocks off with shotguns and six-shooters. He was probably someone with sensitive eyes. Morgan told himself to stop worrying. Everything was going to work out. The most important thing was for the bus to meet the train on time. All sorts of things could happen before it got there—flat tire, engine breakdown, even a highjacking. But these possibilities were remote. The Quakertown bus took this route every evening and, as far as he knew, it had always met the train on time.

Suddenly the heavy-set woman in front of him whirled around and faced Morgan. He was tempted to bury his face in his hands so that she could not recognize him, but instead he stood up and faced her.

"Is there anything wrong, madam?"

"I-I must have been dreaming. It was so real. The bus had an awful accident and we were trapped inside. I was trying to get out and somebody was holding me down so I couldn't move. It was awful. I—"

Morgan eyed her carefully. Her face was definitely not familiar. He felt reasonably certain that this woman did not know anything about him. Of course, her story about the dream might have been a ruse to get a good look at him.

"I can assure you, Madame, that you were in fact dreaming. The Quakertown bus is in good hands and we are going to meet the train on time."

***

The heavy-set woman in front of him had fallen back to sleep again. Just about every passenger had dozed off. Morgan gazed out the window. The rain was really coming down now and the driver was moving his vehicle cautiously. The Quakertown bus traveled mostly on winding country roads, and even experienced drivers had difficulty staying on the road when the weather was treacherous. For the first time Morgan wondered if taking this trip was a mistake. The woman's dream had unnerved him. It was almost impossible to see anything out the window on these narrow, twisting roads. He wished he could be like the other passengers and fall asleep and leave the worrying to the driver. And even if he made it to Kinzer Junction safely, would he be there in time to meet the train?

Morgan tried to shake the negative thoughts out of his head. After all, what he was doing was exciting and mysterious. Amy said people might compare him to Ambrose Bierce, the American writer who at 77 disappeared to either Mexico or Europe and was never heard from again, or to Judge Crater, who left his office in the afternoon and never returned. Susan, of course, would make a fuss when she realized that he had left her, but in his note he had assured her that he wanted nothing but his freedom. She could have everything, he said—the house, their stocks and bonds, her Audi, his BMW, and several thousand dollars in their Cash Management Account. All he had taken for himself was a thousand dollars from their savings account. He felt he had been absolutely fair to Susan.

He found himself wondering again why they had stayed together these seven miserable years. On his part he suspected it was the fear of change. Unhappy as he was, he had a fixed routine and he never dreamed of just picking up and leaving. He sometimes thought he might have had masochistic tendencies and got some sort of perverted pleasure in his daily arguments with Susan. But there were times when the constant tension in their relationship was affecting his work at the bank. Or was he rationalizing? Maybe it was because many of the couples the Morgans socialized with had similar marital problems and he thought this was a basic part of life. After all, he had a good job, an expensive Tudor-style house with twelve rooms—more than they needed—and ample savings.

And yet he might never have slipped out of his house late on a rainy evening, leaving his wife, home, and his prestigious position as first vice president of a prosperous bank if it were not for Amy. Ah, Amy!

They had met under the most commonplace of circumstances. He had stopped in the Kincaid County Library to do a little research on a relatively unknown geometric figure, the *tesseract*, as a favor to the president of the bank, whose pampered son had been assigned a term paper on it and was in danger of being thrown out of Penfield Prep, an exclusive private school, if he did not get his assignments in on time. It was not the first time Morgan had been asked to do little chores for his boss. Sometimes it was humiliating, but it got him the position of first vice president.

Morgan had not the slightest idea what a *tesseract* was, so he began by looking it up in the dictionary. Not finding it there, he wondered if he had the right spelling. He tried it with a single *s* and still couldn't find it. He was in the process of checking a second dictionary when he heard amused laughter over his shoulder. He knew before he looked up that it was a woman. Her perfume was sweet as honeysuckle, yet with a hint of the exotic. When he turned around he saw a stunning young woman with vivid blue-violet eyes, dressed in a white turtleneck and a dark blue skirt.

"They just don't make dictionaries the way they used to," she said, still laughing softly.

Morgan was struck by the amazing beauty of this young woman. Normally a taciturn man except when dealing with bank business, he could not resist the opportunity of speaking to her. Her eyes were twinkling mischievously, and this relaxed him.

"Do you happen to know what a *tesseract* is?"

Amy smiled. "Of course. Doesn't everyone know that? It is a four-dimensional shape analogous to a cube. In two dimensions there is a square, in three dimensions a cube, and in four dimensions a *tesseract*, or hypercube."

Morgan could not suppress his surprise and admiration.

"H-how did you know that?"

Amy moved closer to Morgan, the tip of her skirt brushing slightly against his knee as she sat down. He felt a sudden warm glow all over.

"Elementary, my dear Watson. I am a woman of many dimensions. In some districts I'm known as the *Tesseract Kid*."

Morgan had never had an encounter as casual as this.

"But it's such an unusual word. I thought—"

Amy smiled again. "You thought? Boy, you are one serious guy. You have to be careful. *Thinking* can get you in a lot of trouble. Look what happened to Galileo."

***

And that's how it started. Just a few friendly verbal bouts in the Kincaid County Library. After that Morgan visited the library every chance he could in the hope of running into the *tesseract woman,* as he referred to her in his mind, but to no avail. He even tried to get some information on her from the librarian by pretending she had accidentally left a book with him, but Ms. Ivors, ever conscious of the library's code of maintaining the privacy of its borrowers, told Morgan politely that although she thought she knew the woman he was describing, she could not disclose her name or address. Embarrassed, Morgan smiled weakly and told her he understood perfectly.

And so he kept visiting the library in search of her, as the Chekhov character had looked for the woman who had unwittingly kissed him in a dark room. It seemed a fruitless search until, seeking a way to get away from Susan in the evenings, he hit upon the idea of joining the local health club. He was in fairly good shape but thought he should lose five pounds or so. For a week he followed a regimen of back, leg and hip exercises, fighting off boredom by reminding himself that it was still better than sitting near the sullen stare of Susan in the evenings. Then one night, while on his way to the water fountain, it happened.

There on one of the stationary bicycles, pedaling furiously, her golden hair swishing in rhythm with her flailing legs, was Morgan's *Tesseract Woman.* Despite himself, he stared at her in wonder. She smiled at him.

"Oh hi there. Where's your dictionary?"

"I-I—"

"Your problem, Dearie, is you don't know whether to exercise your brain or your body," she said, sliding off the bicycle and wiping the perspiration from her forehead. "Actually I think cerebral workouts are easier than physical ones, don't you?"

"Do you come here often?" Morgan asked.

"I try to make it three nights a week. I'll be back Monday night. See you."

***

Morgan was there Monday. And several other Mondays, Wednesdays, and Fridays. While working out on the machines he would watch Amy doing stretching exercises on the mat and marvel at her lithe figure. He was so infatuated with his *Tesseract Woman* that it was a while before he realized that in many ways Amy was similar to Susan—in looks and figure. Oh, Susan is still beautiful, he told himself, but what a difference in personality! He had worked up the courage to chat with Amy, at first for a few minutes, and then later for as long as a half hour while they exercised, side by side. It did not matter much what they talked about: just to be with Amy, to breathe her perfume, to bask in her smile was enough for Morgan, who had not experienced anything that might have passed for romance since his first date with Susan when they were lovers instead of antagonists.

When he was home in bed and Susan was fast asleep, he would fantasize what it would be like to spend an evening with Amy, walking arm-in-arm through the streets of the city en route to an expensive restaurant. And after dinner, well…Morgan's fantasy had several variations every time he brought Amy into his secret world.

The fantasies became so vivid that he could barely stand them any more. He had to bring them to fruition. For two weeks he thought of ways to ask her out. He was new to the gym, so no one there knew he was married. Amy, of course, could be married, but he had never seen her in the company of a man, other than the trainers who stopped to chat with her from time to time.

One Friday night after exercising for twenty minutes on adjoining stationary bikes, Amy leaned over and whispered.

"Think we need a break from our workouts?"

"I-er."

"You look like you do, Howard. I know a nice quiet place where we can relax over a few white wines. I'll take a quick shower and see you in the parking lot. I know where you park your BMW."

And so this was the first of several clandestine visits to *L'Énigme,* a cozy little cocktail lounge in Pittstown, a tiny village on the outskirts of Kincaid County. When they were together, Morgan lost all track of the time. He soon realized he was never happier in his life. When he returned home Susan sensed the difference in him and badgered him with questions of his whereabouts, something she had never previously concerned herself with. But Morgan left no clues—no lipstick on his collar or a vague scent of exotic perfume on his body, for the only intimacies he had shared with Amy were the long, sometimes profound, talks on poetry, art, music, literature and the joy of living day by day. So involved was Morgan in each intense *tête-à-tête* with Amy that he never even bothered to ask her last name, if she were married, and if she worked. She did mention in passing that she was a photographer.

Then suddenly his relationship with Amy took a sharp turn. After one wine at the *L'Énigme* she reached out for Morgan's hand and whispered softly.

"Come."

She handed him her coat and he helped her slip it on. To his surprise one of Kincaid County's four taxis was waiting in front of the entrance to *L'Énigme*. The driver opened the door and Amy gestured for Morgan to get in.

"B-but my car is—"

Before he could protest further, Amy slipped her arms around Morgan and kissed him warmly on the lips. The cab driver started up without asking for a destination. He knew where he was going.

***

The bus was slowing down, causing a few passengers to stir in their seats.

"Digby Falls, everyone. Next stop Kinzer Junction."

Five passengers alighted from the bus, including the heavy-set woman who had been sitting in front of him and the elderly man with the cane. Two rather stout women in their early forties boarded the bus, busily talking. They took seats directly behind the driver. Susan had a few friends in Digby Falls, but Morgan had never seen these two women before. He was safe. Just as the bus was about to take off a tall and slender woman in a blue raincoat and flowing blonde hair falling from a man-style fedora climbed aboard. As she came closer, Morgan gasped.

"Amy! What—"

The woman looked at Morgan curiously.

"I beg your pardon?" she asked.

Morgan stared hard at the woman. At first glance he had been convinced that it was Amy, even though she was not supposed to be here. In the dim light of the bus she seemed to have the same high cheekbones as Amy. But her voice was different. There was a thickness in it, the gravelly sound that comes from smoking too many cigarettes. And Amy didn't smoke. Taking a second glance, he realized her eyes were not violet-blue like Amy's.

"I'm sorry, but you looked just like someone I know."

The woman shrugged and turned around to take a seat near the front of the bus, across from the man with the dark glasses. The driver peered out at the Digby Falls bus shelter and started up his bus.

Morgan found himself shaking. Why would he think that Amy would be on the bus when she said she would meet him on the train? Was it because there were times that Amy was unpredictable to him? She often talked of her girlfriend, Margie, from Peggy's Cove, Nova Scotia, who had a small plane and was going to met them and fly them to Canada. Once or twice Morgan found himself jealous of a woman he had never met. But Amy could not be a lesbian, not the way she made love to him. He probably had Amy's image fixed so vividly in his mind that when a woman who looked a little like her suddenly appeared he jumped to conclusions. Did he see this woman as his love because Amy was so vividly a part of his reverie—of the night that she had taken his hand and pulled him in the taxi to kiss him so suddenly and passionately on the lips?

Morgan shook his head. Here he was accusing Amy of being mysterious while he himself was becoming a little strange, seeing images that weren't there.

His mind wandered back to Susan. What would she think when she discovered his note? Would she go to bed without seeing it? Instead of his desk in the library, he probably should have left it on the kitchen table. Since they had separate bedrooms, would she barely notice his absence until the following night when he did not return from the bank? Susan barely noticed his presence anyway, so it would probably not occur to her that he wasn't there.

Morgan had no sense of guilt when he thought of Susan's reaction. He suspected there was a slight possibility she might even be glad he left, although she would never have agreed to a divorce. What would probably upset Susan the most would be the reactions of their friends and neighbors. Keeping up appearances was so important to Susan. She knew so many people. That was why Morgan was nervous sitting there alone in the back of the bus. If some of Susan's friends whom he did not recognize were sitting on the bus...But, then again, if he didn't recognize them, how could they recognize him? Still, there was that man in the dark glasses...

All of a sudden a weird thought struck him: what if *Susan* had a lover? For the first time all evening he smiled. It would be a wonderful solution, but he knew Susan would never get involved with anyone for the fear of creating a scandal. If she ever found out about his affair, Susan's anger would not be directed at Amy as much as it would at him for creating the scandal. If Susan had one love in life it was *Respectability*. If he didn't make that train and Susan found out before he and Amy could get away, there would be hell to pay.

As long as the bus made it to Kinzer Junction on time, it would not matter what Susan did, because the chances of anyone finding him once he got on that train were remote. That's what Amy had told him, and he believed her. Someone who did not know Amy as he did would say she was playing him for a fool. If he dared to ask his brother, Jack would have undoubtedly told him that Amy was after his money or was somehow in cahoots with Susan. But both those theories were ridiculous. Amy herself had suggested that he leave all his money and assets to Susan. And there was no way Amy could ever be involved with his wife. Not after the way Amy made love to him. Yet Morgan had to admit to himself that it was difficult to be objective about Amy. He loved her so. Once or twice he had had a tiny twinge of doubt about her, but that was barely a flicker in his reverie, and the doubt disappeared as soon as he saw Amy smiling at him and felt her warm hand in his. She told him everything was going to work out and before they knew it they would be in Nova Scotia together. He recalled her words. She would be standing on the platform at Kinzer Junction railroad station wearing a bright red chapeau and a veil. That had puzzled Morgan. If the veil were to hide her identity, then why the red hat? Wouldn't that be ostentatious?

But Amy just laughed. "The color of my hat is immaterial. It is the hat itself that would attract notice. Not many women wear chapeaux these days."

"Then why wear one?"

"It will cover up my blonde hair."

Morgan knew it would be pointless to keep quizzing Amy on the red hat and veil. Either she had a reason for wearing them that she did not care to disclose to him until they met at the station or there was no rhyme or reason to it at all—just Amy's way of teasing and having fun.

"Lover, you worry too much. It is going to work out. Once we are on that train, you will be in a world you never dreamed of. I'll have a big surprise for you as soon as you get off the bus. Don't forget to look for the big red chapeau."

He wondered if Amy had had any problem getting away. The last time they met, he had suggested keeping in touch by cell phone, but Amy had said she did not have one. This struck Morgan as strange. Traveling around without a cell phone today was like taking a trip without a credit card, he told her. Amy just laughed.

"I don't have one of those either."

Ever since he got on the bus he had had a strong desire to speak to her. Just to hear her voice would have eased his tensions. But he supposed Amy knew what was best. Perhaps she had declined to get involved with a cell phone because those messages could be traced. Sometimes Amy was quite secretive. She was apparently not married—at least not now. But he never got a straight answer from her.

"If I were married, would I be running away with you, Dearie?"

During the passing moments when he was Morgan the banker and was reflecting on how little he knew of Amy's background—her parents, her work, where she had lived before moving to Kincaid County, he would tell himself that if she were a bank customer he could never give her a loan. Everything was so vague and mysterious with Amy. But Morgan the lover told himself that Amy's opaqueness was the very reason he was so fascinated by her. At times like this he wondered how he could have spent so much of his life in two prisons, the dull bank during the day and the lonely house during the night.

***

The bus turned into the gravel road that led to the Kinzer Junction railroad station. Morgan peered out the window. The train was there waiting. He strained his eyes to see if Amy was standing on the platform. Although he noticed three women at the far end of the station, he couldn't tell if Amy was one of them. The rain-streaked window of the bus made visibility difficult; yet he thought one of the women might be wearing a chapeau, possibly a red one.

"Kinzer Junction," the bus driver called out. "Change here for the train to the city, leaving in four minutes."

Morgan made his way down the aisle quickly and was the first in line to disembark from the bus. He looked over his shoulder. The person with the black cap and dark glasses was trying desperately to get down the aisle, but was impeded by the two heavyset women who had boarded the bus at Digby Falls.

"Get out of my way, damn it!"

That guy must really be anxious to board that train, Morgan mused. Or does he want to follow me? Although he did not know why, Morgan had felt uneasy about the fellow with the black cap ever since he first saw him. Could he have some connection with Susan? Or was he someone who knew Amy and was trying to stop his liaison with her? The driver opened the door and Morgan stepped down quickly.

The rain was turning into softly falling snow, painting a picture postcard of the old railroad station. He decided to run because two of the women had left the platform and boarded the train. As he drew closer, he saw that the remaining woman was indeed wearing a red hat and a veil. It was Amy!

"Amy, Amy!" he cried out, racing to embrace the woman in the red chapeau, who moved toward him and raised her veil.

Morgan stopped short and stared in amazement as the woman pulled the veil over her face and removed her hat, revealing long flowing dark hair.

"S-Susan! How—?"

Susan Morgan smiled at the bewilderment of her husband.

"Yes, Howard?"

"W-What are you doing here?"

"Why, Howard, that's a question I was just about to put to you. What a coincidence!"

Morgan was so unnerved that he could not speak. But slowly it started to come to him. He had made several of his calls to Amy from his house when Susan had told him she was going to a meeting of her gun club. Could she have just *said* she was going out and stayed in the house to eavesdrop? But he had called from the library and had spoken softly. Even if she were in the house she would have had a difficult time hearing him. Or—worse yet—had she had their phone tapped? A long time ago she had mentioned that several of the instructors in her gun club were private eyes. Could she have hired one of them? That would explain how she knew he had planned to meet Amy on the train. But why didn't she just confront him with what she knew before this? It was almost as if she wanted to show up at the very last moment—just as he was about to run off with Amy.

"What's the matter, Howard—cat got your tongue?"

"I—I—"

"You had it all figured out, didn't you, Howard? You glommed all our stocks and bonds so you could take off with your little slut?"

"I didn't take the stocks and bonds or our bank account. I—"

"Don't lie to me, Howard. You're not as smart as you think you are. I have proof of your infidelity—not only in tonight's little escapade, but in something more irrefutable: photographs of the great lover in action."

"What are you talking about, Susan?"

"Don't play dumb, Howard? I've got shots of you and your little slut in—how shall I say it?—compromising positions. Like to take a look?"

She handed Morgan a large manila envelope. His hands shook as he fingered the pictures. There he was in bed with a woman whose features he could not make out in what looked like a shabby motel room. But he had never been in a motel with Amy. It had always been in her place. Something was weird here.

"You can keep them, Howard. I've got several copies. Nice, clear shots, aren't they?

"Where did you get these, Susan?"

Susan stared at her husband derisively.

"Howard, you must think I'm an idiot. I suspected you from the start. And I got a little help from one of my friends in the gun club, so—"

"You hired a private eye?"

"A crackerjack one, as you can see. It was a mite expensive, but if you were not fooling around, I would not have had to hire someone to track you down. And speaking of private eyes..."

Morgan looked over his shoulder and saw the black cap and glasses.

"Would you like an introduction, Howard? You seem fond of the ladies."

"Ladies?"

"You don't think I would hire a male private eye. Haven't I had enough of the male gender with you? Martha Wellington, meet my husband, Howard. You, of course, have seen him before on many occasions."

The "man" in the black cap removed her glasses. Although the light was dim, Morgan could see the face of a woman, a rather pretty woman at that.

"Besides the revealing photographs, Ms. Wellington has compiled a impressive dossier on you, Howard. The next step is to have a subpoena issued to bring you to court on the charges of adultery and theft of valuable stocks and bonds."

The conductor stepped out on the platform to tell anyone standing there that the train was about to leave. Morgan looked vainly for any sign of Amy. He began to think that he had been deceived. She hadn't come. Had Susan got to her? Should he get on the train and look?

"Howard, tomorrow morning you are going to march right down to our stock broker and return the stocks and bonds you stole from me. If you try any funny business, just remember that I have the original negatives of these pictures, *Mr. First Vice President*. From now on you will do exactly as I say or face dire consequences. Is that right, Ms. Wellington?"

The woman in the black cap put on her dark glasses "You heard her, Mr. Morgan. Now step over here, please."

Before Morgan could say a word, the woman grabbed him and pushed him onto the train just as the door was about to close. Seconds later she jumped in behind him while Susan stared in amazement. The engineer gave three snorts on his whistle and the train moved out rapidly.

***

The force of the push sent Morgan into an empty seat.

"What the hell did you do that for, Ms. Wellington?" a stunned Morgan asked as he staggered to his feet.

"You can forget about the Ms. Wellington business now, Howard. Tell me, do I look like a private eye?"

With a flourish she removed her dark glasses and black cap, revealing long flowing blond hair. For the second time in the span of a few minutes Morgan was taken by surprise by a woman who was not the woman he thought she was.

"Amy!"

"It's not Doctor Ruth."

"What...how?"

The train was beginning to pick up speed. Amy sat down beside Morgan.

"First of all, don't I deserve a kiss for carrying off this intrigue successfully?"

Without waiting for an answer Amy cupped her hands around Morgan's chin and kissed him passionately on the lips while the nearby passengers smiled.

"I'm sorry for keeping you in the dark, Howard, but it had to be done. I'll explain everything to you in a minute, but first let me tell you, we're absolutely in the clear. When the train reaches the city, we'll be taking a cab to the little airport outside of town. Margie will be there waiting to fly us to Nova Scotia. We'll be there early in the morning. We'll stay at Margie's house in Peggy's Cove for a few days while we look for a place to rent. Hello, tomorrow! We are about to begin a new life."

"But Susan? Won't she—"

"You don't have to worry about Susan any more. She's got the house, two cars, and most of your savings. When she finds out that you didn't cash in all your stocks and bonds, she'll put up with the little scandal of not having a husband."

"You told her I took all the stocks and bonds?"

"That's how I got her to come to Kinzer Junction in the red hat and veil. I said she would be able to catch you red-handed trying to run away with another woman. She bought that after I showed her those naughty pictures of you and—"

"That's another thing. I was never in a motel with whoever that was."

"I know, Dearie. It was just a matter of head-switching. I told you I was into photography."

Morgan's brain was reeling. "Wait a second. How did you get involved with Susan in the first place?"

"Remember your telling me that she belonged to the Kincaid County Ladies Gun Club? That got me a little worried. I thought she might have found out about us and was planning to do a little mischief with a Colt .45. So I figured I had better join the club and see what was up. I had put in a little stint with the Army, so I'm familiar with weapons."

"And she never suspected you knew me?"

Amy smiled. "It was a strange situation because one day I heard her telling one of the woman cops at the gun club that she thought her husband had a lover and was planning to take off with all her income."

"The cop said he would put her in touch with a topnotch private eye who would get the goods on you. I made it my business to take a place next to her on the firing line a few times and after she got talking to me I let it slip that I was a private investigator."

"And she never suspected that she had hired her husband's lover to spy on him?"

"It was a strange situation, I admit. She was a difficult person to work for. But I got even when I gave her my bill. $25,000. She didn't complain. I guess she figured it was your money. It's ours now. We will have a little mad money before we get jobs in Nova Scotia. I'm sorry for making it so complicated, but I had to get her to reject the marriage that really wasn't one."

Morgan suspected Amy wanted the showdown so he could resolve any lingering doubts as well. He didn't think he really had any, but if he did, Susan's blistering accusations certainly resolved them.

"Well, it certainly was interesting, Amy, but I have one question: why the red chapeau?"

Amy smiled. "I couldn't get a green one."

The train was approaching an intersection. The engineer sounded a long mournful whistle, disturbing the still of the night. Morgan sat back and contemplated how quickly his life had changed in the past few hours. He no longer had a house, car, or income, save for the $25,000 Amy had saved for him. But he didn't care. He felt the exuberance of being free. He smiled at Amy who reached over to hold his hand. They were like kids on their first date. For all he knew his relationship with Amy could end as most relationships of young lovers ultimately end. But right now he didn't think so. Amy seemed to be reading his thoughts. She looked out the window and then turned to Morgan.

"We still have a long way to go, Howard, but let's sit back and enjoy the ride. That's half the fun of it."

Morgan nodded his agreement. Then train began to pick up speed as it rolled across the lonely countryside in the dead of the night, wending its way towards the big city. +++++

IX.
Remembrances of Things Past

And, when the stream
Which overflowed the soul was passed away,
A consciousness remained that it had left
Deposited upon the silent shore
Of memory, images and precious thoughts,
That shall not die, and cannot be destroyed.

—William Wordsworth

ELMER'S GENERAL STORE

It has been almost ten years since I visited Elmer's General Store in Hiram's Corners. When I lived on a farm in nearby Cartersville, I used to pop in there maybe four or five times a week. But after I moved out of state, I never had occasion to go back there, although I frequently thought about the place that had once been such a regular part of my life.

Elmer's had been a favorite hang-out of mine for a long time. I was fond of the atmosphere—the beamed ceilings, wide-panel pumpkin pine floors, the old lanterns hanging from the walls, and the rich smells of the harvest in the fall. I used to enjoy looking out his bank of windows and seeing acres and acres of green fields, orchards, and neatly fenced pastures. It did wonders for my appetite.

Not that the food was special. Ah, but what ambiance. Elmer's was in the heart of the country, surrounded by cattle-grazing fields, red barns, apple and peach orchards, as well as well-kept old houses, some dating back to colonial times and others, picturesque with wrap-around porches and gingerbread flourishes on the cornices, to the middle Victorian period.

When I first walked into this slice of yesteryear I found myself in a room dominated by the pungent aroma of fresh coffee beans being ground in a relic of a red coffee grinder with hams, baskets and old jugs hanging from battered old chestnut beams which still bore their barks. The store had originally been established as an inn in 1764, serving travel-weary guests even before the Revolutionary War. Although he seemed to be in the middle of nowhere, Elmer usually attracted a fairly good crowd— from weather-beaten farmers to screaming little kids, from grimy factory workers to the fashionable, snobby rich who lived in the million-dollar houses in the hills overlooking Moosehead River just outside of town.

I used to wonder at the size of his clientele, considering his store was so far off the beaten track. In its own way, though, Elmer's General Store was in the center of its universe, overseeing Hiram's Corners as the *Sacre*

Coeur looks down on Montmartre. Bergman's Hardware and Dooley's Garage, which used to be a blacksmith's shop, occupied two of the other corners, and Foxworth's Funeral Home was diagonally across the road from Elmer's to the southeast, a coincidence Hiram's Corners' pundits were quick to point out when Elmer's cabbage soup bore a suspicious odor. Aside from Putney's Five and Ten, next to Bergman's, and Sam's Barber Shoppe next to Dooley's Garage, there were few places of business near the crossroads. I suppose some people might include the Old Dutch Reformed Church, about a hundred yards south of Foxworth's, and the 18th century cemetery across the road from it, but it's hard to think of churches and cemeteries as businesses, although I imagine both of them made out better than Dooley and Bergman.

***

For someone who was almost constantly hosting nearly a hundred customers a day, Elmer had nothing of the look of a glad-handing entrepreneur. He never had to worry about offending any of his patrons by what he said because he said practically nothing. Rarely would he trouble his lips to mumble "Hello," "Nice Day," "How are things?" or even "Goodbye." It is true he grunted once in awhile. Old-timers have told me that one grunt meant "How are things going?" and two grunts, which he belched out on those days when he felt the urge to mimic Demosthenes, might be liberally translated to mean, "I hope your family is well. That will be $15.40, please."

Looking at Elmer was like looking at an old yearbook picture. He always seemed the same, dressed in a heavily starched white shirt, blue bow-tie, black trousers, and white apron that rarely got soiled. He had the manner of a bachelor who lined up his handkerchiefs, socks, and underwear in his dresser drawers with military precision. But the old-timers said he had been married and that his wife died shortly after the birth of their only child. Still, it was difficult to imagine Elmer ever being someone's husband.

I am not a betting man, but if I were, I would wager that he never drank. No one who ever had a few belts of booze now and then could be as quiet as he was, especially since he had so many people to talk to.

You would not think anyone as taciturn as Elmer could stay in business so long. Still, most of Elmer's customers seemed content with him the way he was. I guess in this age of noise—from hard rock to talk shows to jackhammers, people find a non-talker refreshing, as long he doesn't overcook their hamburgers or give them the wrong change.

Looking back, I think my main attraction to Elmer's General Store was not the cracker barrels, pot-bellied stove, or tantalizing smells of fresh-baked apple pies. And it certainly was not Elmer: it was Sarah.

***

It was hard to believe that Sarah was Elmer's daughter. As laid back as he was, Sarah was the epitome of *joie de vie* . She seemed always capable of seeing the lighter side of even the dullest of situations. Raindrops made her laugh because they tickled her nose; one of her favorite sounds was the slurping noises of customers slopping down their soup; and she could create a little story just by watching clouds disappear over the mountain tops. I've seen her kick a football more than ten yards on the fly. Fairly remarkable, when you consider that Sarah was only seven years old then.

I got to know Sarah the day I tried to sneak Flaubert into the general store. He was just a puppy then, and I didn't want to leave him in the cab of my pick-up because I thought he might be frightened, so I slipped him under my overcoat. But Elmer, hawk-eye as he was, caught me when Flaubert stuck his head out as I was putting mustard on my grilled cheese sandwich. He gestured with his New England thumb and actually spoke a few words.

"No dogs allowed."

Sarah, who had spotted Flaubert as he was eyeing my sandwich, called out to her father.

"Oh, Daddy, please let him stay. He's only a puppy. And it's a golden retriever."

Surprisingly Elmer, relented.

"All right, Sarah, we'll let him in. But just for a minute or two."

I gave Sarah a grateful smile.

"Would you like to hold him?"

That was the beginning of our friendship. Sometimes when I was walking Flaubert around the parking lot, Sarah would come out to play with him and we

would talk. With her cornflower blue eyes and wavy blond hair she had a quiet beauty about her, but she was a tomboy. She was neither interested in dolls nor baby carriages. What she wanted to talk about was pirates, haunted houses, and baseball. And sometimes she veered off into the philosophical.

"We were studying about belly buttons in school today, only my teacher called them *navels*," she said one sunny winter afternoon. "She told us God gave us navels so we could be hooked up to our mothers by a little string."

"That makes sense," I volunteered.

Sarah looked at me thoughtfully.

"Do you think Adam and Eve had belly buttons?"

"I-I would imagine they did."

"But why?" Sarah asked, wrinkling up her nose. "They didn't have mothers."

I told her she had a point.

"Unless God was their mother," she said as an afterthought. "But maybe God was too busy to be a mother. What do you think?"

"I always heard people talk about God the Father. But there is no reason she couldn't be a mother."

The idea of God being both a mother and father tickled her. She told me it was possible all right, because God was supposed to be able to do anything and being two parents at the same time should be no big deal for him. She let that spin around in her head for a moment and then returned to the question of navels.

"When I was real little, I was probably hooked on to my mother by a little string, wasn't I, Mr. Farley?"

"I wasn't there at the time, Sarah, but I think you have a plausible theory."

"Would that make my mother a hooker?" Sarah said with a straight face and then broke into a high-pitched giggle.

"Where did you learn a word like that?" I asked, feigning sternness.

But Sarah just kept on giggling. "The same place you learned words like *plausible* and *theory.*"

And she jumped up and down to celebrate her little *coup*. Sarah read the unabridged dictionary the way some people read the New York *Times*

***

As I was passing through the outskirts of Cartersville on the little country road that led to Hiram's Corners, I wondered if Elmer's General Store would still be there. The chances were that it would, because when I lived there change came very slowly. And unless another general store or two had sprung up in the last ten years to give him competition, Elmer had no reason for leaving a profitable venture. But would Sarah still be there? She would be about twenty now and probably half way through college. It was possible that she could have stayed home to help out with the store. I wondered what she would say when I told her about Flaubert. I am sure she would remember him. They were great friends. I had been tempted to drop a line to her at the store last month the day I had to have the vet put Flaubert to sleep, but I thought it would only make her sad.

Besides, she might not be at the store any more. When she grew up she might have wanted to escape small-town life. She had so much curiosity as a kid that there was no telling where she might be by now. I wondered if she were married. It was difficult to think of little Sarah married, but for all I knew she could have a child of her own, one who would someday become the little girl who was fascinated by baseball and belly-buttons.

Elmer was coming out of Sam's Barber Shoppe as I arrived at Hiram's Corners. He had aged quite a bit in the past ten years. His face was pale and his eyes were haggard. Surprisingly his white apron that was always spotless was stained the colors of the rainbow. And something must have happened to his left leg because he seemed to be walking in pain. When I looked closer, however, I saw that he was not limping; he was drunk.

As I got out of my pickup, he spotted me. I didn't think he recognized me at first, for he just stared long and hard, as if I were a complicated mathematical problem. Suddenly he lunged backwards, supported at the last moment by Sam's peppermint stick barber pole, and yelled to me:

"Farley, you old bastard! Where the hell did you come from?"

Now it was not usual for Elmer to use even mild profanity, let alone shout out two consecutive sentences. And I never thought that Elmer would imbibe, let alone get drunk. He really took me by surprise, because in all the years I had known him, he had never addressed me by my name.

"Are you all right, Elmer?"

He stared at me again. "All right? Why shouldn't I be? Are you all right, Farley?"

As I approached him, he began to lose his balance again. I caught him just as he was about to crack his head into Sam's barber pole.

***

After his second coffee he began to come out of it and asked me what I had been doing the past ten years. I think I was more shocked that he was talking than that he had been drinking. I told him I had never seen him take a drink in his life.

"You haven't missed much," he said.

Curious as I was, I did not think this was the time to ask him why he decided to pick up the habit.

So intent was I in sobering Elmer up, I had not paid any attention to the place that had been so much a part of my youth. When I finally looked around, I saw that things were just about the same—the old red coffee grinder, the cracker barrel, the pot-bellied stove, and lanterns and baskets hanging from the battered chestnut beams that held up the ceiling. But to my amazement one part of the picture was missing: the customers. The store was almost empty.

Elmer must have guessed what I was thinking.

"Yeah, it's pretty quiet around here lately," he said.

"Lots of people on vacation?" I suggested politely.

Elmer shrugged his shoulders. "On permanent vacations, I think."

He stared into his coffee cup and sat still as a statue for a few minutes. It was as if I wasn't there. I had the strange feeling that perhaps I was an intruder, and that I ought to get up and leave. But as I looked about the lonely old store, I realized that Elmer needed someone with him, even if only to share the silence. I waited a few minutes and then told him about Flaubert. He listened attentively.

"I remember him. He was a nice doggie. Sarah really liked him. She often talked about him after you left town."

"I know. After I had him cremated, I was tempted to gather a few of the ashes—they were like little grains of sand—and put them in an envelope and send them to Sarah. But I guess that was a silly idea."

Elmer straightened up in his chair. I could see that his eyes were becoming more alert now.

"No," he said, "It's not as silly as you think. The only thing is—"

All at once it hit me. The uneasy quiet that pervaded the near-empty store and Elmer's disheveled clothes and haggard eyes. He didn't have to say another word. But he had to tell me, as he had told every one he encountered since it happened.

"Sarah dropped out of college in her junior year. She said she missed the store and the countryside and wanted to give me a hand. Since Sarah never complained about anything, I didn't realize that she was sick. She was like she always was—cheerful and bright and smiling at the customers. Then one morning when she didn't come down to help with breakfast, I went upstairs to check her room. The doc said she died in her sleep. Right by her pillow was one of those big yellow legal pads. She had been working on one of her little stories about the shapes of the clouds overhead. And you know, Farley, it's a strange thing: she didn't look dead at all. She seem so peaceful lying there, as if she was dreaming."

***

Two customers came in and Elmer got up to serve them. They seemed surprised to see him sober, so I guess he had taken to drinking ever since Sarah died. I waved at him and made my way to the door. Before I left I took one last look around at the old chestnut beams and the relics of years gone by. It struck me how so many things were the same as when I visited it for the first time so long ago. And yet I knew, as Elmer knew, that it would never be the same again. +++++

BANNON

You asked for it, Gene; this one's for you

It was only a month, but a lot can happen in a month in autumn. The last of the hurricanes, like air-borne piranhas, had stripped the trees of most of their russet and gold finery, and gathering clouds suggested we were about to have the first snowstorm of the season. I looked at the calendar the book company had sent me featuring the birthdays of famous writers and artists. Today was November 22nd, the birthday of André Gide. I flipped on my computer and called up the notes I had taken to recall that day. It was October 22nd, exactly one month ago. And yet it still seemed so vivid in my mind that I could picture it as if it were yesterday and see Bannon sticking his head in the door of my office, wearing his Irish tweed cap and that tell-tale grin that hinted something was brewing....

"Do you want to skip the college cafeteria and have something unusual for lunch?"

"Why not?" I said, reaching for my jacket.

"It's a nice day; you don't need a coat."

"All right, but I still have to get my car keys. Unless you're driving.

"We're walking," Bannon said.

I looked at my watch. My next class was in an hour. If we were walking, we would probably spend most or our time just getting there and back I couldn't think of any decent restaurant within a fifteen minute walk from the college, and I told him so.

"Who needs a restaurant?"

"Didn't you just say something about lunch?"

"Lunch, yes; regular kind of food, no. Follow me. I'm the head scout on this reconnaissance detail."

Following him was an old habit. We had been following each other around for fifty years from the time we played stickball on Ege Avenue through grammar school, Prep, college, and graduate school. We hadn't planned it that way and there were times we didn't see each other for months or even years, as in the case of World War II, when he opted for the Navy and I joined the Army. But we kept in touch by mail. When I wrote to him about the scratchy surfaces of French toilet paper, he wrote back on soft Navy tissue that if I didn't enjoy his letter at least I could put it to some practical use when I finished reading it.

Bannon became a pharmaceutical salesman after graduate school, and I worked as a newspaper reporter on a daily at the state capital. After a number of years I wan- dered back into Milford, the town we grew up in, to teach English literature at the local college. A year later Bannon quit the pharmaceutical company because he said he got tired of telling people he sold drugs for a living. He took a few more graduate courses and soon became a guidance counselor at Milford State where I work. Once a week we would usually have lunch together. Half the time we'd eat at the college cafeteria, but before we'd go there we would walk around the campus for twenty minutes or so to enhance our appetites. If you ever plan on eating at the Milford State cafeteria, you would be well advised to do the same thing. An ordinary appetite will not take you through that tepid, overcooked fare. without gagging. So the thought of an unusual lunch had appealed to me.

This time Bannon took the path that follows the river and headed straight for the front gates. He didn't say anything, but I could see by the familiar landmarks we passed that we were going to be walking through the town of Milford to reach the site of our mysterious lunch. It was not a picturesque journey because Milford is one of those old mill towns that have lost more than half of their populations and most of their erstwhile prosperity with the arrival of the interstate. The nicest part of the town was the college with its architecture and its 55-acre wooded campus.

Growing up, Bannon and I thought of Milford as being somewhere near the center of the universe. After all, we had Meyers Ice Cream Shoppe with its double-dip chocolate floats on Friday nights, the La Petite on Elm and Main where all the pretty girls from St. Elizabeth's Academy hung out on week nights and on weekends on the outskirts of town, Elysian Fields, home of the Milford Mud Hens, Middle-Atlantic Conference Semi-Pro Baseball champions in 1937, the same year that Bannon hit a three-sewer plate home run in stickball on Ege Avenue, a record that stood for along time.

Thomas Wolfe must have had an unconscious influence on us, because in the more than twenty years that Bannon and I have been at the college, we never had the desire to go home again and visit the haunts of our boyhood days. Oh, sometimes we would drive through Milford to go to the seafood restaurants fifteen miles to the east by the coast, but we had not actually walked through the old streets of our youth since we were kids. And, as I was soon to discover, there is a difference between driving and actually setting foot on the turf again.

Ege Avenue, where we lived two doors away from each other a half century ago, began at the Eagle Grocery Store on the corner of Main and ran for two blocks to Railroad Avenue. The last house on the street by the tracks was the Krumgolds' who owned a tailor shop, my family was next, on our left were the Manns who told us not to trample on their azaleas when we were chasing foul balls because that's what we would become when we died, and then came the Bannons. We lived so close to the railroad that we could hear the trains coming and going to and from the state capital at the other end of the line.

The last train passed by Ege at 10:03 at night. It was almost always on time, right to the minute. I know because I usually had to go to bed at nine-thirty and I would lie there and wait for it to come by, rattling the tracks and shaking our old house a little. I can still hear in my mind's ear the chug-chugging of the steam engine and the shrill, plaintive wail of the locomotive's whistle, breaking the stillness of a lonely summer's night.

I didn't expect the Eagle to still be there, but I had a feeling there would be some other kind of a store, something in keeping with the times—perhaps a video rental shop. But there was nothing. No building, no store, no apartment upstairs where Ray Price, the fastest kid on the block lived. Nothing. Not even a building. All I saw were a few broken bottles and rusty old tin cans loitering about sadly between the Russian thistle, goldenrod, and tumble- weed. I found myself staring into the empty space picturing Mr. Butler reaching behind him for his long tin dipper to fill up our white gallon jugs from his huge milk container. Sometimes he would pour a mouthful into a Dixie cup and give us a little drink for free. I remembered how rich it tasted and how nice and cold it was.

We called the kids who lived on Ege between Main and River Street the Upper Eges and we were naturally the Lower Eges. The houses on Upper Ege must have gone for at least $10,000 in those days—wrap-around porches, gar- dens in front and back and even an occasional driveway for a Packard or Nash. Where we lived the homes were in the $5,000 category, and the porches and gardens were small. When we played the Upper Eges in stickball, most of their team had uniforms of sorts—baseball shirts with *Tigers* printed on the front in orange letters. Only Henny Ragsdale, Billy Stockhammer, Frankie Judge, Richie Edge, and Ray DeTuro, had baseball shirts among the guys on the Lower Eges, and each one had the name of a different team on it. But it didn't matter; we knew who we were.

The Coyles had the biggest house on Upper Ege—a three-story rambling old Victorian with seven gables, just like the one in the Hawthorne novel, and elaborate ginger- bread all around the windows and eaves. It was set back about fifty feet from the street and guarded on each side by two massive elms. Three sisters lived there—Millicent, Dorothy, and Grace. They were all pretty, but the one whom all the guys had a crush on was Dorothy. Most of us were much too young to frame the words to spell out our attraction for Dorothy—everyone but Bannon, that is. He was never shy or reluctant to say what he was thinking and, as it happens with the case of Dorothy Coyle, what just about all of us were ruminating about in the secret echelons of our minds.

"She has the nicest knockers in the seventh grade," Bannon would say with the same matter-of-factness he would employ if he were noting that Montpelier was the capital of Vermont. We never questioned Bannon's ability to produce empirical evidence to back up such a broad assertion. In those days Bannon was considered an authority on matters of this nature, and if he regarded Dorothy's chest as superior to those of all twenty-seven girls in Sister Catherine Eucharia's seventh grade, we just assumed he had done the proper research, whatever that was.

The Coyles' house was there, but the towering elms had been cut down and someone had closed in the beautiful wrap-around porch and made a half dozen rooms out of it. There were four separate entrances to the house now, indicating that at least that many families were living there. The garden had been long unattended and had grown to weed. The wide sweeping front steps from which Dorothy used to emerge in her bright summer dresses, occasionally flashing glimpses of pink petticoats, were now a dull gray and sorely in need of paint.

And it got worse. Some of the lesser houses on Upper Ege had their windows boarded up and one of them, the Kelloggs on the corner of Ege and River, had burned to the ground, probably a few years ago.

"This is lunch?" I asked Bannon.

"Look at it this way, Cavanaugh. When we were little we could never afford to live on Upper Ege. Now if we moved here, we'd be the richest guys on the block."

That was Bannon's way. In all the fifty years I knew him I never heard him complain—not when his fiancée failed twice to show up for their wedding, not when the only new car he ever owned, a flaming red Chevy convertible, was stolen two weeks after he drove it out of the showroom. He said it could have been worse because if his intended had come to the altar with him he would surely have been married. The car theft was a blessing in disguise, he said, because now he didn't have to worry about it getting stolen. He collected the insurance money, bought a broken down shitbox with a loud but reliable motor and went on a two-week vacation to the Gaspe Peninsula where "the air was so clear you would have thought you were back on Ege Avenue in the days when there were more horse and buggies than Model-T's."

"Have you been here lately?" I asked Bannon.

"No. This is the first time since I was a kid—same as you. I don't know why, but when I woke up today I had a burning desire to see old Ege Avenue once again. Sure looks different, doesn't it?"

I nodded. We had crossed River Street and had passed a few more boarded-up houses, this time ones that had once belonged to the poorer people on Lower Ege. Suddenly Bannon stopped. We were standing in front of his house.

Someone must have been living in it, because there were thin patches of white smoke drifting from the old fieldstone chimney. When we were small we used to go into Bannon's house after football games and sit around the fireplace to tell ghost stories. A elderly Asian woman appeared on the front porch with a broom. Seeing that she was watching us looking at her house, we both waved. I took it upon myself to explain the situation.

"My friend here used to live in your house. A long time ago. When we were both children."

The woman looked at us curiously and made a few passes with her broom before she waved back and returned to the inside of her house. I had the feeling that she had not understood a word I had said.

I glanced over at Bannon to catch his reaction, but he was examining the black walnut, whose branches were extending well over the roof of his old home. When we were kids it barely reached the second floor where Bannon slept and where I kissed a girl for the first time in my life.

Her name was Rita Marley and the last I heard she was living in Australia with her second husband and two of her nine children. She was one of the twenty-seven girls in Sister Catherine Eucharia's class, not as voluptuous as Dorothy Coyle, but pretty with her long brown hair and flashing green eyes. I kissed her just that one time, when we were both about twelve years old, in Bannon's little room that overlooked the young black walnut tree.

Bannon had talked his mother into letting him have a birthday party to which girls could come as well as boys. He had wanted an excuse to lure the Coyle girls into his house ever since he was in the fifth grade. His birthday was February 12th, the same as Abraham Lincoln's, and he persuaded his mother that his patron would certainly not want him to be enslaved to the tradition of all-boy rough house parties when the fair sex could bring a touch of dignity to the affair. As soon as all of the guests had stacked their presents neatly on the living room table, Bannon announced the first little game we would be playing. He wanted to make sure he got this in before Mr. Bannon arrived home. His father was much less liberated than Mrs. Bannon.

All the girls put little tokens into an empty candy box—rings, combs, pins and other personal items. Each boy had to close his eyes and pick something from the box. Whosever token he selected he had to take upstairs to Bannon's room for a quick smooch. My knees began to shake when I went up the stairs to kiss Rita Marley who was already there. But she smiled and touched me softly on the shoulder and I wasn't frightened any more. I could still smell her perfume as I descended the stairs. Naturally Bannon had Dorothy Coyle up in that room a dozen times before Mrs. Bannon switched the game to pin-the-tail-on-the-donkey in deference to Ege Avenue morality and her husband's impending arrival.

I don't know if Bannon was reading my thoughts when he returned from his meditations by the black walnut, but when he saw me looking up where his room used to be, he smiled.

"We had some good times in that old house, right Cavanaugh?"

He stepped into the street to take a better look at it, in the process crossing Ege Avenue's middle sewer plate, second base in stickball games. While Bannon closed his fists to swing an imaginary broom stick, I glanced at home plate in front of Krumgolds and then at the third sewer plate, way in the outfield a little before the intersection of River and Ege. When he completed his swing, he bent his knees a little and placed both hands on his chest.

"Are you all right?" I asked. He seemed to be in a little pain.

"Right as the mail, as they say," he said, straighten- ing up and allowing his facial muscles to relax. "It's just that I need to limber up a little before I take a few more swings like that. Say, Cavanaugh, did you notice it too?"

"Notice what?" I asked cautiously.

"It's really not as far as it seemed back then, is it?"

I knew what he meant. When he hit that three-sewer plate home run back in 1937, the three-cent pimple ball seemed to take off like a bird in flight, way over the oaks and elms, until it disappeared somewhere in the Coyles' garden in Upper Ege. Well, at least that is the way we remembered it. But now it did not seem so far from sewer plate to sewer plate, and if either of us could swing a stick without throwing our backs out, we could probably hit five out of ten three-sewer plate shots. Bannon seemed de- pressed at the thought, so I tried to cheer him up.

"Don't forget you probably hit your homer with an old ball. Once a ball has been sitting in the sewer for a while, it loses some of its zap."

That brought a grin to his face. "Remember how you used to go down the sewer head-first and Ray DeTuro and I would hold you by the ankles?"

"That's what you call trust in one's fellow man. You know, we would get as many as five balls in ten minutes of sewer-diving."

"We got even more on Upper Ege. Those rich kids never worked the sewers. Every time a ball was lost they'd just hit up one of their mommies for another three cents."

We were walking the other side of Ege now and were just opposite my house, probably the oldest on the block because it had a flat roof and windows in the front that were as tall as the door. When I was a kid I used to think that kidnappers would break through the windows and come upstairs and get me. I'd tell that to Bannon and he would laugh and tell me that it wouldn't be worth all that effort on the kidnappers' part.

"Look at it from their point of view. They'd have to break the glass, maybe cut themselves, and then climb the stairs to get you out of bed. And after all that, what would they get? The truth is, Cavanaugh, you ain't worth much in the kidnapping market. Now if they had a way of getting into Dorothy Coyle's house, well then that would bring in top dollars."

I climbed up the front steps of what used to be the Dingles' house to get a better look at my boyhood home across the street. Bannon started to follow me, and then stepped down.

"What's the matter?" I asked.

"You know, even after all these years, this house still gives me the creeps. Do you think that Bobby Dingle is around here somewheres?"

I shrugged, but I knew what he meant. Every neighborhood in the world has some version of a Bobby Dingle, I suppose, but the Bobby Dingle of Lower Ege was a notch or two stranger than the usual weirdoes who got their rocks off de-feathering birds and torturing cats. He persuaded me to visit his room once while both his parents were out. His walls were lined with pin-ups—not of Holly- wood movie stars, but of African headhunters and Public Enemies like John Dillinger, Al Capone, and Baby Face Nelson. He had a drawer full of something that I thought were dirty white balloons until I asked Bannon about them. I left when he took an old shoebox from under his bed to show me what looked like a dead mouse. He prodded it with a stick and large W-shaped wings fluttered past my nose, making my hair stand on end. He had trapped a baby bat while it was asleep. It zoomed over my head again and crashed into one of the African headhunters. I raced down the stairs as fast as I could, hearing only the pounding of my feet and the idiotic laugh of Bobby Dingle from the top of the landing. That was the last time I had any social encounters with him, though I would nod and walk fast when I would see him in the neighborhood. He never played stickball, two-hand touch, or any of our street games, and he wasn't interested in any of the girls on Ege, not even the Coyles.

I couldn't tell if anyone was living in my old house or in the Manns next door. The windows were not boarded up, and the grounds had not deteriorated as much as most of those of the other houses on the street. The Manns' azalea bushes, much taller now, were still there and seemed ready to burst forth next May in even greater glory than our early days on Ege. Mrs. Mann evidently had been quite successful in keeping kids away from her flowers. Her admonition that we would all become azaleas in the next world flashed through my mind.

Bannon had walked across the street and was sitting on the stone steps of the Krumgolds, the last house on the block. I didn't know if he was getting winded from our walk, or if the proximity to Bobby Dingle's old house had depressed him, but when I crossed over he stood up, straightened out the kink in his back, and put his right arm around me the way he had been doing for years. I knew this was a signal that he had thought of an old story and wanted my undivided attention until he finished telling it.

"Do you remember who lived on Railroad Avenue just behind the Krumgolds?"

I knew he didn't want me to talk, so I just nodded.

"Herman Schmidtberger. His family moved to the West Coast after he finished grammar school, but he came back to Milford after the war. He would hang out in Sam's Saloon with us sometimes."

Just thinking about Schmidtberger made me smile. He was one of those guys who succeeded in making an art t out of cheapness. For example, as soon as he looked old enough to be served at Sam's, Herman noticed that the bartender always took the money for the first round from the guy on his left and worked his way down. Naturally Schmidtberger positioned himself on the extreme right. When his turn was approaching, he would either cover up his money with a pack of cigarettes and go to the bathroom or suggest they try another bar for a change of pace. It would work for about three or four months, after which Schmidtberger would start hanging around with another crowd in a different saloon.

"Remember the time a big crowd of us went to that new bar in Fox River where they advertised nickel beers, but Schmidtberger for some reason didn't know about it?" Bannon reminisced. "He was using every dodge he could to avoid coughing up any money, because there were about ten of us and he figured it was twenty-five cents a beer as usual. When he overheard someone say that beers were a nickel each, his eyes nearly popped out of their sockets. I can hear him till this day: `Five cents a beer! I'll buy a round.' It was probably the only time that he sprung for any thing except spit in his life."

I glanced at my watch. If I was going to get back in time for my class, we would have to hustle. But Bannon seemed lost in a reverie of the exploits of Herman Schmidtberger.

"He popped in my apartment at two in the morning one time," Bannon recalled. "I was half-asleep watching one of those pitch men selling hair tonic and Herman seemed fascinated by it. He had a premature bald spot in the back of his head and, besides being cheap, he was extremely worried about losing his hair. I guess he thought it would hurt his chances with the ladies. Even though the pitchman had a head like a cue ball, he had the moxie to sell this little 'magical' bottle of gook guaranteed to bring back your hair. For a measly four bucks. Now Cavanaugh, the one thing I've managed to hold onto over the years was my hair. That didn't stop Schmidtberger. Do you know what he said to me? 'How about you and me splitting a bottle? I'll throw in a deuce.' The funny thing was I went along with him. I wanted to watch the expression on his face when he polished the back of his head with that glop."

The roar of the diesel engine of the afternoon train bound for the state capital drowned out the last few words of Bannon's sentence, but I sensed what he had said. I started to say that we had better hustle if I was going to make my class, but the thought occurred to me that Sam had a son who years ago had talked about carrying on his father's saloon business. Even if Sam, Jr. were too old for the daily grind, he himself might have a son. Or a daughter. It was worth a try anyway. Besides, if the saloon was still around, I could use the phone to call the secretary of the English Department to cancel my afternoon class. I would tell her I was busy "doing research with a colleague from the guidance department."

It was a wise decision. Sam, Jr., a little bent now, recognized us right away, even after all the years. We each had three beers and Sam Jr's son joined us for one before we left.

It was the last time I ever saw Bannon.

***

When Bannon didn't come around for lunch the following week, I gave his office a ring. They said he had called in sick that morning. I phoned his apartment later in the day and got his sister. She said he had died an hour ago. A bad heart, the doctor told her. Knowing him as well as I did all these years, I could never imagine anybody saying Bannon had a bad heart.

I shut off my computer and glanced out the window. A light snow was beginning to cover the tops of the trees that lined the path along the river leading to the front gates, the path Bannon and I had taken a month ago when we took our little walk through Milford town. I opened the window to get a better view. The wind whistled across the campus, rattling the signs on the fraternity houses across the way. It looked like it was going to be a cold winter. +++++

LaVergne, TN USA
04 February 2011
215252LV00004B/15/P